COMMUNICATION THEORY

THE GUILFORD COMMUNICATION SERIES

Editors

Theodore L. Glasser, *Stanford University*
Howard E. Sypher, *University of Kansas*

Advisory Board

| Charles Berger | Peter Monge | Michael Schudson |
| James W. Carey | Barbara O'Keefe | Linda Steiner |

COMMUNICATION THEORY
Epistemological Foundations

JAMES A. ANDERSON

THE GUILFORD PRESS
New York   *London*

© 1996 The Guilford Press
A Division of Guilford Publications, Inc.
72 Spring Street, New York, NY 10012

Printed in the United States of America

This book is printed on acid-free paper.

Last digit is print number: 9 8 7 6 5 4 3 2 1

Library of Congress Cataloging-in-Publication Data

Anderson, James A. (James Arthur), 1939–
   Communication theory : epistemological foundations / James A. Anderson.
      p. cm. — (The Guilford communication series)
   Includes bibliographical references and index.
   ISBN 1-57230-083-3
   1. Information theory.   I. Title. II. Series.
Q360.A48 1996
001—dc20   96-12352
                                                        CIP

ACKNOWLEDGMENTS

Several generations of graduate students have both suffered through and contributed to the development of the ideas and arguments in this book. Four worked their way through an early draft and gave their care as a gift to the project: Claudia Clark, Claire Johnson, Linda Lynn, and Karen Webster. Faculty colleagues offered their help too: Stephen Acker, Susan Tyler Eastman, Elaine Englehardt, Joe MacDoniels, Maureen Mathison and Garard Schoening. My friends at the University of Klagenfurt—Klaus Boeckmann, August Fenk, Brigitte Hipfl, Walter Schludermann, Günther Stotz, and their guests Gunther Kress and Jan Jagodzinski—spent hours arguing the issues I discuss here over a glass or two of good Austrian wine. Stephen Littlejohn and Em Griffin, well-recognized students of communication theory, offered useful comments when we were all at the Institute for Faculty Development at Hope College. Geoffrey Baym created the glossary on rainy Sundays and late nights; it should prove to be a great help to the reader new to epistemological studies. My colleagues in the Department of Communication and elsewhere in the College of Humanities at the University of Utah offered encouragement, advice, and references to lines of thought. Melissa Anderson, who teaches chemistry, wrote a comment on every paragraph, reflecting the writing. And finally, Ted Glasser and his anonymous crew forced me to make this book better. To everyone who helped, I offer my thanks, although I probably did not give them all they deserved.

CONTENTS

I

ON READING THIS BOOK

Steve and I are setting rebar in the forms for the foundation for the addition to his Colorado home. Steve is a world-class communication technologist and futurist. He has been reading parts of this book and asks me if a hermeneutic tape measure would be blank. "No," I say, "but it would recognize the difference between a short 8 feet and a long 8 feet," referring to his instruction to set the rebar a short 8 feet from the footer. I cannot resist the pedantic impulse to add that no distance is real except at some level of precision. We agree that the level of precision is a code of the work to be held in common by the workers. The reality of length, then, is a practical achievement.

INTRODUCTION

This book represents a journey forced upon us by the collapse of the epistemic unity that governed nearly all scholarship just a few decades ago. Then, as in nostalgic pockets yet, the dominant intellectual interests were invested in a masculine empiricism and a rugged rationality. We were moving to contain, conquer and control through material, reductionistic knowledge. This knowledge, sentence-based and propositional, was the necessary and largely unquestioned consequence of good methods and right reason.

The voices of dissent, suppressed but not silenced then, are now an unmistakable chorus. It would be remarkable for a colleague not to be conversant with, at least, something from the menu of Kuhnian revolutions, Foucaultian archaeology, Derridian deconstructionism, Lacanian desire, Bahktinian dialogics,

1

Peircean semiotics, German hermeneutics, and feminist theory, as well as a turn-of-the-century longing for the likes of James and Dewey—all of which point toward some form of the social construction of knowledge.

Even if we reject all who can be heard in opposition, the simple recognition that we are not alone on our epistemic island equally forces this journey of exploration. In this journey, we will not come upon the monuments of communication theory until nearly its end. Instead, we will spend most of the time exploring the prior epistemic conditions that provide for a justified belief in any theory. This is a journey through what we must believe to be true before we can demonstrate the truth of our claims.

A colleague of mine remarked, "I don't make truth claims, I only report what I observe." Her comment resonates with hard-bitten journalism or steely-eyed science. Clearly, however, her sentence is itself a truth claim in that it purports to validly represent what she does. How can the contradiction of her claim that she does not make truth claims be true? My colleague can truthfully claim that she does not make truth claims because she believes in an incontrovertible naive empiricism ("what I observe") and an incorruptible representational language ("I only report"). Because of these Lockean beliefs, her sentence is unassailable at the level at which it is advanced. It is, however, an obvious contradiction at the level of its priors.

In the same manner, if we are to understand the bewildering array of the dozens and dozens of theories that populate our journals and textbooks, we will have to explore them archaeologically to discover what must come before. To offer a deliberately provocative example, Marxism and cognitivism share many epistemic components—materialism, reductionism, determinism, an ideological or perceptual consciousness—though they diverge in the way they tell their final story. That one rejects the other is much more a function of their similarities than of their differences.

Plan of the Book

This book is organized around seven defining questions. The questions are traditional and are used heuristically to sort through the complex of ideas and information that forms the foundation of theory development. Traditionally, we hold that a complete theory statement has four claim components. The *ontology* of a theory makes a claim about what is. The corresponding three questions are: What is the nature of the phenomenal world? What is our manner of engagement with it? What is the nature of the individual within that world? The *epistemology* of a theory makes a claim about what we know. The corresponding two questions are: What is the character of the justified argument? What is the relationship between theory and method? The *praxeology* of a theory makes a claim about how it is done. The corresponding question is What is the practice of the practical argument? Finally, the *axiology* of a theory makes a claim about its worth. The corresponding question is What is the presence of scholarship in society?

Chapters 2 through 8 examine the positions and arguments that are available as answers to these questions. Chapter 9 sketches the disciplinary community of communication archaeologically to outline theory genealogies within the intersecting scholarship fields that form the geography of the community. With the sketch of what we could expect to find given an extensive analysis in hand, exemplar theories are further excavated to show how the analytical tools developed under the question rubric reveal a foundation of understanding.

Theory must have an object of its explanation, an explanatory form, a method to relate evidence to claim, characteristic explanations within a scope of performance, and a consequence of value. A foundational analysis of any theory will move toward these ends. Such an analysis speaks to the singular, overarching question What do I have to believe to be true to live a scholar's life in the fashion of this theory?

Style of This Book

This book is necessarily a postmodern text (Rosenau, 1992). "Necessarily" because it is written from the belief that any position is put into place and held there only through effort. The writing continually acknowledges both the deliberateness of its placement and the required sustaining effort by introducing a plurality of voices and by refusing the conclusion of its own claim.[1]

I am asking the reader to explore the consequences of seven prior conditions for the construction of theory. In the course of the exploration I offer alternatives inevitably, but also intentionally, unequal[2] and the consequences that I would draw. It is not necessary for the reader to agree with me. It is sufficient if she or he simply stays the course.

This text is a "writerly text," one that demands that the reader write the ending. Most of our textbooks are precisely the opposite, organized to demand that the reader come to the writer's conclusion. Here, there is a response for everything but an answer for nothing. The writing is much like an unfinished jazz symphony in which themes and their variations are played but remain open to further improvisation. This openness may cause frustration for a modernist reader or the modernist classroom.[3]

Finally, this book is written for communication graduate students and their faculty colleagues. It assumes an audience of widely different readers in terms of their epistemic exposure and degrees of engagement. Because of these assumptions, I have taken on a conversational style to relieve the tedium of what may be my readers' required reading but also to grant myself the freedom to comment on the intentions and pretensions of my own arguments. I have also tried to make the ideas accessible without refusing the asides and allusions that may be more appropriate to the more experienced reader. The work, however, is serious and intends to be dangerous in a manner that shall be explained.

SOME PRELIMINARIES

Whatever the style and whoever the author, a book of this sort can be—and is, in this case—motivated by two circumstances. One I have introduced as the virtual destruction of traditional epistemology over the past three decades. The other has been revealed as those former structures have been torn down. This other is the politicized character of any epistemic position along with the methods of indoctrination disguised as graduate education. We take up these two circumstances as the preliminaries to the main event under the headings of the "motivating argument" and "initiation practices."

The Motivating Argument

The question in epistemology (in fact the only question) is that of certainty. How do we know that we know? The standard answer to this question has been the progressive development of Baconian empiricism and Cartesian rationality. Empiricism, it has been argued, provides us with a foundation of incorruptible evidence. Rationality provides a correctable method of applying that evidence to a conclusion. The scientific method, in fact all proper epistemology within this argument, is seen as a combination of good empirical protocols of evidence gathering and the right canons of logic in claim.

Certitude is assured in this argument because our experience is wholly trustworthy and ultimately gives itself up to one and only one claim through logical reasoning. Powered by the successes of Newtonian and Darwinian science, this argument flourished in the 19th century and dominated the epistemology of the 20th, peaking about midcentury.

There were a number of reasons for its subsequent decline. The mechanical insights of Newtonian physics provided unsatisfactory answers to the questions of the 20th century. The human sciences could not be contained in the physical science model and failed to coalesce around a common epistemology. The trustworthiness of experience was undermined in studies on perception, the mind, culture, and language. Our observational evidence was shown to be corrupted by our theories. Theory itself was shown to be better explained by sociological rather than evidentiary practices. And the evidence we did generate was shown to be promiscuous rather than faithful. The conclusions are stunning: observations are arguments, theories are sociopolitical practices, and truth is plural. There is certitude only in political action (science as well as all other forms of scholarship is as political as the Democratic Party). Teaching theory is an act of indoctrination and theory texts are ideological documents.

Thump! How far we have fallen. A person might protest, "But I don't believe any of that. I believe that valid observations are reliable, that such observations do decide between opposing positions, that language can be literally representative, that claim can be objective, and that our science and scholarship is progressively better at approximating the true." Such is a person's right (particularly in a domain of plural truth), but can we avoid the insidious "Why?" Why, in the presence of now-legitimate alternatives, does one hold to an incorrigible empirical rationality? How is one justified in holding those beliefs? The questions do not imply change or a debilitating skepticism. They call for an explanation. It is this explanation of the quality and manner of the beliefs that are the foundation of our scholarship that motivates the rest of this effort.

Initiation Practices

When we examine the ordinary practices of undergraduate and graduate education, we see that most of us entered into the study of theory through a common hierarchy of events. Typically, we probably started on two curriculum paths called "theory" and "method." We first came to theory through normalized, textbook descriptions of generalized theory frames, most likely within some topical division (e.g., organizational communication or journalism). We probably learned them by their "ism"—cognitiv*ism*, behavior*ism*, functional*ism*, structural*ism*, interaction*ism*, and the like—if we were coming to theory through science.[4] What we were actually given, however, depended on when and where we were taught. There is simply too much to offer for any given time and place.

Usually at a slightly later date we were introduced to conventional methodologies: on the objectivist side, surveys, questionnaires, experiments, and behavioral coding, or, on the interpretivist side, life histories, participant observation, and long-term interviews (and in recent days maybe even some parts of both sets). As objectivism is surely more prevalent, we likely learned about operational definitions, variables, and constructs, as well as about causal, stochastic, and correlational relationships. Our first knowledge claim probably arose from a classroom exercise—usually a survey—designed to show that we knew how to use these methods.

In very deliberate and specific ways we were moved into a field of scholarship, the specific part of which was further bound by particular theoretical frames and conventional methods, within a disciplinary community. As budding theorists of whatever school, we learned the questions to ask and the ways to answer them; we learned the people to read and those to ignore; we learned what was *us* and what was *them*. We also learned that this is a world of limited resources and either our tolerance of others ought not to include our own decline lest our own investment be lost, or, on the other side of the ledger, our loyalties ought not to lead to our downfall.

The next two sections, discuss these techniques of investiture. My purpose is to point to a few of the practices by which we become naturalized citizens of some intellectual community. The writing is only a shadow of the robust sociological analysis possible and intends to open a small space for the rest of the chapters that follow.

Normalizing Texts

Assigned reading within a field is part of our investiture work. Most of what we read are examples of normalized science or other scholarship—science or scholarship written from well inside its paradigmatic boundaries. A published example of this sort, that makes use of a generalized cognitive theory, can be found in Badzinski (1991):

> In comprehending a narrative, an individual constructs a mental representation of the text by integrating explicit and implicit text concepts. Recognizing that the narrations often lend themselves to several plausible representations, vocal cues guide the processor in selecting which interpretation ought to be made. (p. 715)

Nearly every phrase in these two sentences invokes some theoretical notion. What are the actions of "comprehending," "constructing," "recognizing," "guiding," "selecting," and "interpreting," and what is the force of "ought to be made?" What are the objects of a narrative, individual, mental representation, text, explicit text concept, implicit text concept, narration, plausible representation, vocal cue, processor, and interpretation?

It is clear that these sentences cannot be read except from a position deep inside the general framework of cognitive theory. Badzinski's study (I presume) is motivated by an interest in children and stories. She needs no particular theory to pursue that interest, but can move forward from the prevalent understanding of how things work held by the community of cognitive theorists. Her writing necessarily positions the reader inside that understanding. It does not otherwise make sense.

Backgrounding. Even when particular theories do enter into the argument, they do so from a well-established foundation of general assumptions (background principles) that permit the particular theory to be advanced. Just to stay inside the cognitive arena, Eckhardt, Wood, and Jacobvitz (1991) make use of schema theory (their reference is Bloom, 1988) as a way of understanding the results they obtained in studying adults and film. But the introduction of this idea of mental templates that guide interpretation comes late in the article and is in no way necessary for what precedes it. What precedes it are the straightforward applications of the background principles of cognitivism.

My use of these studies implies no criticism of them, but rather is intended to demonstrate ways in which theoretical concepts appear within studies. In these examples, they do so in the taken-for-granted way that is characteristic of normalized scholarship. The reader must appropriate the same background assumptions as Badzinski or Eckhardt, Wood, and Jacobvitz in order to read either study sensibly. One is implicated as a cognitivist from the first sentence on.

Poaching. A similar collusion occurs with the technique of poaching. Poaching makes use of diverse, even contradictory, theories in order to advance a particular argument. The constructs are moved into the argument through what semioticians call "excorporation." Excorporation strips the term from its collective ownership—liberates it, if you will, from its characteristic invocations. The term, while echoing past service, can be put to radical and even subversive uses.

Cultural studies, for example, claims to be atheoretical, and at the same time encourages its members to use whatever theory works to advance the argument to be made (Grossberg, 1993b). This appropriation is often dedicated to the highest professional and emancipatory goals (you need to know it all in order to do good work). Again, however, the reader is ensnared in the actual (albeit denied as theoretical) premises that constitute what is recognizable as cultural studies.

Backgrounding and poaching work to achieve the same goal of acceptance from opposite directions. Backgrounding imposes an objectification upon theoretical constructs. They are "already known to be true" and are not recognizable as theoretical. Poaching problematizes theoretical constructs, while hiding its own, in order that the meaning values of the appropriated concepts can be constructed on the site of the argument. In poaching, theoretical constructs are "custom-made to be true."

Backgrounding and poaching may appear to be faults in a truth-seeking system, but they are simply ways by which arguments can be normalized. And they are necessary ways at that, a point we will take up more than once in later chapters on the justified and the practical argument. Suffice it to say here that all scholarship moves as quickly as possible to normalize its arguments, must promote arguments from some background, and poaches where it can't create or where it anticipates its opposition.

Theory as Practice

Normalizing does, however, deeply complicate the study of theory. Our analysis calls on us to recognize that theory is not only a set of textual propositions so nominated, but the ongoing practices of intellectual communities. Cognitive theory is the work done in its name by members who would call themselves and be recognized as cognitive theorists and scholars. There are textual products of this work, but they are, at best, only markers of the work done.

The pernicious idea that theory can be read instead of practiced is, at least in part, a legacy of the positivist's project. That project intended to show the separation between statements of theory and observation. Most agree that that project failed and that proposition and practice are inextricably intertwined. Theory, then, describes a particular practice of scholarship incorporating leading figures, scriptural texts, characteristic claims, conventional methods, typical performances, and practicing members.

Essentializing descriptions, of the sort we read in undergraduate textbooks, are part of the normalizing process, tidying things up by sorting claims and people and then declaring what they are. What is hidden, of course, is the essentializing effort. Theory is messy, temporizing work in an ongoing struggle to gain mastery and suppress uncertainty. If we were to begin our study of theory at the level of descriptions, we would have come to the show for the closing credits.

Indoctrinating Methods

Our research methods courses indoctrinate us in equally subtle ways. Most research methods classes are engaged entirely on the practical level. At this level students may be asked to give answers such as: "The first four elements in the analysis of a text are structure, synonyms, names and titles, and transitions" (adapted from Cheney & Tompkins, 1988). Or: "The social situation is defined by actors, activities, and place (adapted from Spradley, 1980). Or: "Three methods of measuring attitudes are the adjective check list, the semantic differential, and the equal interval scale" (adapted from Kerlinger, 1973). In learning to give such answers, students can reproduce the methods but not the implications of Burkean, ethnographic, and quantitative analysis, respectively.

By investing themselves in a set of practical activities students are also immersed, often without their informed consent, in a particular way of thinking. (The ethical implications of "required" methods courses is especially interesting from this perspective.)

That "particular way of thinking" does important work. Conventionalized methods are one way of setting paradigmatic boundaries. A paradigm is a large epistemic area (generally cosmological) that contains disciplinary communities bound by a common language, beliefs, and practices. Conventionalized methods are a good part of those practices and contribute as well to the common language and beliefs. One's methods, therefore, mark the individual in definable terms. And, as with most ideological definitions, it happens prior to its recognition and without defense.

The study of methods not only inducts the student into an ideology of scholarship but also into specific theory domains. There is a symbiotic relationship between theory and method. But the relationship is rarely at the level of what we might call name-brand theories. Methods become conventionalized because they support active theory families of the same epistemic genealogy.

Such theory families form a generalized theory domain in which the various members appear to be different and may even compete with one another, but, in fact, have the same foundational belief. In the family tree of cognitivism, for example, we find the branches of belief theory, attitude theory, attribution theory, knowledge acquisition theory (e.g., cognitive mapping), and schema theory.

The branches are not interchangeable, but they are bound by a common dependency on persistent mentalist states, which are the product of experience but remain malleable, and which can be objectively measured because they are the agents of action. If one just says "No" to the notion of persistent mental states predicting behavior, one rejects the entire cognitivist enterprise and steps out of the cognitivist paradigm.

One also leaves behind the methods of attitude testing, opinion polling, personality measurement, value inventories, schemata diagrams and cognitive maps. It makes no sense to test a mental state (e.g., attitude, opinion, personality, value, schema, or cognitive proposition) unless one accepts the generalized epistemological position by which mental states are ontologically constructed and become the explanation for the results. On the other hand, if all that is taught is the testing of mental states, students become paradigmatically invested while being assured that it is only a methods course.

Hierarchical Structure of Knowledge

Our typical initiation processes that the novitiate into the smallest venue of knowledge production. As beginners we focus on a set of practices that when properly reproduced will generate acceptable claim. It is nearly a mechanical effort because the set of methods we learn produces knowledge primarily as the product of a hierarchy of assumptive frames. That hierarchy produces all but the smallest past of this claim.

Let's take an inventory of the hierarchical components we have seen. We have talked about sets of *conventionalized methods* that legitimize certain constructs and relationships; *bounded theoretical frames* (behaviorism, cognitivism, semiotics), which in turn support specific "brand-name" theories; *disciplinary communities* (communication, language and literature, sociology) in which scholarship is materialized; *paradigms* (objective empiricism, cultural studies) that incorporate methods, frames, fields, and parts of communities, and *scholarship fields* (science, literature, criticism) from which paradigms arise and are exported. To this list we need to add the concept of *episteme*.

The Episteme

The episteme is the epistemological epoch that characterizes the intellectual activity in which our particular part falls—for example, Western scholarship is an episteme. The episteme provides for both the dominant and the subordinate, the proclaimed and its contradictions, the unities and the differences.[5] The episteme makes sense out of the local alliances and oppositions between and within fields and paradigms in the same way that capitalism makes sense out of corporate mergers and competitions.

Foucault, who is credited with coining the term (Gutting, 1989), calls our present understanding "the episteme of the individual" (Foucault, 1970). From the Cartesian intellect to methodological individualism to the search for the fundamental building blocks of matter—all scholarship is defined in or against that term.

The "modern episteme," which is said to cover the last 200 years, represents the currently discoverable universe of intellectual activity. (The term "discoverable" includes all the "hiddenness" of past and future epistemes as well as oppositional potentials that reside within the episteme.) For our purposes, the episteme is an additional device that allows us to investigate the world of knowledge and inquiry as one composed of entities in varying relationships.

A Dialectical Structure

As theorists, we are part of a larger structure that accommodates all forms of opposition and complementarity, the authenticated and the dismissed, the nominated and the exnominated. Knowledge is produced in an economy of the true and the false. Who we are is defined in the dialectic of who we are not. Both are required. We cannot understand a paradigm, discipline, or particular theory without investigating what it opposes, excludes, denies, or suppresses. Indeed, the domains of scholarship, arts and letters, sciences, and professions are more easily understood in their demarcations from one another than they are in the profusion of differences that are held within their respective boundaries.

As an example, questions of fact are naturalized within the empirical domain of science and questions of interpretation are naturalized within the hermeneutic domain of letters, despite the postmodern movement of hybrid (or bastardized) forms. Crossover attempts such as quantified content analysis posing as criticism or interpretation masquerading as the empirical are not sustained. One cannot in an unnoted manner ask anything anywhere. Location in this system of knowledge production facilitates some and inhibits other questions, methods, and claims.

Ideological Identities

The value of this ideological analysis is to allow us to see the sociological structure of knowledge as a system of constructed identities and patrolled differences. Any form of scholarship must work to achieve sufficient internal coherence to distinguish itself from other forms. A part of all scholarship works just to establish its collective identity and difference.

That work of achieving identity and difference extends across fields, paradigms, disciplinary communities, frames of theory, and conventional methods. At each level we account for ourselves and for the other. I work, for example, as a scientist, of the small science sort, who also holds an oppositional stance vis-à-vis some aspects (determinism and objectivism) of the dominant paradigm of small science within a disciplinary community, which is only partially defined by science, from a social action frame of theory (part of the trunk of interactionism), which has a history of difference, using conventional methods of ethnography redefined from its objectivist parentage (radical hermeneutics).

To do that work well, I need to know how interpretive ethnography differs from traditional ethnography and how ethnography differs from variable analytic approaches; how social action theories hang together and differ from behaviorism, cognitivism, functionalism, and the others; how communication marks science in the journals and publishers for which I write; how the practices of the dominant paradigm of small science create its dominance (ours is a Hegelian relationship); how small science differs from big science; how science differs from criticism and everything else; and finally how science and criticism (and the rest) are part of the same intellectual universe. Those requirements define more than a lifetime.

They also define more than a book can possibly accomplish. We cannot, therefore, be fixed on a destination but rather must attend to enjoying the journey. Our first step—and our next chapter—concerns the conceptualization of reality.

NOTES

1. Notes do much of this work. There are four kinds of notes in use: reference, elaboration, exegesis, and reflexive. The latter three either advance or comment upon the text.

2. In this regard I have found the example Terry Eagleton provides in *Literary Theory* to be invaluable. Eagleton presents the alternate forms of literary theory in a manner that allows but does not require his conclusion. The rejection of logocentrism—that there is something out there that governs description—means that any description—or rejection of a description—is rhetorical.

3. Note the implicit values attached to postmodernist and modernist. This bit of characterizing may be just a disguise for incompetent writing but actually is written in response to a reviewer who suggested that I rewrite to put the reader "in my pocket." She or he noted the fact that I didn't as a failure; I count it as a success.

4. If you came to theory through literature, you may have learned of New Criticism, Marxist analysis, reader criticism, or reception theory. The role of theory is much the

same throughout scholarly venues: to provide a field of understanding from which to justify methods of study and to advance claims.

5. For example, my study of the history of the human sciences suggests that themes of theory seem to have a center-stage life of 3–4 decades (Leahey, 1994, is a standard historical treatment). Hebb declared cognitivism as the second American Revolution in 1960, although Tolman's (1930) field theory was present some 30 years earlier. In 1995 cognitivism's decline was noted by Waldron. Cognitivism never reached the paradigmatic level in which all others were muted, but it was the most likely psychology of the 1960s and 1970s. (I use it often as an example in this book because its methodologies of attitudes, opinions, values, and other mentalisms are so well known.) One implication of the life cycle of theories is that a practitioner can expect at least one major transition in scholarship over the duration of a career. That transition is signaled by the shift of editors, reviewers, funding agencies, and other points of resource control, as well as by the enthusiasms of students and others on the cutting edge.

CHAPTER 2

THE NATURE
OF THE PHENOMENAL WORLD

INTRODUCTION

The road to Delphi passes through a country side startlingly reminiscent of southeastern Utah. The hills are sparsely covered with small evergreens and the yellow soil shows through. It is a pleasant contrast, but not one I would have expected from my childhood readings of Greek mythology. The location of the spring at Delphi where the oracle gave her pronouncements is now uncertain. What are clearly left to view are the treasuries, monuments, temples, and shops that archive a particular worldview.

Delphi records a worldview where lives were governed by the whims and wishes of divine personages whose own way of being-in-the-world was marked as much by lust and deceit as by honor and wisdom. The oracle was the telepath between the divine community and its human consequence. The messages from the divine about what the Fates commanded and the gods did muddle were never clear. They had to be interpreted, at some point of understanding, when the events made their meaning apparent. Lucky the person who could understand them early enough to profit from their prediction.

Nevertheless, a good number of petitioners must have—sometimes in spectacular ways—given the many monumental testaments of thanks that cover the temple grounds. Delphi represented a whole science—a whole way of knowing—that existed to control a very uncertain world. The methods and texts of Delphi were not unsophisticated, simplistic, or childish; instead, they were elegant and insightful. But from our vantage point they were also wrong.

They were wrong because they were driven by a view of willful, contingent, case-by-case decisions disrupting whatever order could be found in the phenomenal world. As long as the gods provided the final answer, one could not recognize the patterns of regularities upon which one could depend.

This worldview came to an end with the decline of Greco–Roman society, the rise of Christianity, and the earthquake of 451 A.D. that destroyed its infrastructure. But it would take Western civilization nearly one thousand years to learn to describe the phenomenal world in radically different terms. The revolution of the scientific revolution was not a method of study or a set of discoveries but the centering of a way of thinking, present even in classical times, that saw the phenomenal world as material, determinant, and ordered by lawlike regularities. No more cowboy interventionism. If it rained on your parade, it did so because of the confluence of different weather systems, not the disfavor of the gods. (But, perhaps, there's a prayer or two left for good weather.)

The vision of a material, determinant, and dependable phenomenal world has been quite productive. It led us from implication and divination to a rock-solid empiricism in which the real was palpable, not spiritual. That rock of material empiricism, however, has never stood alone on the epistemic plane and, moreover, the 20th century has withstood its rapid erosion.

This chapter explores the underlying assumptions concerning the nature of the world outside the conscious mind as it presents itself as an object of inquiry. The continuum of the discussion lies somewhere between an "actual world" wholly outside the conscious mind, the proper engagement of which will *validate* a line of inquiry, and a "virtual reality" which is a construction of our perceptions, the existence of which is *a result* of a line of inquiry. Further discussion centers on the criterion of the real, the natural or constructed boundaries of phenomena, the domain or domains of phenomena, the relatedness of phenomena, and the nature of those relationships.

To set the stage for this discussion, I would like to draw out the worldviews of two contrasting knowledge practices, those of objective empiricism and hermeneutic empiricism. Both of these positions direct broad-scale programs of inquiry including the scientific and the critical, but they both start and end in very different places.[1]

The First Example: Objective Empiricism

Objective empiricism typically assumes phenomena that are naturally configured, that are perceptually accessible but autonomous of the perception, and that reside in a stable network of relationships in which their characteristics and actions are dependent on other phenomena. Such phenomena are independent objects of analysis which become the subject of our claims. Our claims themselves are reported acts of discovery, which is to say that they accurately describe objects and relationships that are independent of both the discovering observations and the reported claims.

Empiricism of this sort is often materialist or at least holds to a materialist criterion for evaluating claims. Materialism advances solid material bodies as the premier exemplar of the real. Materialists argue that as we move the foci of inquiry away from such bodies, as we do in theoretical physics or in cognitive psychology or in the analysis of meaning, we move further from the analysis of the real. As we move from the real, we lose our ability to empirically validate claim, for there is "nothing out there" that can prove the argument. Arguments over immaterial entities such as attitudes, values, schemata, and authorial intentions are a return to the abuses of Scholasticism, materialists claim (Popper, 1972).

Objective empiricism is usually coupled with reductionism. Reductionism appears in any argument in which one thing reduces to (i.e., is explained or validated by) something else as in these three examples: (1) surface manifestations reduce to a lawlike regularity, (2) the meaning field of a text reduces to authorial intent, and (3) theoretical terms reduce to empirical entities. Reductionism, when applied to knowledge fields, holds that at base there is a single knowledge field (usually physics) to which all others ultimately reduce. (A typical reduction would argue that all the arts and professions reduce to sociology, sociology reduces to biology, biology reduces to chemistry, and chemistry reduces to physics.)

Reductionism is the foundation for the unity-of-science hypothesis. This hypothesis states the belief that all science shares common methods of achieving reliable observation and producing valid claim so that both observation and claim are transportable across knowledge fields. Joseph Hanna (1991) gives us a good description of the effect of this belief when he writes:

> The goal of science is to develop representations of the empirical world that enable us to explain and predict phenomena that are of interest, whether they lie in the domain of physics, biology, psychology, sociology or communication science. Simply stated, the aim of empirical science is to provide objective information about the world. (p. 202)

Reductionism and the unity-of-science hypothesis both depend on a belief in the unity of the phenomenal world. This belief holds that all phenomena—anything that is the proper object of inquiry—have the same foundations. For example, the thought in my head that leads to this sentence can be claimed to be an energy state (called thinking) in the same way that the collected particles of carbon that form the letters on this page are an energy state (called printing). A full understanding of energy and the states it can take (matter, here, is thought of as compacted energy) will lead to understanding both print and thought.

Finally, objective empiricism may also be coupled with determinism. A very early determinist (and anti-Delphian), Leucippus (c. 430 B.C.) states the case in *The Great World-Order*: "Nothing happens at random; everything happens out of reason and by necessity" (Freeman, 1948, p. 91). Material determinism expresses the worldview that all real phenomena reside in causal chains. Each phenomenon is both a consequent of some prior phenomenon and the agent of some subsequent one.[2] Determinism works to exclude explanations based on chance, fate, or choice from the pantheon of valid claim.[3]

A material, independent, determined, and unified world of phenomena provides the axiomatic support for the image of objective science progressing through increasingly perfected approximations of the invariant conditions that govern this world. Theoretically, in this world, there is a point where the practice of science disappears as it is replaced by codified knowledge (i.e., science is no longer the practice of discovery but the reproduction of what is already known).

The Second Example: Hermeneutic Empiricism

A potentially quite different picture of the phenomenal world is drawn from the axiomatic assumptions that support hermeneutic empiricism. Hermeneutic empiricism assumes a world of multiple domains of phenomena with no common foundation. Human engagement of the phenomenal world occurs across these multiple domains. A typical formulation (further developed near the end of this chapter) would recognize us to be first of all material entities in a physical world, but also living organisms giving expression to the principles of animation and sentience, and finally the creators and inhabitants of the domain of the sign.

The assumption of multiple domains, however formulated, strikes at the ideas of a common foundation for all phenomena, reductionism, and the unity-of-science hypothesis. Taking these in reverse order, hermeneutic empiricism gives over the domain of material phenomena to physics and chemistry, gives over the domain of animation and sentience to biological studies, and retains for itself the domain of signification and meaning. The unity of science is rejected because perfect knowledge in one domain does little to advance knowledge in another. (It's a nice move because the only place physics, chemistry, biology, and psychology can be understood is within the domain of signification and meaning.)

Reductionism is often replaced by what is sometimes called "downward causation." In the order of the material, biological, and semiotic domains, the material must precede in time the biological and semiotic and the biological must precede the semiotic, but the semiotic is the basis for understanding both the material and the biological. The material and biological are brought into being as fields of knowledge after the creation of the semiotic.

Further, in reductionism, subsequent fields (chemistry, biology, etc.) are theorem branches of the same axiomatic trunk (physics). In the downward causation formulation of multiple domains, the subsequent domain accepts the axioms of the previous one but introduces irreducible axioms of its own. To put a fine point on it, one cannot understand "significance and meaning" from the field of physics but one can understand "the material" from the field of semiotics.

A much less hierarchical way of looking at multiple domains is simply to postulate them as relatively autonomous fields of knowledge production, all of which contribute to the lives that can be lived. As material, biological, and semiotic entities we are the intersection of these three domains and give concrete expression of them in our daily affairs. Physics as a set of claims, however, does not "speak" to communication as a set of claims, although it would as a political action in, for example, the arena of science funding.

Finally, the notion of a common foundation of phenomena is generally abandoned. Semiotic phenomena are held to be fundamentally different from both the material and the biological. As Popper (Popper & Eccles, 1977) puts it, "Matter can . . . transcend itself, by producing mind, purpose and a world of the products of the human mind" (p. 11). "The products of the human mind," the proper objects of hermeneutic analysis, represent, then, real phenomena of a different sort in no way identical to the biological, electrochemical processes that support them. One may, for example, discover how memory works by studying large protein molecules, but one will not consequently discover the stuff of memories (Hess, 1988).

It is in the domain of the sign where hermeneutic empiricism generally finds its targeted phenomena. These phenomena are, at least in part, a human construction, ontologically dependent on the perspective of their engagement, and reside in ad hoc relationships whose effectiveness is defined in terms of human achievement. Hermeneutic empiricism places an interpretive accomplishment between the object of analysis and the subject of the claim. Claim itself does a variety of political works including that political work which sets the conditions by which the claim can achieve acceptance as true.

The phenomenal world of hermeneutic empiricism incorporates the material, independent, determined, and unified products of the "Big Bang" with the significant, complicitous, improvisational, and localized products of collective human accomplishment. It is a world of material facts and interpretive achievements made meaningful in human action. Claim is a truth-making performance and science is part of the action.

A Close Reading of the Pivotal Issues

Four issues have been raised in this comparison that every scholar must resolve either intentionally or by default. They are (1) the criterion of the real, (2) the unity of the phenomenal world (and of its fields of study), (3) causality and agency, and (4) constructionism in reality and knowledge. We shall take them up in that order.

THE CRITERION OF THE REAL

What is real? Looking to the field of communication studies we might wonder: Is public opinion real or is it an artifact of polling procedures? Are schemata real or are they merely devices of theory? Is the bond of friendship real or is it the product of romantic myth? Is gender real? Is there really violence on television?

The question of what is real has hundreds of answers that help to define a wide variety of answer givers. A casual review would offer up the communities of realism, idealism, nominalism, naive empiricism, Berkeleyism, Kantianism, existentialism, phenomenology, contemporary empiricism, and hermeneutics, as well as semiotics. We can do little more in this section than to lay out a few of the principle lines of argument.

The question itself arises because we know we can be both wrong in our perceptions and imaginative in our thinking. (Of the two, the latter is both the source of and the central threat to valid claim.) Because I know I can be in error as to what is real, I am forced to consider how I know when I am not in error.

The Materialist Solution

The most popular solution has been the materialist criterion. The materialist criterion begins axiomatically with the claim that matter exists.[4] The matter that I indisputably know to exist is that which I can encounter through my own materiality. I can bump into it, walk around it, pick it up, feel its weight. Such objects are material like I am material. Further, I must materially account for them. I cannot pass through the tree in my path no matter how I construct its image or by what language I recognize its presence.

Simple materialism of this sort runs into difficulty when we begin to extend the domain of the real to things with which I have only the slightest contact. Consider stars which I can encounter directly only as pinpoints of light or other things which I can encounter only through some form of instrumentation.

What is the materiality of an "ideological stance," a "media gratification," or a "personality characteristic"? I cannot hold such things in my hand. I can see them only through some frame of analysis or measurement technique. George Gale (1979) offers a reasonably direct test: objects are real if "they interact with and thus share the same world with us" (p. x). (Gale, of course, is trying to solve the problem of how to understand atomic particle traces in a cloud chamber, so his correspondence would depend upon some rule that connects those "products of the mind" with some physical state of the body.)

Ideological stances, gratifications, and personality characteristics are thus conjectures that can be reasonably held as real because we can establish conditions where we expect them to interact with that portion of the material world that we can engage directly (in, say, a line of material action, the presence of a material body in front of a television set, a pattern of material behavior). They remain, nonetheless, conjectures whose status in the real is provisional until the weight of the evidence is such that we would appear foolish to deny that status.

The hinge on which this argument hangs is our ability to establish conditions that necessarily mark their appearance. We may not be able to find alternate explanations for cloud chamber traces, but there may be many alternatives for how we understand check marks on a page of an opinion survey. Those alternatives coupled with our inability to point to unique physical states that define mental products can do much to undermine the material standing of such concepts as public opinion.

Several methods are used to deal with this uncertainty. In the social sciences, the most common method is an appeal to operationalism (Bridgeman, 1927). Operationalism has as its center the operational definition. An object *is* operationally defined according to the method of its measurement. The material reality of a gratification, then, *is* precisely the check marks on a test of gratifications and that of a personality characteristic is precisely the score on items within a personality test. The notion of an "ideological stance" is, of course, a critical notion and not one (as yet) taken up in science. But an analogous test is used in that the presence of an ideological stance is materialized in the formulation of the argument about its interpretation (Hirsch, 1967). It becomes authentic when that argument can be materially produced. (Consider "ideological stance" operationally defined as a set of material, discursive practices of argument.)

Operationalism and its critical counterpart, however, leave us wanting more. A colleague of mine once reported a paper entitled "Physiological Correlates of Attention" in which he related changes in electrical potentials to the appearance of attention devices in a televised segment. One of the Swiss members of the conference asked him how he knew those changes were changes in attention. He replied in true Bridgeman fashion that he did not care whether it was attention or not. What mattered was that the dials changed. The material facts of his study were those dial changes. One wonders why he did not call his paper "The Physiological Correlates of Dial Changes."

I suspect we know the answer. A personality is not the sum of a set of scores nor is an ideological stance its argument, and neither would we be very interested in a paper that purported to be merely about dial changes. Our interest is kindled because these operations "stand for" the material reality of the larger construct. We are, nonetheless, never far removed from the tautology of operationalism—call them whatever you like, dial changes are still dial changes and may be nothing more.

Ethnography faces a similar problem (Jarvie, 1986). Let's assume we are interested in empowerment in organizations.[5] Our problem is to document ethnographically the material practices of empowerment, but how will we know them? Clearly, the only way out of this problem is to assume that the material practices that we do document become the material reality of empowerment in that organization.

The weakness of operationalism and its ethnographic and critical analogies is that these solutions do not independently verify the material reality of what we really want to talk about. The conventions of methodology or discursive form are accelerated to a claim about the real.

Nonetheless, the operational definition, the authentic argument, and the documentation of material practices do present a reality test of some sort. All must conform to professional practices and can be critically assessed in that performance. This conformation may be all that we can hope for as we leave the domain of acts we can observe and objects we can handle to enter the domain of the mind.

The Problem of the Domain of the Mind

Materialism is most forceful in it appearance as a demarcation of science. Science is a "natural epistemology" useful for explaining the material. (Scientism would go on to claim that nothing else is useful epistemologically.) Realms of inquiry that want to wear the badge of science need to pledge their rejection of the nonmaterial.

This pledge, however, becomes quite burdensome if the common topics of one's study are group dynamics, relationships, meaning, cognitive structures, and the like. We are, in fact, quite unwilling to say that a friendship relationship is not real. We can see the obvious consequences of its existence in the actions of friends.[6] Where, then, does this relationship exist? For many, it exists as an element in the world of the transcendent human mind.

From Hume (skepticism) to Kant (transcendental idealism) to Husserl (transcendental phenomenology) to Peirce (semiotics), there have been lines of argument that sought to liberate the human mind from Locke's empirical prison. Locke (1690/1974) wrote that the human mind was a blank slate upon which experience traced its message. Genuine knowledge was empirical and *only* empirical. Hume (1748/1974) argued that the human mind offered devices of understanding of its own, for example, the idea of cause. Cause is not empirical but must be understood in the relationship between two empirical events. Kant (1781/1964) offered two intuitions (space and time) and 12 categories of a priori understanding (unity, plurality, totality, reality, negation, limitation, substantiality, causality, reciprocal action, possibility, existence, and necessity). For Husserl (1929/1964) all knowledge begins in experience but comes to its fruition in the eidetic, intentional grasp of human consciousness. Finally Peirce (c. 1897/1960) holds that the phenomenal world is understood in terms of a three-part relationship between the sign, its ideational object, and our recognition of the relationship between the two. It is the third of these elements that creates the unique field of human understanding.

All four of these positions—which are here gravely understated—lead to the same conclusion that the material world alone will not answer our questions (see Carruthers, 1992, for some of the current discussion). We must also understand human consciousness (Fuller, 1993b). Faced with the demand to enter the conscious realm, how do we maintain the materialist criterion of the real? We must necessarily give up this criterion when we reject the physicalist's claim that each conscious state is isomorphically related to a brain function.[7] That rejection is routine in studies admitting perceptual processes, holding to cognition, dependent on ideology, and the like (Anderson, 1994).[8] What, then, can we offer for a criterion of the real?

The Answer of Objectivism

Objectivism has been a typical substitution. Objectivism is a form of material realism that holds to an independent, determinant, and knowable world in which a clear distinction can be drawn between the object and an individual's cognitive grasp of it.[9] And while many who claim objective knowledge would disclaim a rigid materialism, none would deny objectivism's central claim that there is necessarily "some permanent, ahistorical matrix or framework to which we can ultimately appeal in determining the nature of rationality, knowledge, truth, reality, goodness, or rightness" (Bernstein, 1983, p. 8).

Objectivity derives from this philosophy. Objectivity refers to any set of practices in which the "effect of the subject"—the public consequence[10] of any particular mind in its particular time and place—is sought to be reduced. Objectivity depends on an independence between the (observing) subject and the object. What is true of the object is what remains after all "effects of the subject" have been removed. Objectivity is achieved when the focus of our inquiry is treated as an object with the same sort of "bump into it, walk around it, pick it up" reality of a brick.

The measure of objectivity is intersubjective agreement. Newell (1986) states the general case: "What makes a line of inquiry 'objective' is not the topics the inquiry is about, but the practices of adjudication and confirmation with which the inquiry is conducted. Objectivity becomes a product of proper method" (p. 27). Kerlinger (1973) more practically recommends that we "think of degrees of objectivity as degrees of extent of agreement among observers" (p. 492).

We can see the practical clarity of this criterion: if I am uncertain as to what I hear or see, I ask others what they hear or see. If they agree with my observations, I presume something is there to cause them. There are difficulties, of course (there are always difficulties). Not the least of these is the meaning of "agreement" when observers have been trained to hear or see in a particular way, which is the local case in any coding procedure and the general case in each tradition of scholarship. Has the training simply extended "the effect of a particular mind?"

Objectivity in the worlds of theoretical terms and critical texts (linguistic or behavioral) hangs on the doctrine of meaning realism. Meaning realism is little more than the concept of literal meaning—that this word (or picture, action, sound, etc.) in this location has this and only this meaning. Meaning realists such as John Reichert (1977), E. D. Hirsch Jr. (1967), Robert Bales (1951), or Bas van Fraassen (1980) hold that each word (or act) in the configuration of an unambiguous text refers to a single ideational object (by virtue of the determinants of behavior, the structure of language, or of the intent of the author, or of some other imperative; see Cummins, 1989; Harrison, 1991). For the meaning realist, this veridicality is the referential character of signs. In the case of scientific (and "competent" commonsense) terms for the phenomenal world, the ideational object is also an empirical object. This identity is the representational character of signs.

Meaning realism is the basis of any claim concerning the absolute character of content. Claims that a narrative is "violent," "pornographic," "informative," or "entertainment" are all realist claims because they are based solely on the characteristics of the content.

Meaning realism is also the underlying belief of all sign-based (language, pictures, etc.) objective tests. If the meaning of an item on such tests depends on the interpretation of the reader, then the value of the response is unknown, because the analyst cannot know to what ideation the reader is responding. Therefore, if the test is to be objective, its meaning cannot depend upon the reader.

Objectivism, as considered here, is an extension of the material criterion. Most excursions into the consciousness, including Freud's partitioned subject, Marx and Engels's dialectical materialism, Jung's archetypes, French and American cognitivism, as well as Althussar's ideology coupled with Gramsci's hegemony, retain the objectivist criterion. Autonomous and anonymous forces and conditions (not identifiable with any exclusive subjective act) work to produce a common human consciousness with particular expressions much like the genetic code produces different individuals of the same species.

Contemporary objectivism owes a significant debt to the positivists (particularly the logical positivists discussed in Chapter 3), but the two are not synonymous. Adherents of the varieties of objectivism do share a common belief that the part of the material universe that resides within the realm of unmediated human experience represents an epistemic primitive that is directly evident. But divisions begin almost immediately on such questions as: How large is the realm of unmediated human experience—does it include mental states (Hess, 1988; this reference and those that follow are exemplars of some answers)? What is the role of the a priori—what do we know before experience (Chisholm, 1982)? How does language affect what we experience (Hanson, 1958, 1972; Lewis, 1946)? How secure is the doctrine of meaning realism (Quine, 1953/1961/1980)?[11] The answers to these and other questions help create the variety of positions that we encounter in our journals and classrooms.

An Excursion into Objectivity and Subjectivity

Objectivity, as we have seen, is a protection against the biases of the individual.[12] It is the use of a collective defense against the "effect of the subject." Objectivity is best contrasted with idiosyncracy (or solipsis) rather than with subjectivity. Subjectivity is also a collective enterprise that involves the invocation of a subjective stance. The subjective stance is a matrix of collective accomplishments that establish the reality substrata upon which particular truth claims can be rested. Individual claim makers speak from this foundation, but their work is collectively authenticated and is not idiosyncratic. Subjectivity, then, is not the same as the "effect of the subject."

I hope to point out the important differences among objectivity, subjectivity, and the effect of the subject with the use of the following example. I have constructed this example from two positions critical theorists adopt when attempting to deal with the issue of the possibility of multiple and conflicting interpretations of a text. Let us begin with John Reichert. Reichert (1977) argues the objectivist position in claiming that "when two interpretations of a work are actually in conflict with each other, either the work is fundamentally ambiguous or at least one interpretation is wrong" (p. 26).

For Reichert, an interpretation is a statement of the meaning of a text, and the meaning of the text is a factual consequence of the manner of its encoding. The analysis of meaning is directed objectively by the characteristics of the text. Multiple interpretations at odds with each other but nonetheless valid can arise only from a text that itself is similarly conflicted. Reichert's text is an object of criticism. Criticism is that object revealed. This sort of criticism is called "logocentric" (Derrida, 1972).

Paul Armstrong (1990) argues a different theoretical position. He states that a text is never autonomous, never the master of its own interpretation. Instead, it is heteronomous—a bounded field "of different possible meanings each correlated to a particular method of interpretation" (p. 22). There are, then, facts of the text that are the object of interpretation. Nevertheless, "texts are nothing more than objects of actual or possible interpretations. Anyone who searches for the 'text itself' will find a never-ending series of construals of it" (p. 23). This sort of criticism is called "hermeneutic" (Gadamar, 1960/1989).

These two positions exemplify the contrasting states of objectivity, subjectivity, and idiosyncracy. Objectivity in interpretation is achieved in Reichert's scheme when said interpretation is true to the text. The text is the object and the criterion of interpretation. Idiosyncracy occurs when the critic substitutes his or her own interpretation undisciplined or improperly disciplined by the facts of the case.[13]

Subjectivity occurs when the text is the subject of interpretation and brought into meaningfulness through a particular interpretive method, itself made sensible in the matrix of reality accomplishments (the subjective stance). The valid interpretation is true to its method and matrix. An idiosyncratic approach is one that cannot be recognized as competent criticism (i.e., one that has no professional identity).

Do objectivism and subjectivism conflict? They do, but not as opposites (one can give up objectivity without taking on subjectivity).[14] Both objectivity and subjectivity admit to the same textual facts—this word rather than that word, this pictorial component rather than that one. Objectivism claims that these facts are *determinants* of all valid denotative meaning revealed by the textual object itself; subjectivism claims that they are the *resource* of a valid meaning revealed from a given subjectivity.

Objectivism seeks to treat nonmaterial entities as objects with the same autonomous, corrective status as our aforementioned brick. Objectivity comprises the practices that allow us to do that. The arguments from subjectivity hold that any objective fact is produced through consensual achievement. Facts are the product of cultural and sociological processes, not a reading of their essential character. Objectivity, from subjectivism, is a particular subjective stance that seeks to hide the considerable efforts by which its claims can be made true.

Summary of the Objectivist Criterion of the Real

We have now arrived at the set of assumptions about the real that dominates the major portion of work in communication (some 60% by some estimates): (1) There is an independent and singular material world that gives rise to physical and ideational phenomena that are naturally defined. (Example: Public opinion is the set of attitudinal positions held by individuals in a society.) (2) These phenomena are autonomous and ahistorical in their reality. (Example: Public opinion as a phenomenon exists even in the absence of public opinion theory and has existed since the genetic moment of human cognition that provided for it.) (3) The objects and entities of this material world exist in determinant relationships that persist across time and place. (Example: Attitudes are a product of human cognition, and attitudinal positions are the results of socialization processes and media messages.) (4) Language (as well as any unambiguous sign) is *in itself* referential and its references to phenomena can be traced. (Example: The word *attitude* has as its reference an actual cognitive state that itself is the result of an actual physical state.) (5) Further, language (or any sign usage) can be representational in that its points of reference can be used to map the characteristics of objects and entities. (Example: The public opinion measured in polls exists as an independent entity in society.)

Hermeneutic Solutions

The enormous success of the physical sciences, which took the human domain from the energy of fire and the power of draft animals to atomic energy and the power of artificial intelligence in less than 500 years, created a dominant model for all forms of inquiry. The presuppositions of materialism, determinism, and objectivism became the foundational claims of rigor and validity. Throughout, however, there has been a persistent resistance to scientism (the claim that all knowledge is scientific knowledge). That resistance has increasingly focused on "establishment" science in the realm of human affairs.[15]

For our purposes, I have gathered these various forms of resistance under the single heading of "hermeneutics." Hermeneutics is the practice and study of interpretation. Hermeneutic approaches in inquiry have some fundamental dependence on interpretation within its "what" (existence), "why" (causation), "how" (practice), or "value" (ethics) claims. In this section we are concerned with the presence of interpretation in existence claims and the criteria of the real that result.

The General Form

The first move of the general form is to separate the material from the social, and then to realize that in the social reality is a conferred status. Weber (1903/1949) states that the culture of social life "is a finite segment of the meaningless infinity of the world process, a segment on which *human beings* confer meaning and significance" (p. 81). What becomes real, then—in the sense that it can be known—requires an interpretive act that punctuates the infinite process that will become our history. That interpretive act creates the "data"—the objectified elements of the social world—we consider to be real.

This move declares the real to be dependent on the particular cultural strategies that constitute the social life in which their reality may appear. We have now rejected a singular, independent, and autonomous reality as the object of our study and substituted a multiple, contingent, and subjugated reality in its stead from which multiple, contingent, and subjugated epistemologies must result. "Multiple," in that sentence, references the separation of the material from the social—one does not explain the other; "contingent" recognizes the historicity of reality—its production in the here and now; and "subjugated" notes the dependence of the real on human accomplishment.

The second move positions the understanding of human behavior as a communal achievement founded in communication practices and full of significance. It is a move that denies both an unmediated engagement of the phenomenal world (it is, rather, managed through language) and any mechanical configuration of human action (it is, rather, the meaningful products of human agency). Bakhtin (1986) captures the notion in a two-line statement: "The human sciences—sciences of the spirit—are philological sciences (as part of and at the same time common to all of them—the word)" (p. 161).

The third move is the recognition of the participation of the activity of inquiry per se in what we consider to be real. To quote Weber again:

> All knowledge of cultural reality, as may be seen, is always knowledge from *particular points of view*. When we require from the historian and social research worker as an elementary presupposition that they distinguish the

> important from the trivial and that they should have the necessary "point of view" for this distinction, we mean that they must understand how to relate the events of the real [material] world consciously or unconsciously to universal "cultural values" and to select out those relationships which are significant for us. (pp. 81–82)

We will come to know, then, whatever multiple, contingent, and subjugated reality that is held in place through social processes *subjectively* (embedded in the active matrix of reality constructions) in the collective processes of inquiry and in the private processes of personal experience. The point at which the real becomes the real is the vantage of its declaration (Johnson, Dandeker, & Ashworth, 1984). Further, that point is an actual, historical point, fully locatable. At this point, we deny the possibility of ahistorical, objective social knowledge. Social knowledge is local and culturally particular, although the cultural locale may be very large.

The final move is more contemporary. It is the claim that inquiry is part of the practice by which the real becomes the real. In most cases, this practice is reactionary in that it serves to maintain what we already know to be true and thereby retain its position in the social structure to which it contributes. Foucault (1987) argues what must be done to move inquiry from the reactionary mode to enlightenment:

> This work done at the limits of ourselves must, on the one hand, open up a realm of historical inquiry and, on the other, put itself to the test of reality, cf contemporary reality, both to grasp the points where change is possible and desirable, and to determine the precise form this change should take. (p. 171)

Here the analyst is more than a discoverer; she is an agent of emancipation. Reality is no longer anonymous. It is the collection of signature products that result—for Foucault—from power relationships, but for Wittgenstein from living action.

This fourth principle of hermeneutic reality states that those of us in the profession of inquiry make choices as to the reality we both serve and study. But the signature on the bottom line is not personal: instead, it is collective. Private choices are always trivial (although they may be made into something). Personal choices of an empowered member of a strategic collective may be positioned to account for the choices of others both within the collective and beyond it. Both the empowerment and the consequence are collective enterprises.

A Word about Interpretation

The epistemological significance of interpretation is simply that it is a human accomplishment. By that I mean that once it is agreed that a human achievement participates in reality, the essential break with foundational empiricism has been made. It is on this essential characteristic that I justify the global use of the term.

There is substantial disagreement over the character of this achievement, ranging from the deep, transcendental certitude available in Husserl, Hegel, and Polanyi to the contingent struggle of James, Wittgenstein, and Derrida. This disagreement has collective, temporal, and closure dimensions we shall visit as we go along.

Hermeneutic Varieties

The reach of a hermeneutic net defined by some dependency on interpretation in any of the what, why, how, or value claims is quite wide. Not all the fish enmeshed will even be fish. One or two of the principles may be suppressed, and differences will occur within the principles. Variations will occur across the scale of the collective action required for reality production (e.g., from all members of a language community to a work group in an organization), the transcendence of significance (e.g., the stretch between Whorfian structuralism and Barthean floating signifiers), the scope of subjectivity (e.g., the critical community, all New Critics, the positioned critic per se), and the culpability of participation (e.g., people who study racial differences reflect racism, maintain racism, advance racism, are unwittingly racist).[16]

Name-brand varieties (following in part Schoening, 1992) would include (references are to contemporary exemplars): phenomenology (Lanigan, 1992), hermeneutics (Caputo, 1987), pragmatism (Rorty, 1982), social theory (Giddens, 1984), cultural studies (Williams, 1981), interpretive sociology (de Certeau, 1984), language theory (Jameson, 1972), feminism (Harding, 1986), social semiotics (Barthes, 1974), social action theory (Taylor, 1986), and a growing number of combinations. With this very large number of interpretive communities, names are contentious, border patrol is hopeless, and crossovers continuous. Members, however, often see real differences.

Summary of the Hermeneutic Criterion of the Real

The hermeneutic reality criterion can be summarized as: (1) The "real" of social life transcends—but does not deny—the material and is the product of the human mind in collective action. The "real" requires some set of material practices for its production and for recognition as the real. (Public opinion can be seen as the joint production of public opinion polls—which define what is the opinion and who is the public—and media coverage of those polls.) (2) The material practices of reality production center language and significance as well as communication and meaning as their primary devices. This centrality is seen in both the questions raised and the answers given. (Public opinion is not a causal agent but legitimized public discourse.) (3) The real is revealed from some vantage point. The revelation tells us as much about the point of view as about reality. (Pollsters are entrepreneurs; the questions they ask make them money.) (4) The revelators are themselves part of the reality production process. (The study of public opinion—especially those studies that claim its preexistence in the public—confirms its status as real.)

Summary: Criteria of the Real

When Buller, LePoire, Aune, and Eloy (1992) investigated the relationship between rate of speaking and level of compliance as mediated through a path of attractiveness and obligation, they were working from a materialist/objectivist criterion of the real. All of the elements are present: independence, autonomy, anonymity, ahistoricity, determinacy, referentiality, and representation, as well as operationalism and objectivism. Attractiveness, for example, is a real force for these analysts that can be considered as independent of any given measure of attractiveness, autonomous of any results of attraction, anonymous of any particular agents of attraction, and not limited to concrete attraction events (ahistoricity). Attractiveness is the result of other conditions—here, speech rate—and causes other circumstances—here, obligation (determinacy). Its theoretical conceptualization references an existing force (meaning realism and referentiality) and the researchers' measures represent its actual action in the study. Attractiveness was operationalized in a "15-item semantic differential scale" (p. 295) the intersubjectivity of which (its objectivity) was documented by Chronbach's *alpha* and the citation of other applications.

On the other hand, when Goodall (1991) writes of "living in the rock and roll mystery," he presents his own demonstration of the interpretive turn. He offers a lived reality that is multiple, contingent, subordinate (made meaningful), subjective, shot through with agency, accomplished discursively, and accountable for its insights.

He has captured a radical image of these elements in the introduction to his interpretive ethnography:

> These are the senses of the power and pull of mystery, the whisper of its voice and sensuous lull of its prose rhythms, the surround for the private investigations that constitute the public music of this book. Mystery is used here in both straight and delinquent senses, to denote both a way of expressing and a way of experiencing what I will call the rock n roll of social life. Why I call the form of social life I examine *rock n roll* (and even spell it this way) is part of the reading, part of the rhetorics of motive, part of the assemblage of semiotic clues, that join you and me, reader, in working out the terms of this mystery. (p. xi)

To offer only two distinct examples in this summary is a concession to space demands, but it cannot be allowed to mask the many significant and sometimes subtle differences across what is considered real. Differences are more useful, however, for understanding disagreements across venues of theory and less useful for understanding the real within a theory.

Toward that end, it is important to remember that the explanatory object of any theory is always considered real in some fashion whether by its persisting materiality or by the momentary effort of the theorist. Our first task, consequently, for understanding the real within any theory is to ascertain what the theory intends to explain.[17] Then the question to ask is what reality criteria does this explanatory target pass—what must be believed for its existence?

THE UNITY OF THE PHENOMENAL WORLD

In the Delphian world, pananimism—the notion that all things have an animate spirit—unified the phenomenal world. We were all in our own way expressions of the spirit. Not to oversimplify but certainly to oversimplify, the Cartesian mind–body duality was part of the work that directed science toward the material and allowed the human soul to retain consciousness and agency. This solution was an uneasy political compromise between the growing power of science and the gradually declining power of metaphysics and religion. The boundaries of the material became the demarcation zone of what was science and what was not.

A Materialist Unity

During the ensuing three centuries since Descartes, the realm of science was enlarged from astronomy and falling bodies to include human action and consciousness as well as life itself. Part of the success of science was the demonstration that much of what were thought to be metaphysical processes were indeed material ones. In the very recent past of the first half of the 20th century, elements of science claimed it all, asserting that what can be valid knowledge must be scientific knowledge (epistemology naturalized). The realm of knowledge became unified and along with it the realm of the phenomenal world.

This position has never been without its opposition (e.g., Hume, Swift, Kant, Peirce, Husserl, Weber, James, Horkheimer). This opposition has been encouraged by the apparent failure of the materialist thrust to significantly reduce the disruptions of social life (or so it is claimed). Whatever the reasons, we can certainly note an increasing presence of approaches (as well as the "rediscovery" of previous oppositional positions) that depend on fracturing the unity of the 1940s and 1950s into multiple domains. This opposition dominates postmodernist and poststructuralist writings, although such writings do not dominate the field of communication and have very limited presence in the human sciences generally. (The position has done wonders for criticism and the critical review of science, however).

The unity or disunity of science depends on our conceptualization of the phenomenal world. John Dupre (1993) states the case well:

The conceptions of an ordered nature and a unified science belong naturally together. If there is some ultimate and unique order underlying the apparent diversity and disorder of nature then the point of science should be to tell the one story that expresses this order. (p. 221)

Dupre goes on to note that there are other unifying forces as well. There is a sociological unity in which disciplines attempt to legitimate lines of inquiry by designating them as "scientific," thereby claiming to be the same sort of enterprise as, say, quantum mechanics (see Hanna, 1991). And there is a methodological unity in the "mathematicization" of evidence and claim that helps us to better understand both the presence and vigorous defense of quantification and statistical analysis, which is math's common appearance in communication studies.

The Disunity of Inquiry

Once we step off the platform of belief that human life is explained with no reference to the mental, we leave foundational materialism behind. When we reject a world shaped only by universal, anonymous forces, we walk away from the foundational determinism of an ultimate order. In doing so, we reject the cornerstones of scientific unity. This rejection takes us into a world where there is something other than an "infinitely divisible substance" organized in a "single universal order," although there may that as well.

The belief in a phenomenal world that has multiple domains implicates a belief in multiple epistemologies, the adoption of a critical stance toward science, and the production of a methodological pluralism. We briefly turn to each.

Multiple Domains

Popper's (Popper & Eccles, 1977) formulation of multiple domains posits three worlds: (1) the world of physical objects including nonsentient living objects; (2) the world of sentience and subjective experience; and (3) the world of the human mind, particularly language and argument (p. 16). Dupre (1993) offers a similar arrangement, separating biology from physics and chemistry and then moving on to the mental. My own formulation runs something like this (adapted from a speech given at Baylor University, 1990)[18]:

We are first of all material entities in a physical world. We are as governed by the grand laws of mass and energy, structure and relationships as any other physical entity. The first domain of human life, then, is the material. The material domain provides the evidence of our *existence*. It establishes many of the brute facts of that existence. Experience in this domain is as a nonsensate element in a system of mass and energy. Explanation fitted to this domain can take advantage of its regularities, relative lack of exceptions, and the similitude of independence that those regularities give to our observations and our descriptions of those observations.

We are also living organisms giving expression to the principles of ecological animation. The foremost of those principles is our ability to initiate rather than to be solely the consequent of change. Rocks change when forces work upon them but not by necessity—not by the demands of being rocks. Living entities change because change defines them as living. The second domain of our existence, then, is the biological. It is within the biological that we find *act*. And in act, our experience as a player—an entity that can modify the outcome of the forces working upon it—comes into existence. Explanation appropriate to the biological domain must make a clear space for the exception, the evolutionary sport, the genetic mutation, the spontaneous appearance, which can change the character of the relationships within this domain.

We recognize with taken-for-granted certainty the requirements of being the material, living entities that we are: "Star Trek" to the contrary, we cannot pass through a solid wall. Two of us cannot occupy the same space (though it's often pleasant to try). We are bound in the relationship of the stimuli of life demands and our instinctual, reflexive responses. We cannot continue without food, water, shelter, reproduction.

As educated women and men we have at least a nodding acquaintance with the sciences of these two domains: physics, chemistry, biology, botany. These sciences have offered great understanding of the world and our being in it. We marvel at their accomplishments, enjoy the progress of their applications, and, yes, suffer their unintended consequences.

But these sciences are not enough to approach a complete understanding of our being-in-the-world. We cannot understand human life by studying only the material and the biological. We inhabit yet another universe, the universe of the sign. This universe is populated by the chemical and energy exchanges that become the sights, sounds, tastes, odors, movements, pressures, and temperatures of our languages, pictures, sculptures, music, noise, perfumes, performances, comforts and pain. This is the universe in which cultures and great societies arise. It is the universe of our communities, of our collectivities, of our relationships between self and other. This universe is the semiotic domain.

It is within the semiotic domain that we make sense of ourselves, our world, and our manner of being in it. The semiotic domain is characterized by the principle of signification and the process of communication. Signification is the punctuation of the continuous exchanges that constitute sensate experience. Signification produces the sign, and it is through the sign that the human mind—that point of recognition of self and other—comes into being. Signification liberates us from the ongoing present by creating a past and a future within the realm of human *action*.

Multiple Epistemologies

Whether the multiplicity is formulated in objects, sentience, and language, or in existence, act, and action, the argument of multiple domains entails the provocative claim of multiple ways of knowing. In a very shortened form, the argument states that our ways of knowing the material world (the world of objects and existence) will be inadequate for the production of knowledge about the semiotic. There is not, therefore, a single science but multiple sciences (Roth, 1987; Turner, 1986).[19]

Each of these epistemologies will necessarily need to develop their own criteria of the real, their bases of validity, even their separate logics, as well as the utilities of their claim. The outpouring of publications in the 1980s and 1990s declaring the interpretive turn, some era of post-ness, or some form of reconstituted empiricism may be the current tokens of this effort. We have a shopping mall of science—a consumerist economy of inquiry—with a product for every desire. The task is to avoid both nonproductive narcissism and irredeemable skepticism while recognizing the struggle to establish a center for the community of one's own work.

A Critical Stance toward Science

It is a defining characteristic of this era of inquiry that there is no epistemological position that is immune from critical attack. Significantly, it is critical attack mounted from within the fortress. It is the inside character of the attack that leads us to conclusions of chaos in inquiry (or ferment in the field). The angels are divided. There is no sacred; it is all profane.[20]

The hypothesis of the *dis*unity of science allows us to more productively understand this postmodern critical stance. Indeed if the struggle is to define a center on which to stand, then part of that effort has to be to establish one's own domain and the limits of the other. The dominant must be reduced to withstand its honorific seductions. Establishment science must be sufficiently delegitimized to produce the space of alternatives. Quantification and statistical analysis will come under attack to break the methodological hegemony of a mathematical ideology.

These are the moves of separation and identity.[21] It is a pluralist attack on epistemological monism (and an illustration of the enduring David–Goliath narrative). We are certainly reforming ourselves into multiple communities and much of what appears to be new is that reformation work. The communities that are arising are present expressions of a lengthy history that is evidenced in the rediscovery (reinvention) of, say, Peirce (1831–1915) and American pragmatism or Chladenius (1710–1759) and hermeneutics.

Multiple Methodologies

Methodologies are here defined as the set of conventionalized practices that marks the membership of scholarship. These are the practical activities that are carried out in the name of scholarship as the practitioners and their supervisors/gatekeepers know it. Methodologies are multiple even if the practical activity is understood by the same name—participant observation under the objectivist criterion is meaningfully different (action is self-evident, observation is neutral, language is referential, description is representational, subjectivity is suppressed) from participant observation under the hermeneutic criterion (action must be interpreted, observation depends on perspective, language is rhetorical, description is political, objectivity is denied)—and even if enacted similarly. Multiple methodologies are a necessary consequence of multiple epistemologies because methodology is a "method of knowing," the technique of knowledge production. The technique of knowledge production must be driven by what counts as knowledge.

But what of the arguments for the use of "multiple methodologies" in a single study? Certainly such studies make use of recognizably different activities in their investigations, but their methodology—that is, their method of knowing, what counts as warranted evidence in claim—remains the same.[22] In some cases, the call for "multiple methods" is politically motivated as a coopting move to deny a difference or to entail legitimation. I offer no positive view of these latter arguments. They are either unwitting or deceptive.

Unity of Science or Multiple Domains?

One's prior beliefs concerning materialism and determinism establish the basis by which the choice between the unity of science or the multiple domains of inquiry can be made. One need not wholly reject either materialism or determinism to endorse multiple epistemologies. It is simply necessary to reduce them from universal. Popper (Popper & Eccles, 1977) can, therefore, hold to "products of a transcendental mind" without denying the resources of neural activities such as orientation, sensation, and memory, and he can further accept a material and determined world of physical objects.

Theory is often silent on the issue of materialism. Cognitive theorists regularly finesse the question by defining key mentalist concepts with other mentalist concepts (e.g., schemata are defined as sets of rules for interpretation). One has to discover their position by their practices of analysis. Theories that motivate the use of scales, behavioral coding or case studies represent objectivist extensions of the materialist criterion. Such theories are interim theories that await the breakthrough that will describe the connection between brain states and mental activity (if I can measure an electrochemical potential directly, I do not need attitude scales).

On the other hand, theories that locate their descriptions in a collective enterprise such as society or culture or language or action look at the material consequences of nonmaterial agents (Giddens, 1984). Once society, culture, language, or action has arisen, there is no benefit in looking inside brain cases. The explanation will not be found there.

Both of my preceding examples are deterministic. Both attempt to explain current behavior/action on the basis of some prior, manipulatable state. Non-deterministic theories require some form of agency or uncaused cause. (This comparison is the topic of the next section.)

The further one moves away from materialism and determinism, the less tenable is the argument for the unity of science. Claims that the human sciences are not the same as the material sciences or that the boundaries of scientific and critical genres of inquiry are blurred are representative of this movement. We will consider the implications of this movement in all of the remaining chapters of this book. They are substantial.

THE CAUSAL FABRIC OF PHENOMENA

The issue of causality is principally a "science" issue (but not wholly absent in hermeneutic approaches). Causality and its associational relatives are at the center of all theories in traditional science arguments except the purely onto-logical ones (i.e., questions of what is). The recognition of association in a patterned sequence allows the analyst to anticipate outcomes (to predict) and to intentionally accomplish (to manipulate and control). A prior belief in the causality of all phenomena—the belief that all phenomena are both the result of some agent and the agent of some result—establishes the principle that all things have an explanation beyond the simple observation of their existence. This principle—that although material presence is considered self-evident, cause must be recognized, perhaps in difficult ways—motivates the professional activity of inquiry. It also establishes the primacy of the analyst in the field of knowledge. Laypeople cannot know as the professional can.

Causality

Theories that are classically causal hang on Mill's principles of necessity (if no X—agent, then no Y—consequence) and sufficiency (if X, then always Y). Because few human events appear to meet these criteria, few theories are classi-cally causal. Most argue a conditional relationship where the appearance of the agent increases the likelihood of (or sets a probability concerning) the appear-ance of the consequent. (There are a number of issues concerning conditionals, probability, and knowledge certainty that are debated but have little practical force. In practice, any finding that offers probability results beyond chance is considered evidence in support of its conditional theory.)

Causal Determinism

What makes a theory deterministic is the causal chain that explains the element of interest. What varies is the reach (how many subsequent events are governed) and the scope (how many different conditions does it govern) of the causality in question. (A modesty of claim invokes a short reach and a narrow scope.) True determinism would trace the chain to the "Big Bang" itself. Typical determinism focuses on its own few links, leaving the rest of the chain unexamined (but not denying the chain either).

Open Systems and Agency

Both open systems and agency remove us from deterministic argument. An open-system argument involves the acceptance of an uncaused cause, an act of creation, or an intrinsically unexplainable initial condition. Agency involves an un- (or at least under-) determined choice and as a characteristic of the individual posits "the ability to do otherwise." All such causes, conditions, choices, or abilities must be irreducible for a nondeterministic argument to be truly present.[23]

Explanation within the system or surrounding the choice will most likely remain causal or conditional but the linkages will be short and interruptable. Explanation will make no assumption beyond its focal episodes (e.g., the way this committee meeting came together is not predictive of the way other committee meetings may come together.)

Agency and open-system arguments greatly increase the work of the analyst and reduce analytic power. Work done here does not eliminate the work to be done there, and there is no final set of principles to move toward. Explanation is neither reductive (moving toward a finite set of principles that cover all occurrences), nor progressive (a claim that more closely approximates that finite set of principles). Explanation is local not transcendent.

We can clearly see the relationship between determinism and the unity of science. If there is an underlying order, then it ought to be the business of all inquiry to discover it. Similarly, we can see the relationship between multiple domains and agency. There seems to be a difference (so the argument would go) between consequence in rocks and consequence in humans within certain realms of analysis. Both humans and rocks are subject to gravity, but rocks don't appear to anticipate the fall.

The Special Case of Chaos Theory

Chaos theory has engendered a certain excitement for the study of human behavior. The importance of chaos theory is that it breaks the connection between determinism and prediction. Chaotic events such as weather systems or committee meetings are fully determined systems that are, nonetheless, low in predictability because they are exquisitely sensitive to multiple agents of exceeding frailty. Such agents are well beyond any ability to measure because of their weak signal and momentary nature (the beat of a butterfly's wing changing a convection current within a weather system is one example).

Chaos theories allow the analyst to tell us a fragmentary but true story of what *happened* without being able to tell us what *will happen*. Incompleteness and postdiction are necessary characteristics of chaotic theories. Most arguments out of British social theory—especially those that do not use agency—represent the full determinism, acceptable incompleteness, and valid postdiction characteristics of chaos theory, although those theorists would probably resist that description.

Causality: A Summary

The assumption of transcendent cause—cause for all time and all places—within a definable field of such causes has been the basis of the Movietone image of science since the age of rationality. Realms of inquiry outside the boundaries of science have attempted either an imitation of this image (e.g., structuralism, formalism, or intentionality in criticism) or performed in open defiance (e.g., the move against representation in art) of this image.

The image is, of course, only an image used by the ardent to promote scientism and by the opposition to produce a strawman foe. Science is much less sure of itself than this image suggests. Causal explanations remain, nonetheless, the gold standard against which all others are measured. Standing against its achievement are the problems raised by open systems, agency, historicity, subjectivity, interpretation, local and partial knowledge, as well as the acts of creation that social constructionism represents.

CONSTRUCTION OF REALITY AND KNOWLEDGE

Many of the contemporary theories in communication depend on some belief in the constructed nature of reality and knowledge (e.g., intercultural, structuration, social action, and ideology/hegemony theories).

Construction of Reality

Reality construction references acts of human creation (and also the human engagement of reality that is the topic of the next chapter) that bring into existence circumstances of the same force as self-presenting events. Such circumstances are commonsensibly recognized as real with the same intransigence as the reality of our brick. They are the "of course its true" circumstances of everyday life. (That common sense recognizes them inappropriately—e.g., "false consciousness"—again motivates a professional inquiry.)

Is the reality of friendship, for example, primarily the consequence of social practices and would it disappear if those practices ceased? Or is it the consequence of a specifiable pheronomic chemistry that would persist regardless of the social practices of its expression? Similarly, is gender an economy built on the trivial differences of sexual characteristics or is it a biological mechanism, with trivial cultural variations, evolutionarily encoded to ensure genetic diversity in the species?

The answers one gives to questions like these help to identify one's position on the constructionism issue and provide the direction inquiry should take as well as the limits of change within the representational social practices. In the answers that we work, we are once again managing the relationship between the material and the social/mental. Is there a supervenient relationship between the material, the biological, and the cognitive realms of human activity (is each of the subsequent realms an expression of the previous one)? If so, then constructionist activities are a screen for what is actually happening. If not, then constructionist activities are their own proper object of inquiry.

We can see that constructionism is tightly bound up in all the issues of this chapter that revolve around the real, materialism, unity, and determinism. For example, constructionism is the basis for considering reality to be multiple, contingent, and subordinate rather than singular, independent, and autonomous. In what follows, we will explore these arguments across five different dimensions (a somewhat arbitrary selection): the semiotic, the phenomenological, the pragmatic, the cultural, and the actional.

Semiotic Constructionism

Semiotic processes are considered to play an active role in reality construction in three ways: by punctuation, by semiosis, and by extension. Punctuation involves the question of the independence and/or the autonomy of phenomena as addressed within the problem of boundary recognition versus boundary production. The constructionist issue begins with the presumption that reality is presented to us in a continuous albeit variable stream of exchange rather than in discrete entities. Objects appear to us by virtue of the differences within that stream. Those differences are punctuated as boundaries. The argument arises over the mechanism(s) that controls that punctuation. To the extent that it is controlled at the point of reception, rather than "out there in the phenomenal world," reality construction enters the scene.

Most constructionist punctuation claims are used in explanations of the processes of perception (cognitive theories) or of the role of language as a reality construction device (hermeneutic theories). (You might remember the figure–ground illustrations like the faces/vase that are used as examples of perceptual boundaries. A common language example is that different parts of the electromagnetic spectrum are coded as the "same" color name by different language groups.) In either case, punctuation stands against the claim of *self-presenting events* and argues instead that reality is, at the very least, a composite of encoding and decoding.

Semiosis is the method and moment in which an event is recognized as meaningful. It is the moment (and the methods of attaining that moment) when a perception (a mental event with significance) enters into its potential as an agent of action. At a traffic signal, for example, sensory/perceptual processes will recognize a light stream as "green"; semiosis will recognize a "green light."

Semiosis has much the same standing as interpretation and is used conceptually to explain the consequential differences that occur across reception events involving ostensibly the same content. In these explanations, content is the factual foundation for the production of an interpreted (or activated) text. The agency of content is not its facts, however; it is the produced text. Most of these explanations emanate from hermeneutic camps, although some radical perceptual arguments make use of something similar.

The constitutive aspect of semiosis is managed in several different ways, from cognitive theories that make use of it in socialization processes; to critical studies that use it in polysemic ideological encoding and decoding; to social action theories that apply it in the "local and partial" interpretations of "cultural agents." The radical break across these sorts of applications of the constitutive aspects of semiosis is the availability of a true (or rightly interpreted) text. As one moves toward the radical in hermeneutics, the objective text recedes and interpretive difference advances. In the end, meaning becomes rhetorical and texts nominated as true are so placed via the political rather than the veridical.

In no case, however, is semiosis considered to be under individual control. One does not get to decide for oneself what shall be meaningful. Instead, semiosis is governed by organic perceptual processes, the socialization processes of cognitive structure formation, culturally processes of subjectivity, or the contextualization of action. Harrison (1991) shows this important distinction in writing that the determinacy of textual meaning is founded on the principle that "these signs standing in these relationships to one another in this context, can bear these possible interpretations but not those" (p. 36).

There is, nonetheless, a remaining act of agency (a semiotic excess, if you will)—guided but not determined—residing in the materialization of the singular of "these possible interpretations" that occurs. It is the particular materialization that is the constructionist act.

Finally, there is the issue of extension. Semiotic extension refers to the proposition that the signified (e.g., what a word might stand for) is not a material object (the word *tree* does not stand for a tree[24]) but is itself another sign invoking another signified. Eco (1977) likens this effect to that of an encyclopedia where one article calls forth another article and another until all the volumes of the set are implicated.

This "web of significance" applies to all sign usage. The sight of the tree outside my window is not the tree but a sign of the tree. Its signified is not fixed to the aspen in my frontyard but invokes the whole semiotic system. Signifiers are, therefore, said to "float" (Barthes, 1974). The action that contains them to a particular referentiality is constitutive.

Phenomenological Constructionism

Edmund Husserl's (1907/1970) philosophy of intentional consciousness has been cited both as a cornerstone of modern hermeneutics (Mueller-Vollmer, 1990) and as the source for the science of phenomenological insight (Lanigan, 1988). For Husserl, the real arises in the spatial, temporal relationships of the ego in the material world. What is real is materialized in intentional action. Genuine knowledge ensues not from the external, objective study of the material but from the reflexive analysis of the intentional relationship.

Husserl posited a transcendental phenomenology by declaring a set of inborn, universal intentions that allows a common human experience of reality and that is the true object of inquiry (Landgrebe, 1981). Lanigan (1988) argues that it is the extensive work of Merleau-Ponty (e.g., 1962) that establishes the existential (rather than the transcendental) character of modern pheno-menological analysis. This existential character redirects phenomenological analysis from a search for universals to an examination of the intentionality of lived experience (Sobchack, 1992).

Phenomenology seeks to explicate the consciousness of human experience. It moves from a description of the experienced, to a reduction of the experiencing to its genuine elements, to an interpretation of the experiencer (Lanigan, 1992). It is constructionist in that reality is the product of the human consciousness working (i.e., intentionally directed toward) the material. It is not idiosyncratic, however, in that an explanation must be developed for each individual. Rather, consciousness is subjective—an identifiable stance emanating from collective rules of intentionality. We arrive, then, at an understanding of the subjective consciousness of lived experience.

Pragmatic Constructionism

American pragmatism founded in the writings of Charles Sanders Peirce, William James, and John Dewey (and more recently in W.V.O. Quine, 1953/1961/1980, Donald Davidson, 1980, and Richard Rorty, 1982, among others) has been characterized as forming a point of resistance to British empiricism on the one hand (Roth, 1993) and Cartesianism on the other (Murphy, 1990). Roth writes:

> When one moves from British empiricism to American pragmatism, . . . one finds oneself in a quite different atmosphere. There is no inventory of the mind, a sorting out and cataloguing of discrete and separable sensations and ideas as the building blocks of knowledge. Nor is there a sharp separation

between mind and object as introduced in modern philosophy by Descartes and continued to some extent by Locke and Hume. Atomism gives way to continuity, diversity to unity, discreteness to interrelation, isolation to inter-action. (pp. 10-11)

The pragmatic notion of experience is one of interpenetration, an active interrelationship in which experience arises out of action in the phenomenal world. Experience is not passive reception but is the product of acting upon and being acted upon. No "blank slates" here to be written upon, this is a human agent cocreating a reality with its own markings.

John Murphy (1990) presents us with Peirce's argument against Cartesian-ism which he notes "opposes the spirit of Cartesianism with what might be called the spirit of experimentalism" (p. 11). Murphy lists three experimentalism principles: it denies (1) Descartes's "philosophy of doubt", (2) that "the ultimate test of certainty is to be found in the individual consciousness," and (3) that "a single thread of inference" (the philosopher thinking well) is the method of truth (pp. 11-12).

Pragmatism substitutes instead a method that begins with belief that is to be acted upon (and from which pragmatism establishes its name), the validation of intersubjectivity, and a line of attack that is multiple and varied. Belief, chosen not determined, is to be multiply tested in its interaction with the phenomenal world. Belief advances to knowledge according to its public success. Knowledge is not a passive discovery but an acknowledged manner of acting upon the phenomenal world (Joas, 1993). As Dewey argues, there is no single reality; instead, there are as many realities as there are acceptable epistemological lines of action.

Once again we must note that this is not individualism. No one of us gets to decide the manner of coconstructing (in fact, individualism is expressly denied). Lines of epistemological action are institutionalized. Knowledge is public accomplishment based on joint agreement not private inspiration.

Cultural Constructionism

Cultural constructionism works from the assumption that one is born into an ongoing system of understanding that is cosmological in its effect, reaching into every aspect of life. The source of this system may be outside (as in structural-ism) or inside (as in structuration) human action. This cosmological system encodes its ideology everywhere. (This QWERTY keyboard upon which I write, for example, archives the primacy of technology demands over human conven-ience.) This encoding sustains hierarchical arrangements of power that are enforced by the "realness" of the ideological hegemony. (In capitalism, it is right and true that crimes against private property are crimes and that professional sports players should make more money than police officers.)

In strict structuralist formulas, ideology is no different from "big bang" determinism—our present state is the playing out of forces initiated in the first coming together of human society. We are all ideological products, enacting out our present state of enlightenment as we should. We are back to inquiry as a practice of discovery. It requires the declaration of our ability *either* to resist (de Certeau, 1984) the demands of ideology through which resistance we can produce a temporary individual or collective emancipation *or* to restructure ideology itself (Apel, 1980) through which restructuring we can advance social justice (Habermasian communicative action) or simply produce a new set of emancipated and subjugated subjects (Foucaultian change). (For a quick read on this comparison, see the articles by Habermas and Foucault in Rabinow and Sullivan [1987]).

British and American cultural studies, as well as the critical studies of the Frankfurt School, all have representatives of the trapped despair, dangerous change, and cautious utopian optimism that colors cultural constructionism.[25] In addition, organizational culture studies (the organization as manifestation of its own culture) have taken these same lines of argument down to a very local level and even advocated "packaging" cultures for creativity and success (for a reader's introduction, see Putnam & Pacanowsky, 1983).

Actional Constructionism

A long-standing debate in philosophy focuses on the relative prior status of essence and existence. Determinism establishes essence as prior to existence: We are born into a world in which the future is already encoded in forces already in action. In deterministic formulations, essence determines existence. Constructionism adjusts this relationship by arguing that existence must be directly taken into account in any understanding of present reality. (Note the beliefs to be acted upon in pragmatism and the innovative acts of resistance and restructuring of cultural constructionism.) In constructionist formulations, existence at least modifies essence.

Actional constructionism takes us further down the existentialist road, seeing reality as the product of cultural agents acting in the world.[26] The meaning of all things is materialized in action. And action is always a local improvisation that is partially representative of all possible improvisations. Such improvisations have consequences, always real, with some unintended and many unanticipated. It is in this act and consequence that reality as we know it is achieved. Reality is always historicized (instantiated), excessive (beyond an effective prediction and control), and abundant (in production).

Actional constructionism sees (human) reality in the pragmatist's terms as a production of the interaction of human action in the phenomenal world. It sees human action in the culturist's terms as performed by a cultural agent in both senses of the term as an actor *for* and an actor *of* cultural expression. And it understands human action in the semiotician's terms as a sign of what is going on. It certainly appears to be the most derivative, and may be the most constructionist. Action is a creative performance materializing institionalized understandings. Stabilizing institutional inertia is balanced against the requirement of opportunistic local expression. Every continuation requires a constitutive act.

Knowledge Constructionism

Constructionism is often considered a slippery slope that leads to yet another slippery slope (until one realizes that it is the ride not the destination that counts). The basis for this concern is that constructionism relativizes knowledge. It releases knowledge from any rock-bottom foundation of objective phenomena or universal experience and recognizes it as a set of institutionalized agreements.

This says nothing more about atomic theory than atomic theory is a Western European contrivance that takes into account both the patterned regularities of the phenomenal world it intends and the Western European manner of being-in-the-world. It is more or less true to both, but neither truth can be spoken singularly nor is it the only truth that can be spoken about each.

For constructionists, inquiry is driven by the same political interests that background any activity. There is no innocence here, but good things can emanate from the mundane. Knowledge is, therefore, always subjective (from a locatable—not a personal—position); there are no Archimedean points (not even this one) from which to move the universe.

This argument has a number of implications (not the least or which is how do I manage the sureties of my life given the uncertainty of my knowledge) which we will take up in the chapter on justified argument. For now it shall suffice to presage that work and to ponder some of the questions this chapter has been about: What is the real? And what is my knowledge of it? At the same time we need to prepare for the questions of the next chapter: How do I know I know? And when do I know that I know? These questions have captured the imagination of authors from the earliest writings to the exploding scene of the present. The answers you come to make a difference.

NATURE OF THE PHENOMENAL
WORLD: A SUMMARY

In this chapter we have been looking at four issues: What is the real? What are the domains of reality? What is the structure of the reality domain(s)? And what are the sources of that structure?

We have found that positions on the real vary from a narrow materialism in which only objects count to a very broad pragmatism where attributable action verifies the reality of belief. If we apply this range to communication theory or research directions, we will find none that meet the strict materialist criterion in which explanation begins and ends in the material. Theories that motivate behavior coding and ethnography certainly begin in material practices, but they quickly jump to some nonmaterial understanding that directs the patterns of activities. Most of our theories make use of the objectivist criterion in which conventionalized measurement (where one's actual performance is of technical interest only) stands for or is held to be predictive of material practices.

The explanation for the results on those measurements is typically the existence of some cognitive structure—again a nonmaterial ending. These nonmaterial endings may be held as interim conditions—practical solutions to the state of one's science—that will be abandoned once the mind–brain connection is more thoroughly understood. But other formulations appear to be uncertain of this outcome and imply, at least, some embrace of real mentalist states that transcend the material.

Hermeneutic theories hold that reality is some composite of the material and the conscious and that human action is both productive of and directed by that composition. A consciousness greater than its material foundation is a real presence in all such theories and is itself a proper and necessary object of any inquiry.

Arguments concerning a transcendent mind generally activate arguments in support of the multiple domains of reality. It follows that rejection of the materialist criterion of the real would force an image of reality where materialist successes in one area will not hold the promise of success in another. By proposing a semiotic/conscious/mental domain whose foundation is somehow a human achievement (whether by material practices—structuration, existentialist theories, reception criticism—or by inborn characteristics—Kantian logic, phenomenological interpretation, Chomskian linguistics, structuralist criticism), theorists craft new epistemological standards for inquiry.

Those standards may or may not break with the determinism that commonly appears with materialism. The break with determinism requires acceptance of original creative events—events that are their own explanation (events sometimes derided as miracles, as in the Harris cartoon). Theories that offer unexplainable initial conditions or acts of agency are nondeterministic although they may be causal within the consequences of chance and choice.

We looked at five of these constructionist positions (semiotic, phenomenological, pragmatic, cultural/critical, and actional). These five fall along the essence-to-existence dimension with semiotic and phenomenological being expressed primarily on the essence-is-prior-to-action side and the pragmatic and actional moving toward the existence-provides-essence end.

We now have four tools by which to evaluate theories. What is the explanatory object and how is it held to be real? In what sort of domain does that object exist? What is the structural character of that domain? Does creation or agency appear within it, and if so, how does it function? (Exemplar applications in which names are named are given in Chapter 9.) These interrogations can be applied to any sort of theory: aesthetic, critical, ethical, literary, scientific. They all must hold something to be real in some way with some explanatory value which itself must obliterate or manage creation.

NOTES

1. The argument of these two contrasting views is itself dependent upon the assumption of epistemological pluralism (Roth, 1987). Epistemic monists (e.g., Phillips, 1987) would, of course, claim that one or the other has to be true or both have to be false. It could not be that both would be true. If one is a monist, one works for the suppression of pluralism. If one is a pluralist, one claims monism as an agent of suppression.

2. In Laplacean cosmological determinism, it was believed that any state of the universe predicted every other state. Quantum mechanics and the Heisenberg Principle (i.e., that one cannot know both position and momentum with equal certainty) began the refutation of Laplace which has continued with the theory of black holes in which information about prior states is actually lost. Nonetheless, Laplacean determinism is a necessity if there are to be laws, as traditionally defined, in knowledge.

3. Determinism and determinacy gets talked about a lot in this book. I need to distinguish several different forms: determinacy, indeterminacy, undeterminacy, underdeterminacy, and overdeterminacy. *Determinacy* refers to a relationship where A causes B so that A determines the appearance of B. *Indeterminacy* is a relationship where the cause of B cannot be resolved. B is presumed to be caused but the cause cannot be known because of, say, the presence of multiple causation or causal events too small to be recognized as such (chaos theory is of this sort). *Undeterminacy* is an event that is uncaused. It is self-presenting, an uncaused cause. Neither indetermined nor undetermined (when speaking of relationships among elements) means unknown. They both refer to a specific type of relationship. *Underdeterminacy* refers to a relationship between A and B where B has a choice in the outcome motivated by A. (We say either that agency inhabits the consequent or the consequent can refuse the antecedent.) One says that data underdetermine their theory in that the scholar *must* make a choice of which theory to use to account for those data. *Overdeterminacy* is a term from cultural studies and it refers to the naturalized choice of one interpretation over another. Overdeterminacy is an unreflective instance of agency.

4. Berkeleyism (Berkeley, 1710/1974) probably came as close as any position to denying this axiom. His axiom, "To be is to be perceived" does not appear to require the prior, independent existence of matter. There is also the idea of the "brain in a vat" (Pollock, 1986). This is the idea that we are only minds—disembodied intelligence—in a virtual reality.

5. If instead of ethnographic methods we were doing survey research, we would develop an instrument to measure empowerment and distribute it to the organizational members. Assuming a competent effort in measurement design, empowerment by definition would be what we measured.

6. American behaviorism was and is a clear effort to avoid "breaking the pledge." To continue the example in the main text: Behaviorism would demand that friendship

be nothing more than the unique actions recognized as friendship. Friendship actions would be recognized as those supported by the stimulation of particular reinforcement centers in the brain. The result is a fully materialist science of human behavior. It has foundered (been delayed) on the failure (difficulty) of the physicalist project.

7. See Davidson (1980) for this argument.

8. The writing of this book has its own history that the autocitations such as this one document.

9. As with any attempt to fix the boundaries of an "ism," this one too is bound to fail. Megill's (1991) short introduction allows one to get to several of the issues quickly.

10. Perhaps this is the moment to remind ourselves that epistemology is concerned with public knowledge, not private thoughts or individual beliefs.

11. For readings across the practical dimensions of these questions see Diesing (1971) (a logical positivist position), Phillips (1992) (a recent recuperation of positivism greened), and Anderson (1987) (a cautionary tale).

12. The thrust of our current work is about objectivity, but the notion of subjectivity is central to its understanding.

13. When an argument is nominated as idiosyncratic it is dismissible as "mere opinion" or as one's "personal stance." It is refused entry into the domain of public knowledge. Even in this postmodern age of multiple epistemologies we still reject work deemed incompetent. When an argument enters the public arena, I may not agree with it but I have to account for it. I don't have to account for your opinion unless or until it is invested with authority.

14. From a subjectivist point of view, objectivity is simply an undeclared and unexamined subjective stance. Through its deep and extensive conventionalization, objectivity is able to deny itself and all others. From an objectivist point of view, subjectivity is the interposition of an ideational mask between material reality and valid claim. The mask, at best, adds nothing, but typically distorts true understanding.

15. I am deliberately positioning the hermeneutic arts and sciences in a Hegelian relationship with establishment science in the manner of Winch (1958). One denies the dominance of establishment science with great risk. Further, my reading of the hermeneutic literature (and indeed some of my own contributions) show it to be replete with distinguishing moves that diminish and legitimate other and self, respectively. Nonetheless, the differences that we argue appear in the hegemonic relationship as it has been constituted. Attempts to reconstitute it (Hesse, 1980) are precisely that. (See also Bernstein's [1983] discussion of Winch and Hesse, pp. 24–34.)

16. Notice the absence of the word "report" in that list—as in "reporting it like it is" in order to maintain the contributory aspect of inquiry. One cannot report it like it is because reporting is a constructive act. Reporting contributes to the "it" reported. The "beingness" reported is not fully prior to the report.

17. Our first example in this summary comes out of cognitive theory as applied to compliance gaining and is concerned with the character and action of cognitive states. The second comes out of a less defined interpretive sociology whose concern is the significances of everyday life. Both are mentalist but the first is fixed (material state of attraction) and the latter procedural (material practices of significance).

18. I would ask the reader to note the change of voice here as the writing moves from text to oratory. One can experience, I hope, the avuncularism of the text and the

advocacy of the oratory. Both voices are deliberate constructions as is the voice of any writing.

19. How the human sciences during the first 6 decades of the 20th century developed primarily along a single epistemological track is a story the science historians and sociologists are just now beginning to tell. Tales of outright suppression (in promotion, tenure, publication, and leadership) by philosophic and science communities are being told on the Internet lists. It is interesting that there was an active debate up to the 1920s which was reduced to a murmur for nearly 30 years. It is my belief that our present contentiousness is the "normal state" of human inquiry and that the tranquility of the 1940s and 1950s was enforced.

20. I write these lines less than 24 hours after appearing on a television talk show in which Freud was a fraud, Kinsey an abuser, and social science was proclaimed "freeze-dried in the era of self-gratification." Wonderful stuff. That show, however, was a dismissible attack from without the walls.

21. There are, of course, sympathetic criticisms of quantification and statistics that do not imply their rejection (e.g., Anderson, 1987). I am not referencing such arguments here but rather those whose abomination is numerical and those that glorify numerate rigor in reply.

22. Triangulation (Jicks, 1979) is a good example of this "multiple-practices/same-method" distinction. Triangulation is often presented as the use of multiple methods to "fix the true object" of one's analysis. The analogy is to the navigational practice of determining an unknown location from its position relative to two known positions. Such an argument applied to the nonmaterial depends on the prior beliefs of something "out there" to fix on and to objectively measure.

23. Deterministic theories will often use "random events" as an equivalent uncaused cause, but in such theories random events are unknown events not unknowable events. A random event in a deterministic theory will ultimately be reducible to a consequence given greater knowledge.

24. If humanity were to be extinguished, the material trace of tree (the thing one bumps into) would remain but all trees as human semiotic objects would instantly vanish.)

25. The following works are instructive: Hall, 1982; Hardt, 1989; Horkheimer, 1968/1972; Horkheimer & Adorno, 1944/1972; Jensen, 1986; Radway, 1984; Slack & Allor, 1983.

26. Exemplar works are: Anderson & Meyer, 1988; Hodge & Kress, 1988; Sigman, 1987. As I am the Anderson above my essentializing text is undoubtedly more personal here.

CHAPTER 3

OUR MANNER OF ENGAGEMENT
OF THE PHENOMENAL WORLD

INTRODUCTION

Whatever the phenomenal world is, an independent question arises as to the nature of our engagement with that world. The question of engagement involves three components: (1) a common object that we can (2) identify and reidentify and (3) describe and redescribe (Solomon, 1987). The (1) ontological component raises again the issues of the previous chapter, for the basis by which an object (material, ideal, semiotic, intentional) is both an object and common must be answered. The (2) identification component deals with the character of the instrument of observation. The observing entity must not only be able to observe but to *consistently* observe the *same* object (which must exist independently of its observation) and obtain the *same* results. Finally, the (3) description component implicates the nature of language or other systems of communication. One's private observation is of no value to the course of knowledge until it can be exchanged. The referential and representational values of the system of exchange thus comes into the discussion.

The end points of the discussion around these three issues are generally seen as fully trustworthy experience or "brute sense data" in which the phenomenal world impresses itself directly upon us on the one end and full existential constructivism or some "unique mediation" by each individual in an achievement of private understanding on the other. All ordained discussion falls well between those points, however (Brown, 1987). Four positions are usually distinguished as the four corners of contemporary empiricism:

1. *Traditional empiricism* (Carnap, 1928/1969; Hempel, 1952): All intelligence is singular in nature and engages the phenomenal world in the same

manner. This world is directly accessible to good observation and right reasoning (all things to all knowers). Dolphins, humans, and extraterrestrials will all come to the same justified conclusions about the phenomenal world that exists in the same manner for all of us. Errors are correctable at any level of intelligence. Within this perspective, the engagement of the phenomenal world can be considered a process of isomorphic transduction (exact reproduction from one field to another) in which normal sensations are the recognizable foundation of perceptions and normal perceptions are true. Subsequent behaviors can be read as responses to sensations in a reliable representation of their effect.

2. *Perceptual empiricism* (Goldman, 1986): Intelligence is species-specific, but each member of a species lives in the same phenomenal world and engages it in the same way. There is a material foundation to all understanding, though that understanding will be marked (all things to each set of knowers). Our intelligence is human but all humans, if properly trained against bias, can reliably engage the phenomenal world and craft justified claim from that engagement. Errors in human knowledge are correctable by better (i.e., less biased) methods. This position is mostly a restatement of Position 1 above, although it does admit to a human representation rather than to universal intelligence and does concede that perceptions can be in error. (This concession can also be used to underscore the need for a professional inquiry.)

3. *Constructive empiricism* (Davidson, 1980, 1984): Human intelligence is in ways dependent on (mediated by) collective accomplishments, and therefore any given intelligence is partial. The parts are additive, however. Further, the phenomenal world is greater than its material foundation and plural because phenomena arise in separate domains (the sum of material and achieved things to the sum of human knowers). Both our engagement of a phenomenal world and our justified arguments about it are at least partially dependent on cultural memberships. Nonetheless, our engagement of a phenomenal world can be considered as a mapping of a P-world onto human understanding. The map can be culturally inflected and does indeed mediate our understanding but does so with literal signs in valid claim.

4. *Postmodern empiricism* (Rosenau, 1992): Finally, human intelligence is both a combination of the semiotic and the sensory as well as partial, but here the parts are nonadditive. The phenomenal world is not only greater than its material foundation and plural, but it is also greater than what can be known from a given vantage point (some things to some groups of knowers). What is there and what we know about it are problematics reduced by ideology and political action. Actual errors are unknowable; claims about errors advance on ideological and political grounds. This position would hold to public knowledge as an articulated understanding marked by the authority, voice, and process of its articulation and by the collective semiotic resources in which understanding can be expressed.

The variations run, then, from the unity of the phenomenal world and of intelligence generating a single epistemological method, to an increasing diversity starting with a unitary phenomenal world but multiple intelligence generating a single but human epistemology, to a phenomenal world of multiple domains engaged by human intelligence resulting in multiple epistemologies coded to the multiple domains, and ending with the most diverse stance of multiple domains and partials of human intelligence resulting in multiple, partial epistemologies. Along the line, we have moved from capital-"T" *Truth* to *human Truth* to *human truths* to *partial truths.*

This is a big slide and the ride is given by the answers to the following questions: What is to be known? How is it to be known? And who is the knower? Our work on the first question is the stuff of the previous chapter. Here we take on primarily the method of knowing with some introduction to the character of the knower.

Our method will be to first consider the implications for theory of the four positions just articulated and then to take up the specific issues of (1) empiricism in positivism and beyond, (2) poststructuralist social theory, and (3) criticism in the land of the floating signifier. Again my intent is to lay out some issues with the understanding that I've made my choices and yours don't have to agree, but also with the understanding that the issues themselves are useful interrogators of the character of theory.

FOUR CORNER IMPLICATIONS

In his 14th month my enthralled grandson is standing on the first step of the stairs to the bedrooms of my house. He has discovered that in this location he can reach the light switch. (His own house has only one level.) I watch him as he enjoys the action and sound of flipping the switch up and down. At first, his attention seems to be entirely focused on the switch. At the top of the stairs and about half-way down the hall a light flashes on and off as he works the switch. I observe him as he comes first to the recognition that the light is flashing and then that he controls that event with the switch. He giggles with such excitement that he nearly falls off the step.

What has he experienced? Without attempting a detailed analysis, he has discovered the tactile and auditory event of the light switch and the visual event of the light flashing on and off. But he understands something more. He understands that they are related not just in the space of the hallway or in the synchrony of their time but as cause and effect. (My evidence for this claim is that he begins to vary the timing of the switch and to anticipate the light change when he changes the switch. This is as powerful a piece of evidence for Kant's presuppositions as any I have encountered.)

It is the recognition that experience is some sort of composite—however that composite is defined—that has led to a general rejection—in principle but certainly not in practice, as we shall see—of the singularity of the relationship between the phenomenal world and our observations of it. That rejection casts us out to sea on the question of what that relationship might be.

The question is fundamental and it has a number of guises. It is the basis for all the questions concerning the forms of validity in measurement. It is in the formula for operational definitions; it underlies any coding procedure; it is at the heart of ethnography and criticism; and it is certainly the question of the sign and its meaning. It is my intent now to take up this question in this last form: the relationship between a sign and its meaning. My reason for this choice is that once we step aside from brute sense data—that one-to-one relationship between "out there" and "in the head"—we are forced into the semiotic domain.[1]

In some way or another our observations are not simple reproductions of the phenomenal world but instead are signs of it. If those observations are the signs of the world and not the world itself, then we must face two classes of questions: What is the manner of their construction? How do they invoke meaning? We can engage these questions at any level from the most physiological to the most discursive.

Let's pose these questions in terms of some specific examples. What is the evidentiary force of the grandson example? Is it only a solipsism (a single person's view of untested reliability), is it merely anecdotal (a nice story but lacking rigor), or is it the professional observation of a trained ethnographer (a legitimate claim)? Did I see what I claimed to see? My grandson standing on the stair? Probably there would be little argument. My grandson's moment of recognition of causation? Probably there would be much more contention. Why? Because the claim references an unobservable mental state and requires us to take implicative action. It is what Harrison (1991) calls "dangerous knowledge."

Another example: Presume a content analysis in which the researcher is determining story topics and the number of column inches devoted to each. How do we determine story topic? There is no single observation that allows us to make that claim. Topic is an overarching judgment made up of various forms of evidence: words used, their relative frequency, their placement, syntax, and the like. These are the signs of the topic. (The procedural mask of this question is intercoder reliability. Any time researchers use multiple coders, it is likely because the observations are considered vulnerable.)

Let me offer a final example. Wayne Beach (1990) argues in his article on conversational analysis that

> coding methods inevitably function to gloss (and perhaps even misrepresent) the phenomena accounted for with empirical findings. The key issue, however, is the nature and degree of glossing that occurs, and the implications such glossing holds for understanding how interaction gets organized. (p. 222)

How does he know this? If every engagement of the phenomena is an encoding and every coding glosses and perhaps misrepresents, what coding is the standard by which we judge the gloss of others?

A SET OF INFORMING QUESTIONS

The problem for Beach, and for us all, involves the recognition of an authentic engagement of the real and its distinction from both a defective engagement and an engagement of the imaginary. The problem is summed up in the relationship between a sign and its meaning and is illuminated by two sets of questions.

The first question set concerns the realm of symbol production or the move from the cognitive interior to the semiotic export. The second set concerns the realm of symbol interpretation or the move from the exterior sign to some conscious or performative understanding. These two question families concern the manner in which material facts produce a signifying potential (the sign), the character of the semiotic object (our understanding of it), and the nature of the relationship that mediates sign and signified (how our understanding is connected to the sign), as well as the possibility and the extent of our control over that relationship. These four interior concern are raised at both points of focus within communication, the production of the sign in a publically accessible manner and the understanding of the sign in some subsequent decoding.[2] We start with some questions from each side which will direct our analysis.

In the realm of production, the questions might be posed as: What is the unformed resource, for example, of the observations that Beach would like to make or of the words on this page? Who or what is the maker of the sign? What is the site of the work of encoding? What are the resources of this encoding? How are those resources made available to the meaning maker? What is the necessity of intent? What is the formulation of an intent to mean? What is the recognition of the resources to accomplish that intent? How is its satisfaction accomplished (encoded in sign choice)? And where is its realization?

In the realm of interpretation, the questions might begin with: How is the sign recognized as a sign? What are the structural/genetic/learned/idiopathic components in that recognition and subsequent interpretation? Who is the meaning maker? What is the site of interpretation? What role does production intentionality play in sign recognition and sense making? What is the character and moment of semiosis? How are the resources of semiosis engaged? What is the nature of the product of semiosis? What is the conclusion of the interpretive event or task?

There are, of course, extensive literatures on nearly every one of these questions, and we will do no more than touch the surface of each. One way to begin this analysis is to take the central points along the range of our four communities from which answers have been developed. These centroids (if you will) can be plotted across the degree of determinacy in sign character, encoding, decoding, and interpretation. (Comparisons of this sort can be found in Outhwaite, 1987; Teichman, 1988; and Terwee, 1990—among many others.)

Traditional Empiricism: The Remains of Brute Sense Data

We might begin at the most determinant position, one that has been dubbed "the physicalist position." This position echoes the naive empiricism of Bacon and Locke in that the phenomenal world is conceived as a set of natural signs that represent a set of true conditions. (Teichman, 1988, provides a fair review of this argument.) In this position, the character of the sign is wholly reputable and is responsible for encoding, decoding, and interpretation. Language and other constructed signs can be literally true. Something can be meant and encoded without error, given an act of nature (nature gives itself directly) or the proper level of linguistic competence (language can be referential and representational). Semiosis is the "natural" decoding operation of the sentient instrument that is a trustworthy observer of the sign and its encoded meaning. Interpretation is an elaborated understanding of the sign in its setting and the purposes we have for it. It is directed by right reasoning.

This physicalist position was gaining strength by the close of the 16th century, and it is a fundamental argument of empirical science still today. It has resisted efforts completely tear it down but its erosion has been in progress since the partitioning of the mind by Freud and Jung and the partitioning of reality by American pragmatists and European scholars.

In the fields that touch on communication studies, behaviorism was and remains the obvious restatement of the primacy of the sign as agent. Many studies in communication, particularly effects and literacy studies, reflect the behaviorist tradition and are conducted "as if the brute sense data position were true" while the authors would probably demur that "of course it's not."

The "as if" portion of that claim is upheld by any study that (1) holds that content has a definitive, literal, or governed meaning, (2) treats content as the delivery system of that meaning, (3) declares content to be the agent of some consequence in an audience, and (4) treats the audiences as a reactant. Such studies have adopted an "as if" stance on the physicalist's site. The researcher first asserts both an ontological and praxeological claim by declaring content to be something—for example, violent, pornographic, scary, informative, or persuasive— to someone else. The subsequent behavior of the someone else is attributed to the content exposure. Examples of these "as if" studies would include the classic Berkowitz and Rawlings (1963) and Bandura, Ross, and Ross (1961, 1963) studies, as well as recent ones by Phillips (1983), Rosenthal (1986), Wilson (1991), and Zillmann and Bryant (1982)

Perceptual Empiricism:
The Introduction of Perception

By the close of the 19th century, the general belief in the unmediated character of sense data gave way to the recognition that human understanding required a perceptual process to intervene between sensation and cognition. Continuous sensory data had to be perceptually organized for us to experience the world's phenomena. Encoding was no longer conceived as wholly dependent on the character of the sign and there was consequent slippage between encoding and decoding, so that the sign and its interpretation were no longer one. Perceptions were (and generally are) nonetheless considered to be authoritative representations of actual phenomena although error and bias can occur.

There arose a large class of studies that examine the perceptual process—the whole Gestalt school, for example. These studies hold perception to be an orderly, reliable process with predictable failures (any of the bent-line perceptual tricks) and problem areas. (As an aside it should be noted that any declared failure has to be judged against a more privileged perception. A line, therefore, is straight to the ruler but bent to the eye and the choice of which one is true is conventionally made.)

Perception has also been used to indicate a "taxonomic" response. Studies of this sort have titles like "Perceived Fright Values of Horror Films by 8-Year-Olds" or "Perceived Attributions of Gender-Differentiated Characters by Adult Males" (for an actual example, see David, 1992). The implied argument is that there are either real fright values or attributions that can be compared with those of, say, 8-year-olds or that there is no objective basis for claiming any fright values or attributions, and consequently the ones expressed by the respondent groups is a characteristic of their ideational taxonomy (for an example, see Frost & Stauffer, 1987).

This form of taxonomic claim is further developed in studies that use "relevance triggers." These studies (e.g., Inyengar, 1979) attribute differences in outcomes to devices that serve to position the respondent (usually by reminding him or her of some doctrinal or attitudinal stance).

Both are arguments that one's (the respondent's) vision of reality is marked by social conditioning,[3] but at the same time, because the researcher can determine the real or the objective, such markings can be resisted by the well trained. That this good training can be extended to others is one of the principal tenets of media education (Anderson, 1980). It is seen in training efforts to produce the skills that result in the right perception of deceptive or otherwise inappropriate media fare.

Perceptual processes are also the underlying support for interventions in which one message (and resultant understandings) is to form the basis of the perception of some subsequent presentation (see Donohue, Henke, & Meyer, 1983). Such studies are an extension of the forewarned-is-forearmed principle.

For example, children who had the opportunity to handle real earthworms prior to their exposure to a film clip that depicted a giant earthworm monster had reduced fear responses (Weiss, Imrich, & Wilson, 1993). The prior exposure was seen as directing the effect of the film.

The precept that perception is a requirement of human understanding has general acceptance among the scientific community. Its application, however, varies widely.

In the majority of effects studies, its operation is either ignored or considered to be a constant across all respondents. This transparent perceptual process is effectively a return to brute sense data. When perception appears in effects studies, it is often used as a marker of respondent typification by class, gender, race, education, and the like (e.g., Zemach & Cohen, 1986). These typifications are accomplished by differentiated responses to material that in itself is considered perceptually neutral across these categories of influence. The operation of perception, then, is considered a constant across type.

In some studies, (e.g., Vidmar & Rokeach, 1974), the issue of perceptual error or bias is also inserted. Perceptual bias must necessarily imply some alternative nonbiased position from which it can be viewed. Usually this position is that of common sense (which is the property of the researcher).

Relevance triggers and intervention studies offer a more complex application arguing that perception can be shaped at the moment of reception of the focal message. The *step beyond* these studies is the argument that perception must be shaped (and is, therefore, in each and every case somehow shaped) at *any* moment of perception. While adherents of this view have typically not taken that step, the potential of taking that step shows perception to be the social science equivalent to deconstructionist subjectivity—the relevance trigger as interpellation.

Perception puts the character of the message in play at the point of reception. Beyond the rules of competent production, the perceptionist has little to say about the message as encoded. In most perceptual analyses, that encoding is fully justified by authorial intent (it is a different community that introduces polysemy). It is an interesting position that allows the researcher or critic to declare what is true while exploring the diverse perceptual activity of the respondents or audience.

The legacy of naive empiricism is clearly seen in the loose and friendly way in which perception offers its presence to research. It imposes no requirement to account for its operation, but one can use it if desired. Researchers are free both to hold to perceptual processes and to presume that they have no effect, that treatment messages can change perceptions but research protocols will not, that others are subject to perceptual derivations but researchers are not, and that the untrained are biased and the trained are true. A more difficult presence would require, at the least, researchers to abandon any claim of what a message is prior to its interpretation by a target audience and would compel the analysis of that interpretation in any study of effect.

Perception remains, at this writing, a theoretical device to solve anomalies that have arisen in testing the central empirical claim of a generally unmediated engagement of phenomena, material and semiotic. There is little evidence as to its material operation. As Bolles (1991) notes, "Not only do we not know how perception works but we haven't a clue as to how it might work" (p. xi). Its character in theory and method is firmly in our own hands.

Constructive Empiricism: Creating the Semiotic Object

In most perception studies, we are looking at the perception *of* something. There is a material, factual object with a reality independent of the perception per se. This is the independent character of the signified. For example, Pettersson (1988) speaks of a "figure" that becomes the number 13 when placed in a sequence of numbers and the letter B when placed in a sequence of letters. It, however, preexists as a figure before it is perceived as a number or as a letter.

The theoretical break between material and semiotic objects—and the break between the private and public processes of encoding and decoding—comes with the claim that the figure's existence as a figure is also a perception. Indeed, all objects are the product of the sign. The material facts of their existence are the bounded persistences of reflection, refraction, absorption, and the like. Those boundaried persistences become what can be known when they are coalesced into a semiotic object. (A relationship of persistences becomes a chair only in the presence of a mind, although the relationship continues even in the mind's absence.)

This move changes the phenomenal world from a world of material objects to a polysemic world of material semiotic potentials. In this latter world, there are material foundations for what is seen, but what is seen is always the product of the mind (Gibson, 1966, and Sacks, 1993, call this the creation of a perceptual self).

While images of Berkeleyism and trees falling soundlessly in the forest may dance in our heads, there are positions in this constructionism that work in the same way as the physicalist's brute sense data. One need only posit universal rules governing the relationship between material potentials and resultant semiotic objects to return us to the beginning. We start to move toward the "Wonderland" of Lewis Carroll—where meaning is clearly in doubt—when we release the semiotic object from the universal sentience (or at least universal human sentience) of Peirce and Husserl and (1) cultural processes enter into the equation, so that the same material foundations are used to produce culturally different semiotic objects (culturally different boundaries of color is the example I have offered); (2) the semiotic object is greater than the material foundation can warrant (the idea of semiotic excess, of the sign invoking the sign); (3) the material foundation is itself a set of human practices that must be understood semiotically (the idea of justice).

We move closer to the Red Queen—where meaning is under local control—by defining the semiotic object as the set of socially determined understandings in play for some material foundation (what Crapanzano, 1992, calls "centering") within some cultural era or, more radically, some community of understanding. By putting what is signified in play, we affirm the social construction of reality and open the door to different ways of thinking across generations and communities. The result is that collectives of the same ostensible language group use the same material resources of semiosis to achieve in their well-practiced and naturalized methods different worlds of everyday life. (Morely's [1980, 1986] work in caste-based understandings of soap operas is a good example.) The sign remains reliable (within limits of perception) *within* a community but not *across* communities.

Questions remain as to the size, scope, quality, and character of reality-defining collectives and how one enters into them. Where one finds an answer in this liberation of the jointly held mind to create the reality of its understanding is the defining point of theoretic and methodological ontology.

Whatever one's ontological position, the constructionist ferrying of objectivity from the phenomenal world into the realm of collectively governed cognition changes a number of fundamental tenets (a good development of these is in Seung, 1982): reality is no longer universal or only material and is determinate only within community boundaries (even if the boundaries encompass us all). The individual is no longer the measure; the collective stands in that place.[4] We no longer perceive a preexisting object but create a perception out of possibilities. The adjudication of error is no longer determined by reference to a standard independent of the researcher. In sum, the trustworthiness of the sign as well as its ability to drive an interpretation are reduced to collective boundaries, and encoding and decoding are volatile practices because they migrate across those boundaries.

Postmodern Empiricism: The Final Deconstruction

Remembering that the Peircean sign is composed of a material trace (natural or composed), the object for which it stands, and the acknowledged relationship between the two (Nöth, 1990), our work to this point has been to consider the manner in which the material trace is recognized in perceptual processes and the methods of social construction by which the semiotic object is formed. Throughout those two analyses, once the material trace is grasped in perception, its object (however achieved) is presented in a reliable relationship. I have called this "the trustworthiness of the sign." I believe it reasonably represents, along with perception and social construction, a significant boundary among different theoretical communities. We are about to cross that boundary.

Our philosophic guides are the likes of Schleiermacher, Dilthey,

Kierkegaard, Heidegger, Gadamer, and of course Derrida, but we also gain direction from American pragmatists, social interactionists, and interpretive sociologists. In crossing the boundary we abandon any transcendent relationship between sign and meaning. Instead, we focus our efforts on understanding how a sign is always in the process of becoming meaningful, always in the process of creating the relationship between what can be recognized as the possibility of understanding and what can be understood.

Within the fractious community that harbors the likes of Derrida (*Speech and Phenomena*, 1972), Barthes (*Pleasure of the Text*, 1975), Eco (*A Theory of Semiotics*, 1976) and Caputo (*Radical Hermeneutics*, 1987), this position of the other side argues that signs are contingent means of managing the flux of the present. Signs rather than being referential are encyclopedic. They reach out in every direction in an infinite potential that can be but partially realized in any instance. Signs are the command to make meaning in a collectively recognizable, local performance of sense making.

What something means, therefore, is answerable only in the present, only at the site of considerable efforts that provide for its construction and must be answered anew at the next asking. That answer will have to take into account the tension between collective efforts to sustain meaning (through persistent and overlapping performances) and the necessity of its local and partial expression by some agent[5] of that collective. These requirements in no way deny that retinas respond to light energy in predictable ways, that brains reliably recognize the stimuli of their perceptions, and that minds are shaped by culture and the practices of socialization. They simply claim that retinas, brains and minds are not enough to understand meaning (Sherrif, 1989). One must also understand action, for it is in action that meaning may become.

Now before we all drift out of sight, the methodological consequences for this theoretical stance are (1) to establish the framework of ongoing effort that permits meaning construction as the target for our methods; (2) to nominate methods that reveal onsite the material practices of that effort; and (3) to recognize that the facts revealed are themselves the product of some other framework. Using collective resources, the agent meaning maker achieves some local understanding. *That* local understanding can be repeated elsewhere and by others but *that* repetition requires its own work.

Hermeneuticists have divided along two lines: One, following a structuralist trail, has held to a belief in the primacy of language in constituting consciousness (Bleicher, 1982; Connolly & Keutner, 1988; Manganaro, 1990). The other, more existentialist, has held to action as the means by which the self appears. This theoretical division has shown itself in the practice of scholarship by the appearance of textual-based critical analysis (Carey, 1989; Grossberg, 1984; Huck, 1993) and performance-based interpretive ethnography (Anderson & Goodall, 1994; Anderson & Meyer, 1988; Goodall, 1991; Rose, 1990).

When scholars abandon the trustworthiness of the sign, they are faced with the continuous study of the methods of collective resource production, one's access to them, the subjectivity of agency, the authority of action, and the voice of its extension. All the while they are called to realize that they are the authors of this knowledge and subject to the same analysis. As with the villainess in *Fatal Attraction* nothing is finally submerged, but, knife in hand, it rises again and again.

An Overview of Positions

We have looked at four more or less separate positions from which to compose answers that might address the questions posed at the start of this discussion. They are the physicalist, the perceptionist, the constructionist, and the action-alist arguments of traditional, perceptual, constructive, and postmodern empiricism respectively. The physicalist view is one of an organic machine reliably responding to independent empirical phenomena that drive isomorphic representations of consciousness. Language is a genetically based system of representation of phenomena and preexisting categories, as well as the extensions of both.

The perceptionist can occupy a broad region, at one end very close to the physicalist, noting only certain discrepancies in the reception and interpretation of sensory information, at the other end, speculating on perceptual realities only loosely connected to sensation. Language remains a genetically based system of representation of phenomena and preexisting categories but can be enlivened (or corrupted) by perceptual variation.

The constructionist draws the conclusion the perceptionist resists: If perception intervenes between understanding and the phenomenal world, then we must be active participants in coconstructing the world we believe in. Language has physical foundations and formal structures, but its system of representation is a practical human achievement—a given in which we all enter and contribute.

The actionalist takes the step beyond metaphysics and puts it all in play. In the actionalist project, the struggle for meaning is the work of everyday life and the placement of meaning is the successful expression of power. Language is physical, structural, and representational, but its meaningfulness is not in genetics, structures, or representations (any combination of signs can be made meaningful) but in its material presence in action.

A COLLECTION OF ANSWERS

Tables 3–1 and 3–2 present our initial questions concerning the relationship between sign and meaning in realms of sign production and interpretation. The tables provide shortened references to the questions and rather cryptic answers that allow us to see the points of difference but that do grave injustice to even a marginal articulation of these complex issues. This injustice is somewhat rectified in the sections that follow, which enlarge the answers provided.

The Realm of Symbolic Production

Just as a reminder, the questions that inhabit the realm of symbolic *production* were: What is the unformed resource of the sign? Who or what is the maker of the sign? What is the site of the work of encoding? What are the resources of this encoding? How are those resources made available to the meaning maker? What is the necessity of intent? What is the formulation of an intent to mean? What is the recognition of the resources to accomplish that intent? How is its satisfaction accomplished (encoded in sign choice)? And where is its realization?

Unformed Resources

The major contrast is between the physicalist–perceptionist pair and the constructionist–actionalist pair over what is prior to the semiotic. For both the physicalist and the perceptionist, the semiotically unformed resource of understanding is a verifying phenomenal world that can be engaged in a objective fashion. Signs have meanings independent of their creation. The shadings between the two deal with the degree of mediation involved in the engagement of this objective reality.

TABLE 3–1. In the Realm of Production

Questions:	Traditional Empiricism	Perceptual Empiricism	Constructive Empiricism	Postmodern Empiricism
Prior resource	Empirical reality	Perceived reality	Semiotic achievements	Collective achievements
Meaning maker	Autonomous rationality	Perceiving subject	Situated subject	Acting subject
Encoding site	Individual	Individual	Ideological collective	Agent in collective
Intent	Required	Required	Utilized, not required	Part of the action
Resources	Genetic	Genetic & cultural	Human accomplishments	As available in action
Intent accomplished	Proper encoding	Perceptually encoded	Rhetorically encoded	Coherent action
Intent realized	Proper decoding	Perceptually decoded	Rhetorically decoded	Local utility

TABLE 3-2. In the Realm of Interpretation

Questions:	Traditional Empiricism	Perceptual Empiricism	Constructive Empiricism	Postmodern Empiricism
Sign recognition	Adequate stimulus	Adequate stimulus	Difference boundaries	Difference boundaries
Sign interpretation	Hard wired	Hardware & software combo	Practical accomplishment	Actional accomplishment
Meaning maker	Sensory system	Perceiving subject	Situated subject	Acting subject
Site of interpretation	Individual	Socialized individual	Ideological collective	Social action
Semiosis	Sensory engagement	Perceived stimulus	Ideological engagement	Action engagement
Semiosis engaged	Liminal stimulus	Cognition initiated	Collectively managed	As initiated in action
Authorial intent	Directs interpretation	Directs interpretation	Point of comparison	As required by action
Semiotic product	Isomorphic representation	Perceived representation	Positioned interpretation	Contingent interpretation
Interpretation conclusion	Moment of sensation	Cognitive recognition	Enactment of subjectivity	Enactment of acting subject

For both the constructionist and the actionalist there is nothing prior to semiotics in understanding (see Wertsch's 1985 overview of Vygotsky and Bakhtin). What we know of the phenomenal world, we know semiotically. Meaning is a cultural production. The differences between this pair have to do with the security of meanings. For the hermeneut, meaning is never secure but instead always open to innovation, opposition, and resistance.

Meaning Maker

Answers to this question show a steady decomposition of the monadic self. From the universal representor to the nominated, contingently acting subject, the meaning maker becomes more and more collectivized and requires more and more description to understand that instrument of sense making. For example, while it is true that a person wrote these words, the question remains as to whether he was acting autonomously or as a cultural agent or as a tool of collective action.

Encoding Site

Again our pairs split, this time over the primacy of the individual and the collective. The left hand holds encoding to be the creative act of the intending individual. The right hand holds that the encoder is a clerk of the collective whose invention is wholly derivative. (And here I note the move from private to public forecast in Chapter 1.)

The Questions of Intent

For the physicalist and the perceptionist, the role of intent in symbolic production is to establish the motive for production and the "right meaning" for the text, as well as the basis for judgment concerning its proper encoding and decoding. This position requires a belief that intent is prior to the text and extractable from the text. (For an extended discussion of the necessity of intent, see Arvamides, 1989.)

Intent need serve no validating purpose in domains of the constructionist and the actionalist. For the encoder, intent may well arise after the symbolic product has been formed and may subsequently be revealed in the ongoing action. For the decoder, intent is a device used to advance a particular claim of meaning or to execute some interpretive performance. In both cases, intent is an invention not a determinant.

The Realm of Interpretation

Here, our questions concerned sign recognition, the components of that recognition and its interpretation, the meaning maker, the site of intepretations, the role of intentionality, the character and moment of semiosis, the resources of semiosis, its product, and conclusion.

Sign Recognition

For the first two categories of scholars, sign recognition is a function of the incoming information. The concept of an adequate stimulus is one that excites the sensory nerve. It is that excitation which is recognized (never mind the obvious problem here) and its object source reproduced or perceived.

For the latter two categories of scholars the incoming information has to be punctuated to be recognized. Objectification is the first step of interpretation, provided for and driven by collective resources.

Sign Interpretation

Sign interpretation shows a decomposition similar to that of the meaning maker. We move from the universal electrochemical operations of neurons (which is the singular definition of literal meaning) to an increasing differentiation and collective implication of the interpretive performance as a local and partial product of the acting agent.

Meaning Maker

As in the production realm, the physicalist is clearly separate from the rest on this question, as that position works for system rather than subject answers. The remaining positions will necessarily construct a responding subject, self-contained for the perceptionist, collectively invoked for the constructionist, and implicated in social action for the actionalist.

Site of Interpretation

An inside–outside split characterizes the difference between the left and right pairs. For the first, interpretation "happens" in the individual through sensory or cognitive processes. For the second pair, interpretation is a collective achievement prior to the individual whose role is evocation or enactment.

Semiosis

Semiosis—that moment of semiotic understanding—occurs for the physicalist at the moment of neural response, for the perceptionist at the formation of a perception, for the constructionist at the moment the sign is ideologically positioned, and for the actionalist as the moment of becoming in action. Our first pair offers a "behind the eyes" definition that is strongly dependent on the individual as the acting unit. Our second pair sees semiosis as a collective process in which the individual participates but cannot achieve on his or her own.

Semiosis Engaged

The physicalist defines semiosis engagement as the moment a gate-passing stimulus is presented. That is insufficient for the perceptionist, who believes that cognitive structures (variously called values, attitudes, or schemata) must be brought into play. Therefore, for the perceptualist, it is the implication of these structures that signals the engagement (and for some, the terms) of semiosis. Both of those definitions are far too interior for many constructionists and certainly for all actionalists who want to emphasis the "out front," material practices of the collective as requirements and directives of what we can come to understand.

Authorial Intent

True decoding in the physicalist and the perceptionist camp must follow the requirements of authorial intent, be it natural or human. Decodings accounting for intent in the remaining two camps are simple variants of the possible with no particular veridical standing.

Semiotic Product

We divide our pairs on the issue of representation versus interpretation. (An interesting discussion of representational meaning can be found in Gillet, 1992.) Neither constructionists nor hermeneutists may innocently claim representation. There is, for neither, nothing independent of the semiotic to represent. A sign is the interpretation of another sign. Any representation, then, is a practical accomplishment of semiotic maneuvering.

Physicalists consider representation necessary, and perceptionists consider it righteous. Physicalists gave up the little of representation they were going to with Kant's priors. Perceptionists generally hold that there is always an independent factual (albeit sometimes trivial) expression available to reconcile perceptual differences.

The Conclusion of Interpretation

Interpretation concludes at a definable moment for the first pair. This moment is defined as the instant of sensation and of cognition, respectively. The definitive character of the moment is a significant division, for at its conclusion the interpretation passes from consequent to antecedent. As an antecedent it is the motive for subsequent behavior. It is this theoretical moment upon which the whole effects and attitude literature hangs.

There is no such moment for most of the remaining theorists. Interpretation is an emerging process, not an instant. Its activity certainly subsides but need never end. Interpretations are not the independent cause of some subsequent action; rather, they are accommodated within the larger performances of ideology or everyday life. (Under this rubric, one does not stop at a traffic light because it is red, but because one is driving.)

An Analytic Summary

Much of our problem in dealing with the trustworthiness of observation has to do with the immense range our observations can cover. If you were to put a chair in my path as I walked along, I would undoubtedly fall over it if I were to fail to account for its position. But all of my failings and fallings would not lead me to recognize the object of my distress as a chair. That recognition happens *some place else* outside of the material. How we structure that some place else is prior to and an act of theory construction.

Another example: "The quick brown fox jumps over the lazy dog" is a competent sentence, but it is not a sentence in the way this is a sentence. Typists and keyboarders immediately recognize it as the device for testing a keyboard and their skills. Because of its use, it signals no exchange intent (I'm not telling you what the fox did). The writing that I am doing now is telling you how to make that sentence meaningful, but I have no idea of whether you will follow, ignore, resist, or oppose those instructions.

Our respondents are faced with exactly the same problem when given an item such as:

Friendships involve the exchange of deeply held information.

Agree Strongly	Agree	Agree Slightly	Neutral	Disagree Slightly	Disagree	Disagree Strongly

The sentence beginning with "Friendships" is also not a sentence in the way this one is. It invokes a different set of rules for how it is to be made meaningful. Once a selection has been made by a respondent, the sentence, as it is handed to the researcher, becomes an observation on the entity called "friendship." It changes character from an item on a test dealt with according to testing rules to a research observation dealt with according to doing research rules. We now know the sentence beginning with "Friendships" in three different ways: (1) as an example in this text, (2) as an item on a test, and (3) as an observation in a study. The materiality of the sentence itself clearly does not change, but the action in which it is involved certainly does, and consequently so too does our knowledge of that sentence.

The issues we have been discussing in this comparison of our four communities does not involve the question of whether members from each would fall over a chair in their paths. Assuming equal inattentiveness, each would. The issues have to do with the manner by which one's theory deals with nonmaterial entities like friendship and the contextual responsiveness of our methods of observation. We have seen, then, four different ways in which these issues are handled: (1) the physicalist's material isomorphism (which is entirely silent on the semiotic); (2) the perceptionist's intersubjectivity (where perceptual biases are controlled by concurrent observations of some number greater than 1); (3) the constructionist's collective ideology (which ranges from an emancipatory "some ideologies are better than others" to a nonutopian "everything is dangerous"); and (4) the actionalist's ideology in action (where meaning is an ongoing activity).

We see relatively little of the physicalist position in our journals, although studies of brain wave activity or of the character of an adequate stimulus or of liminality or of the orientating reflex are representative. The perceptionist's intersubjectivity is the dominant position in quantitative analysis, for it provides for the objective criterion. Constructionism is well established in criticism and in media studies, and most of it is of the emancipatory sort. Finally, the actionalist position is appearing in ethnographic or life-world studies that center on organizational culture or media analysis.

We will note that the lines of argument concerning engagement follow closely the lines of argument of the previous chapter. They are, however, two different questions, and the answer to one does not necessarily predict the answer to the other. Consequently, not only do we have to decide what is real, we also have to decide how we engage that reality. Theories can and do mix and match.

We now turn our attention to three specific cosmologies of engagement: empirical positivism, structuralism, and subjectivist criticism.

EMPIRICISM: POSITIVISM AND BEYOND

Positivism is a knowledge argument whose roots are usually traced to Auguste Comte (1798–1857). Comte's claim was that we could have positive knowledge in middle-ground theory, though we might not know how it all began or might end. Positivism as a doctrine in the philosophy of science reached its apogee in the form of logical positivism. Logical positivism was a project of a group of philosophers who collectively came to be known as the "Vienna Circle" and who were writing in the 1930s and 1940s.[6] Though their history is just now being written, they appear to have been unusually influential (accusations of the suppression of others have surfaced).

The Terms of Logical Positivism

In contemporary comment, logical positivism has become a caricature of opposition, with all sorts of "Evil Empire" characteristics attributed to it (perhaps because of the actions of its disciples). Nonetheless, its principles are straightforward and would generally be considered hallmarks of good science. Positivism begins by separating theoretical statements from observational ones. Observational statements are ones that meet the materialist criterion. The are self-presenting events about which we can have positive knowledge. (Positivists, as do most of us, would summarily dismiss an idealism or skepticism that would call that criterion into doubt.)

Because they concern self-presenting events, observational statements are independent of theoretical statements. A competent observer entirely ignorant of theory will see what there is to see (the "positive" of logical positivism), although she may not properly understand it. Theoretical statements are to be modeled on mathematical (the move toward mathematical unification of science) logic (the "logic" of logical positivism). Finally, the two—observation and theory—are to be connected by "rules of correspondence," a concept in line with Bridgeman's operationalism. (For a practical discussion of these principles, see Diesing, 1971.)

Theory building can progress in either the observational or the theoretical realm. Observationally, one might determine the logical characteristics of particular phenomena and their relationships as the basis for moving to theoretical statements of higher generality. Or one might develop a theoretical relationship and then examine what theory entails and observation declares.

For example, based on my observations of organizations, I might claim: "In hegemonic relationships, the expression of power requires the presence or anticipation of resistance."[7] (This is a statement of necessity but not of sufficiency; i.e., I make no claim about what initiates the expression of power.) In this theoretical statement I have moved from the relatively small number of organizations I have studied closely to a statement of great generality covering all organizations characterized by hegemonic relationships. My theory would fail (i.e., require rethinking) if I found one hegemonic organization in which power was expressed without the presence or anticipation of resistance. (Or, it might require an "exception" statement, such as " In hegemonic relationships the expression of power requires the presence or anticipation of resistance *except when that expression is ritualized.*")

On the other hand, thinking about my initial claim, I might decide that there has to be a strength relationship between power and resistance. I would then propose: "The greater the expression of power, the greater the potential for resistance." (There is a change in agency here: power is now driving the equation.) To document the validity of this statement, I would have to return to my organizational sites to examine confirming (or disconfirming) instances. Note that for a logical positivist, my theory is at a very low level as I still am using ordinary language and I imply a relatively low powered mathematical logic (it only has nominal and ordinal qualities).

My theory requires a number of rules of correspondence. I need to provide a correspondence rule for "hegemonic relationship," "expression of power," "presence of resistance," and "anticipation of resistance." Further, each of these in turn has its own requirements. What is hegemony? A relationship? An expression? Power? A presence? An anticipation? Resistance? In practice, I will explain no more than what I have to until I can rest on the background assumptions from which this theoretical position can arise. (If hegemony is not well known, how could I even pose it?)

Let's take "expression of power" as an example. Breaking it apart, I might first define "expression" as an observable set of meaningfully coherent practices (within the domain of power). I might define "power" as the ability to execute intentional action (i.e., to do what I intend to do). Putting them back together, I might get something like: "An expression of power is an observable set of meaningfully coherent practices in which there is a prior intention and the ability to achieve that intention."

I would then have to operationally define all of the "entities" in that sentence. For example, I might define "sets of meaningfully coherent practices" as the responses to a questionnaire that asks managers to list their major responsibilities (e.g., "I manage staff activities"; "I perform profitability analysis") and then to indicate the practices understood as belonging to that responsibility (e.g., "I give out daily assignments to staff members"; "I collect monthly sales data"). In this example, "managing the staff" is the set and "daily assignments" is one of the practices made meaningful by its membership in that set.

It is certainly clear that I have a lot of work to do to move this theory into observationally testable statements. But it is also clear that work, though hard, is entirely possible. There is already in place a set of conventional procedures (questionnaires, experimental protocols, etc.) that will give me the solutions.

The Move to Empirical Adequacy

Unfortunately, the critical analysis of these conventions does not reduce the uncertainty of the quality of the correspondence rules I have proposed. You might, for example, question why the responsibility list is evidence of a meaningful practice set. I can craft an argument in its defense, but because the argument necessarily involves a move from a lower to a higher inferential level, it always ends up in an irreducible ontological claim (it is, because it is!). One of the weaknesses in the logical positivists' project, then, has been that rules of correspondence are not themselves self-presenting events (it is not self-evident that my responsibility list is indeed a measure of a meaningful practice set) but are instead theory-laden directives of what to look for and what to find.

In fact, the collapse of logical positivism as the dominant position has been described as the result of the failure to demonstrate the independence of the realm of theory and the realm of observation. What has been denied is the ability to make theory-free observational statements. In a study of group decision making, it is factually determinable whether a sentence was spoken (granting all necessary assumptions). But to claim that it was spoken is all that the facts will allow. Once I code it as a "one-up" statement (e.g., Rogers, 1989; Rogers & Farace, 1975) in order to study dominance and submission in decision making, I am knee-deep in theory.

Well, yes, but sentences do get spoken and listeners react to them in ways not supported by the facts of the speaking. One's best argument for a rule of correspondence is that it works to reproduce or model some part of the phenomenal world. It does in its domain what the theorist said it was going to do. We can concede that a correspondence rule is theory-laden but we can insist that it is also empirically entangled—what van Fraassen (1980) calls "constructive empiricism."

Nestled inside constructive empiricism, the requirements for my theory on power are eased considerably. It entails that there is something there that I call "resistance" that is at least concurrent with the appearance of something I call "power" and that I will be able to show you that relationship by a set of rules I can clearly state. I do not have to hold that resistance as I have described it is real—according to the requirements of scientific realism—or that I know the phenomenal something(s) called resistance in any way other than as my theory allows—according to the requirements of observational independence. (See Quine's 1953/1961/1980 discussion of these two dogmas.) All I have to do is to demonstrate that the correspondence rules do not of themselves generate the results. The rules need only be "empirically adequate" in such a way that they "preserve" some empirical component (van Fraassen, 1980).

In adopting this most reasonable of positions, we leave behind the rigidity of the logical positivists but enter the rabbit warren of underdetermination. Underdetermination describes the permissive relationship between theory and the phenomenal world that this test allows. It holds that multiple theories can develop around the same phenomena, each having equal standing, each being empirically adequate.

A *Time* magazine cover story on infidelity provides the basis for an example of the relationship between data and their role as evidence in theory. That cover story (August 15, 1994, p. 51) reports a study in which college students were asked one of three questions (Date me tonight? Come back to my apartment tonight? Have sex with me tonight?) by "attractive" members of the opposite sex. The study found striking differences in affirmative answers across gender.

Half of both the male and female respondents agreed to date the questioner that evening; nearly 70% of the male but only 6% of the female respondents would go back to the questioner's apartment; and 75% of the male respondents but none of the female respondents would have sex with questioner.

The article goes on to use these data in a sociobiological explanation in which genetic programming of mating strategies is used to explain the differences. In the genetic explanation, the only thing that counts is advancing the gene pool successfully into the future. For the good of the species, however, men and women have been encoded with different criteria for the selection of their mates. For the male, the choice is directed by the prospective mate's ability to bear and care for her offspring. For the female, the decision is based on the prospective mate's ability to fertilize and to protect. These separate encodings are used to explain the response differences across gender in a physicalist argument from traditional empiricism.

Each of the other forms of empiricism would produce its own characteristic argument. Perceptual empiricism would typically use differential socialization processes to explain the same difference. In this sort of theory, men and women would be seen as invested in different cognitive structures concerning sexual activity that translate into a different interest in casual sex.

The critical side of perceptual empiricism might well posit a sexual economy having its origins for feminist theory in patriarchy, for Marxist theory in class division and for some forms of critical theory in the commodification of the person. Men and women would be described as attaching object and use value to one and other respectively and consequently having a different economic relationship within sexual activity.

Within constructive empiricism, a social constructionist might be far more interested in the work the article is doing to justify male and female infidelity. The headline of the cover says, "It may be in our genes." If it is in our genes, then we can hardly be blamed. I would expect a "genetic defense" to appear in those cases where infidelity has some legal standing.[8]

Finally, in postmodern empiricism, a social action theorists might focus on the question-asking process itself, finding an explanation in the (presumably) very odd circumstances that the study presented.

We can arrange these positions in complementary or competitive fashion. In the complementary arrangement, the sexual economy is founded on the genetic demand and hierarchically turned by gender, class, or materialism. That hierarchy is translated into different socialization processes that produce different meanings for sexual intercourse for those differently enculturated. Those different meanings are instantiated in social action episodes called social science. Social science is itself a player in the social construction of reality. Everybody gets a bit of the action, and we can even make a connection to hard science too.

In the competitive arrangement, each of the theorist groups wants to provide the complete explanation. We are not going to understand infidelity by considering socialization processes; rather, we will understand socialization processes by understanding their genetic foundation and—given the Human Genome Project— institute change by genetic alteration. On the other hand, appealing to a genetic foundation undercuts the reformist motive of critical theory. The goal of bettering society through knowledge is taken out of the hands of the scholars whose tools are political action. They become technologists. Finally, if it's genes not meanings, the social actionist and constructionist are left playing with words. The competitive arrangement is a zero-sum game, but the payoff is high. There is, consequently, a very strong demand to move one's own theoretical position into the forefront. The author of the article and the editors of *Time* have served traditional empiricism well.

This example of alternative explanations shows empirical adequacy to be a relatively easy test. Empirical adequacy requires only that the argument "serve the data" and not be self-fulfilling. Here, some action that can be called "infidelity" needs to be explained, which I have done in four different ways.[9] There can be no reduction across these explanations because the observational evidence is not independent of the explanation itself. What the data are—an expression of genetic preordination, a sexual economy, social action, or reality construction—emanates (is dependent upon) from its theory and cannot be translated into another theoretical domain (Duhem, 1954; Roth, 1987).

This is the argument for the incommensurability of theories. This argument (Tudor, 1982) holds that there is no test that itself is independent of theory. Theory choice must ultimately be a political choice because there is no method that allows us empirically to choose one theory over another. This is an unacceptable position for many empiricists, but that is an argument we will pick up in Chapter 4.

I have called empirical adequacy a most reasonable position, and the reader we may wonder why. I have done so because it allows us to do three things: (1) It allows us to deal with a conjoint reality of signs and things, falling neither for the materialist belief that only things count nor for the collective foolishness that "it's all a matter of interpretation." (2) Within one's own argument, the analyst can act as if it were all true. Certainly, if I am crafting an argument concerning power and resistance in organizations, I have to do the best I can and then just go for it: make the claim, suppress the doubts, anticipate the counterarguments. And (3) one does not have to declare any other position to be false (and none but my own can declare my position false). The analyst can make the argument even in the presence of counterpositions. My argument can be as true as yours.

These three characteristics seem to describe the way we are currently acting (note my authorial move toward empirical adequacy here). Weiss et al. (1993), for example, introduce their own approach with this disclaimer:

> The issue of children's responses to frightening mass media can be studied from a variety of perspectives. For example, researchers working from an interpretive perspective might examine the ways in which different children deconstruct the meaning of a particular frightening episode (see J. Anderson, 1981; Anderson & Avery, 1988; Delia, 1977). Other researchers have begun to document individual differences in response to arousing media content (e.g., Sparks, Spirek, & Hodgson, 1992; Spirek & Sparks, 1993). (p. 42)

This paragraph doesn't suggest that "anything goes," of course, but it does suggest that there are other legitimate approaches to be recognized.

Empirical adequacy and the underdetermination of theory help us to understand the proliferation of theories that marks all forms of scholarship in human inquiry. Empiricial adequacy and underdetermination both turn on the rejection of naive empiricism and the strict requirements of logical positivism. That rejection depends on a prior belief that direct engagement of the phenomenal world expresses itself in banal terms; useful theory must necessarily mediate our engagement. In this mediation, the action of the phenomenal world will punish some theories as false but will permit all that can be true in their fashion.

Beyond Empiricism

Positivist arguments (logical or not) are built upon a foundational empiricism in which our unmediated engagement with the material world stands as a validation of the claims of science. The renunciation of a direct, unmediated engagement cracks this foundation. Empiricism is no longer a secure standing place. Additional arguments will move us beyond empiricism by holding that not only is it not secure, it is also not enough. There is more to the world of human action than can be encompassed in a world of things: we are also forced to deal with a world of meaning. Rochberg-Halton (1986) puts it succinctly: "Meaning forms the very basis of society, not instincts or genetics, materialist economics, or asocial psychological laws and . . . the foundation of meaning is the sign" (p. 43).

The step beyond empiricism requires us to somehow or another manage our inquiry into meaning. Structuralism and its successors in ideological analysis and cultural studies offer one approach. Semiotics and its relatives symbolic interactionism, pragmatism, and social action theory take us in another direction. The two sections that follow take them up in that order.

STRUCTURALISM

Terence Hawkes (1977) in a sympathetic review claims that structuralism involves,

> the realization that despite appearances to the contrary the world does not consist of independently existing objects, whose concrete features can be perceived clearly and individually, and whose nature can be classified accordingly. In fact, every perceiver's method of perceiving can be shown to contain an inherent bias which affects what is perceived to a significant degree. A wholly objective perception of individual entities is bound to create something of what he [sic] observes. Accordingly the relationship between observer and observed achieves a kind of primacy. It becomes the stuff of reality itself. Moreover the principle involved must invest the whole of reality. In consequence, the true nature of things may be said to lie not in things themselves, but in the relationships which we construct, and then perceive between them. (p. 17)

Structuralist theories, then, make use of some prior organization—for example, structures of the mind (Jameson, 1972), structures of culture (Lévi-Strauss, 1967), structures of language (Bloomfield, 1933), or structures of knowledge (Piaget, 1970)—as a screen between the phenomenal world and our understanding of it. The meaning of things is held in these prior structures that themselves may be the product of genetics or human effort. Structures reveal themselves in human action according to the manner in which they explain the seemingly endless surface variations of human life.

Structuralist theories are rationalist, determinist, and reductionist, and are sometimes separatist (multiple domains) but may be materialist (e.g., in a move to genetics) although language and/or culture are their usual end points. As such, these theories have been attacked for being just those things. Nonetheless, and despite this being called a poststructuralist age, structuralism continues to be prominent in developmental theories (structures of capacities and aptitudes), cognitive theories (mental structures), ideological theories (a structure of ideas), cultural analysis (structures of significance), and in any theoretical position that uses an essential form as prior to and the explanation for action or understanding.

Part of the French[10] structuralist project was the destruction of the individual as autonomous agent which Foucault saw as the emblem of the modernist episteme. The "independent intellect" was to be replaced by the individual as cultural agent, simply an expressive tool of language and ideology. It appears to me that structuralism as an intellectual movement foundered when Derrida dared to ask the others from whence they were writing and Barthes took us into the endless play of signifiers cut loose from their signified moorings (Culler, 1979; Sarup, 1993).

INTERPRETATION, AGENCY, AND THE PRODUCTION OF MEANING

That one can no longer write from an unmarked structuralism is not to argue the demise of structuralist arguments or of structuralist theories. It is to say that attention turned to other lines of thought, again largely French in origin, and especially to the theories of Althusser, de Certeau, Bourdieu, and Baudrillard, as well as to a rediscovery of Sartre. The turn away from structuralism also led to a reillumination of Peirce and the American pragmatists James and Dewey, to a new examination of the language theories of Bakhtin and Wittgenstein, and to a renewed interest in the Germanic hermeneutic tradition through the works of Heidegger and Gadamer. This volatile mix is characterized by concepts of oppression, acts of resistance and opposition, the rejection of innocence; the tension between the collective and the individual and among the goals of enlightenment, emancipation, and struggle; but at its center is the question of meaning—its production, ownership, placement, control, suppression, and destruction.

As far as the topic of this chapter is involved, this community works as if the evolution of human action is well beyond the point where the physicalist will have much to say except regarding the technical operation of the instrument. The perceptionist is an attenuated development and even the regularities of the material world are part of the stuff from which meaning is made. In the strong program, scholarship (science, criticism, and all forms of inquiry) is in the knowledge production game. The truth of its claims lies in its power to instantiate a claim as true.

At this point we are not too far away from previous positions in structuralism, and perhaps neo-Marxism. Empiricism recedes and discourse ascends as in those positions. The change occurs in the reconfiguration of the discursive subject through the reclamation of agency. This is not agency of the free-will sort (a distinction we take up in some detail in the next chapter). It is rather an agency that materializes collective understanding in local and partial expressions.

I hope to exemplify this distinction through the use of various forms of critical analysis. Let's start with content analysis. This is the end point of many social science attempts at criticism and the beginning (in the guise of "close reading") of most critical analyses. Content analysis takes an unreflective stance vis-à-vis the facts of content: *this* word, *this* act, *this* sentence, *these* colors, and more complexly, *those* themes, *those* topics, *those* metaphors. I call the stance "unreflective" because the means by which this word is this word or this sentence is this sentence or this topic is this topic are themselves unexamined. A semiotic event is considered "natural," beyond human intervention. Content analysis of this sort will invoke the objectivist criterion (agreement across observers) to demonstrate the "naturalness" of its facts.

The product of this analysis is the frequency of events within a set of nominal categories and occasionally an examination of the relationship among those categories. The aim is to talk about the factual characteristics and/or structure of the piece (or medium) as a way of understanding the meaning it contains. Meaning is contained in the factual characteristics, codes, themes, topics, metaphors, and structures of the work. Meaning is independent of the author and reader and can be factually determined within a formal transcendence. (If a critic were to try to find a home for this sort of analysis, that critic would probably go to Russian formalism or to the Prague School.)

A different approach would claim that meaning is not a product of textual form but rather the expression of the transcendent mind. (Don't go too fast here, I'm not close to reception theory, yet.) It is the mind, not language, that sets the rules for coherence, order, pleasure, understanding. Content must conform to those rules if coherence, order, pleasure, and understanding are to appear. We are still missing authors and readers and meaning is still factual, but its "factness" now resides in neuronal (or mental) structures rather than textual structures. This is generally the doctrine of New Criticism (Richards, 1925) and cognitivist efforts at textual understanding (e.g., Kellermann, 1989).

To hurry, somewhat, to a conclusion, what happens if we abandon a priori structures and bring in authors and readers (as well as critics) as the explanation for meaning? Our first discovery is that the text becomes a contested site of meaning with privilege being claimed for authorial intent (the true meaning of a text is what the author intended it to mean; see Hirsch, 1967) but also claimed for the reader in reception theory (e.g., Radway, 1984).

Deconstruction's response has been to argue that the text is a constellation of rhetorical strategies and maneuvers (Berman, 1988) whose meaningfulness is a separate achievement by author, reader, or critic. And finally, in what is yet to be called "post-deconstructionism," Barnes (1988) argues "that it is possible for criticism legitimately to tolerate incompatible (genuinely and not seemingly incompatible) interpretations for a single work and for critics to directly challenge and defeat other critics" (p. 2).

If we were to compare structuralist arguments with those of the preceding paragraph the principal distinction would come down to, on the one hand, structuralism seeks the meaning to be *extracted,* and, on the other hand, interpretation seeks the meaning to be *constructed.* The meaning to be extracted is governed by the structural rules of language or the mind and the text is the archive of those rules; the meaning to be constructed is governed by the rules in place at the site of the construction and the text is one resource of that effort.

Inherent meaning positions (like structuralism) grant great privilege to the analyst. These beliefs about meaning allow the analyst to declare the meaning of a textual fragment used as a treatment, the meaning of a response item on an attitude test, or the meaning of an experimental protocol, and to declare meaning in any condition where the text is taken factually (at face value). Signs are trustworthy. These theories depend on an unmarked engagement of the semiotic, a transcendent semiosis, a universal meaning making.

Constructed meaning positions grant privilege to the struggle for meaning. The result is that analysis becomes a very messy business (appropriately so in my belief). Claims about meaning are never finished, never without doubt. Signs "float" until fixed in some action. We end up with Barnes's argument that a claim can be both true and not true at the same time. These theories depend on a contingent engagement of the semiotic, a local and partial semiosis, a historicized meaning making.

Meaning is a crucial argument in contemporary scholarship. From Quine's (1966) early claim that we don't know what we are talking about to Derrida's (1982) argument that meaning is an expression of power, from the unreflective conventions of measurement to the elitism of false consciousness, to multiple truths coupled with significant defeat, scholarship is built on separate foundations. The character and place of meaning are useful tools for understanding these differences.

A SUMMARY OF ENGAGEMENT

The issue of engagement is the set of conditions under which our observations of (1) whatever it is we consider to be real are (2) themselves trustworthy—trustworthy so that we can repeatedly depend on them to be true (true in the sense of Wittgenstein's hand or our brick)—and (3) can be re-presented referentially under the control of the trustworthy observation.

No one believes that anyone's observations are always and everywhere true. But many have held that a scientist or a critic has a "special way of looking" that can purify his or her observations of error. This special way has been called "the scientific method" or "critical analysis." When a scientist or critic fails inside these frames, it is a failure of application not of observation.

Others will argue that, beyond private knowledge, all observations are examples of Wittgenstein's language game (see Wittgenstein, 1972) in which the conditions under which observations are true are always a collective achievement. Pushing beyond Wittgenstein, observations are trustworthy because of our efforts to make them so, not because of some inherent character.[11]

The question of trustworthiness implicates the question of representation: What does an observation represent? I recently completed a questionnaire from a graduate student (working under the supervision of a thesis committee, a condition that allows the work to be both avowed as real science and discounted as educational exercise) in which I (as a department chair) was asked how often"I praise my team members for work well done." (I answered, "nearly always.") The observation, as we know, is the check mark. The question is What does it represent? The manner in which we each answer that question of representation makes it possible to do certain things or not, make certain claims or not, know certain things or not.

One can ask the same representation question of the organizational ethnographer who claims to have seen, for example, an act of gift giving in an otherwise ordinary corporate transaction (e.g., Browning & Henderson, 1989). How do the facts observed represent the action claimed? We have looked at four answers: (1) Because they do (meet the materialist criterion); (2) because they do (meet the materialist criterion) and others agree (intersubjectivity); (3) because they meet our collective understanding of such things and I, as authorized speaker, say so; or (4) because they are so understood (meet our collective understanding), I (authorized speaker) say so, and I am enacting knowledge (acting agent).

In the last part of this chapter we examined a response to the demise of logical positivism in the form of constructive empiricism with its test of empirical adequacy, which allows all four of our answers to be true, albeit incommensurably. We looked at structuralism as the screen between the phenomenal world and our ability to observe and describe it. Finally, we considered how the attack on structuralism has centered meaning as a key construct for understanding how engagement is employed in particular theory constructions.

NOTES

1. There will be a recognizable and deliberate use of semiotic theory in the sections that follow because it is powerful in this analysis and because there is, consequently, no deceptive pretense of some metatheoretical understanding of how observation works.

2. The private experiences that you and I have separately have no standing as public knowledge until they are made jointly accessible. In none of this discussion am I con-

cerned with private knowledge except in its implicit standing as the common foundation of public knowledge. There is good reason for confusion on this issue. For the more common cognitive and semiotic theories, both processes of encoding and decoding occur within a single individual. That private process often stands as the transcendent analogue for the public process of knowledge production (the Cartesian criterion of the good intellect), with damage to both as one centers on perception and the other on argumentation. Unfortunately, we will be forced to slide in and out of these private and public processes as the different positions will require, but in the end the difference will become a valuable marker for us.

3. And sometimes more darkly by racial characteristics. See Anderson, 1992.

4. Fuller (1993b) provides the steps by which knowledge devolves to the collective starting with the Cartesian position, "I am in a privileged position to know what I mean and that puts me in a privileged position to know whether it is true," and ending with the most deconstructionist position, "Not only am I in no privileged position to know what I mean, whether it is true, or who is and is not part of my audience, but also the audience itself is in no privileged position to determine who does and does not belong to it, which implies that my identity as speaker is at best fragmented" (p. 121). We will get to that last step in the next section. Here we are at Fuller's fourth step: "I am in no privileged position to know what I mean, whether it is true, or even who is and is not part of my audience. In fact the audience is in a privileged position to determine my own identity as a speaker" (p. 121).

5. The word "agent" is used in both senses of the term: agent as a participating cause in its own right and agent as a representative, here of collective interests.

6. My colleagues in Austria tell me that the ideas of this group of philosophers became far more important in America than they were in Europe.

7. This is an intentional claim not just an example and is a line of argument being developed by Rodrick (1995) in his doctoral work.

8. The television program "Northern Exposure", for example, used a similar genetic explanation in one of its story lines to excuse Chris's (the DJ character) boorish behavior. The narrative was a good example of how scientific explanations circulate in society.

9. Here are two examples of what can be self-fulfilling arguments: I get three marriage counselors to write down all the ways that marriages can be different. Looking at their collected statements I think there are eight different marriage types involved. I then write 10 statements for each of the eight categories which I give to 50 married couples and ask them to rate their marriage on the degree to which it is represented in each of the 80 statements. Factor analysis shows that eight different marriage types appear.

Working from a Marxist orientation in studying organization culture, I presume that efforts by management to empower employees will be read as another middle-class project at achieving bottom-line goals. I can find no evidence of this reading in the discourse of employees. I conclude that this absence is an excellent example of false consciousness.

Note that both of these examples might also be examples of genuine findings.

10. Members of this group are generally reckoned as Ferdinand de Saussure (semiology), Claude Lévi-Strauss (anthropology), Roland Barthes (literary theory), Michel Foucault (structure of knowledge), Jacques Lacan (psychoanalysis), and Jacques Derrida (deconstructionism). However, the late arrival of Derrida (1967) and the later

writings of Barthes and Foucault have also been identified as the transition to poststructuralism.

Indeed, Foucault (as well as Barthes) is an enignmatic figure in structuralism. He is currently being reclaimed from the structuralist camp by postmodernists (see Hekman, 1990) primarily because his writings have great value. To argue that he belongs here or there is an argument without conclusion. It causes problems when authors write over the boundaries of epistemic periods.

11. The move to advance reliability claims as validity claims are a very good example of conventionalized methods which "make" observations true (see the arguments of Latour, 1987).

CHAPTER 4

THE NATURE
OF THE INDIVIDUAL

In the various domains of communication research, individuals are our subjects, respondents, informants, associates, and colleagues. They are the repository of traits, the expression of social forces, the materialization of roles, and the acting agents. They are our statistical aggregates, the surrogates of us all, the objects of study, and the targets of explanation. Individual intentions justify our critical claims; we give voice to the otherwise mute in our ethnographies and reception studies. The individual is everywhere but most often nowhere as we work our naturalized, authorial invisibility and enforce a faceless fecklessness on our respondents.

The individual is an integral part of all communication theory and research methods. The manner of the constitution of the individual motivates its appearance in particular theories and methods. This chapter decodes those constitutions that are materialized in our theories and methods to illuminate the building-block concepts by which the individual is made to appear. It presumes (1) that the individual is not self-evident, (2) that instead a conceptualization is required, and (3) that the conceptualization-in-place does particular epistemic work.[1]

As is typical of foundations, claims implicating the individual most often incorporate the accomplishments of (1) through (3) without comment or question. I propose to use two devices and a set of four models in order to break this silence. I will explain the devices first.

DEVICES

The paragraphs that follow develop two analytical devices or tools that I feel are useful for constructing the models that follow. They also serve as a preface to the issues that I believe are central to the differences in the character of claim that distinguish the research we read.

The First Device: Identity, Subjectivity, and Agency

The first of the devices develops a litmus test of differences out of the concepts of identity, subjectivity, and agency.[2]

Identity

Identity is both an inward- and an outward-looking concept. As an inward-looking concept, it provides a consideration of the existence of a unity, a coherence that extends across time and situation. This unity can be (1) the essentialist self that remains at the core of all particular manifestations, (2) the integrated personality that is predictable (and a therapeutic goal), (3) the impulsive "I" of Blummer's Meadian symbolic interactionism, (4) the quarrelsome Freudian troika, (5) the hyphenated self in its many conceptualizations, (6) the acting agent, or (7) the serial identity of attributes and traits.

As an outward-looking concept, identity is that constellation of characteristics and performances that manifest the self in meaningful action. This identity is the something(s) that can actually be observed to which the concept of a self might be attached. Different theorists will treat this action identity differently. Some will postulate this identity as a sign of cognitive preconditions or of social/cultural/genetic determinants. Others will hold this identity as the expressive site of a larger sociology. And still others will read this identity through lines of action that have recognizable eidetic qualities.

Together, the inward and outward components of identity—the core and its manifestations—answer the question of "Who is the I" in self–other configurations and definitions of the person.

Subjectivity

Subjectivity presumes the existence of cultural paradigms of the self. These paradigms are the concepts of gender and class of cultural studies, the roles of symbolic interactionist sociology, and the figures and characters of narrative. Within these realms, identity always appears within some nexus of subjectivity.

Subjectivity is presented as being both evoked and invoked. As evoked, it is called into place by the actions of others, the power of society, or the force of culture. The degree of anonymity in the evocation and the view of an imposed subjectivity as oppression separate lines of thought that use evocation. Symbolic interaction's use of the "me," for example, holds subjectivity as necessary for any expression, oppressed or emancipated (Meltzer, Petras, & Reynolds, 1975).

Subjectivity can also be read as invoked in opportunistic attempts to position oneself. (My writing in these paragraphs attempts an authorized voice.) One's invocation is often coupled with a concomitant evocation of the other. (My invoked, authorized voice attempts to evoke the compliant reader.)

Agency

Identity pursues the transcendental character of the individual, that element (or elements), its material presence and acting force, that allows us to talk about human nature as generalization. Subjectivity begins a move toward historicizing the individual as a production of a particular time and place (albeit potentially grand in its scope). Agency will allow us to complete this historicity by pointing to the local agent in action.

Agency describes the character of acting (doing) and particularly the question of immanence in human action. Part of the upheaval associated with postmodern thought has resulted from the return of agency from its exile and the reintroduction of immanence in explanation. Most of the history of modernist psychology (1850–1950) has been a drive toward determinism in which the appearance of agency was removed from explanations that instead depended upon transcendental social and material forces.

In the modernist formulation, human agency has been seen as the product of genetic traits (sociobiology), physiological characteristics (structuralism), social forces (structural functionalism), socialization processes (cognitivism), and conditioning schedules (behaviorism), among others. This deterministic move has been explained as a reaction to a metaphysical free agency.

Free agency is based on the concepts of independence, open access, right reasoning, and free will. Free agency was a central concept of the Enlightenment and represented a radical redefinition of the self as it appeared either in libertarianism (Cartesian autonomy) or in communtarianism (the self in the service of other) and formed the replacement for the submissive will of Pope's "great chain of being." In free agency, the human mind has an open access as an independent agent to an objective reality. It can discern and evaluate alternatives properly through right reasoning. And it can choose an alternative without bias induced either from intrinsic sources (e.g., the drives for survival or reproduction) or extrinsic ones (e.g., social forces that negate one alternative over another). Such is the vision of the independent and autonomous self.

There is, however, considerable space between free agency and full determinism. This space gets delineated by the redefinitions of independence, access, objectivity, right reasoning, and the willful act. It is this space that we now examine under the triad of freedom, autonomy, and choice.

Freedom. Freedom deals with the conditions of an objective access to reality. Freedom appears most clearly when genuine alternatives to a current course of action are present and known. Theories divide over the character and production of alternatives and the dissemination of knowledge about them. Feminist theories, for example, have pointedly demonstrated both the alternatives available only to white males and the "old boy" routines that control knowledge of them.

One's personal sense of freedom, then, is controlled by the conditions of alternatives and the information held about them. The collective participates in one's sense of freedom through its manipulation of the social and material conditions of alternatives, both authentic and inauthentic, and of the information concerning those conditions.

Autonomy. Autonomy concerns the independence of judgment. It participates in freedom in two ways: (1) in the determination of the authenticity of alternatives and (2) in the determination of the rightness of a choice. In free-will formulations, each of us has an equal opportunity to access the choices reality presents to all. As soon as we order access and knowledge hierarchically, the autonomy to choose is also ordered. Those with a greater power to declare their own choices have a greater autonomy within their domain of freedom. The parent who says, "You can do your homework or clean up your room" offers freedom but little autonomy of choice, for the authenticity of the alternatives remains fully under parental control.

Autonomy plays a similar role in the declaration of the rightness of choice. Autonomy, here, speaks the story of right and wrong. The freedom to choose in a condition where the consequences are capricious (as in a dysfunctional relationship or organization) is no blessing but instead a constant source of terror. Freedom becomes a secret test of the worth of the choosing individual. These shifting grounds of autonomy place any action—freely chosen or not—at risk. Determining who holds autonomy's power to declare value in a choice situation is crucial to understanding this power.

Choice. If freedom is the presence of genuine alternatives and autonomy is the independence of judgments concerning the genuineness and the rightness of those alternatives, what, then, is choice? Choice can be defined as the ability to do otherwise. No matter what one's theoretical perspective, it is generally agreed that any course of action will often lead to points where alternatives are presented (the first requirement of choice). For the determinist, these points arise only where the determining forces are weak or in conflict. At these points, nonetheless, the individual still does not participate in the resolution. It is the situation that changes to motivate one behavior over another. True choice in strict determinism occurs only in the unknown, and then it is simply uncontrolled, random behavior (and therefore beyond scientific explanation).

From an agency perspective, the action of choice is in some part a self-initiating event and can be understood only as an individual choosing (Pearce, 1994). Asking why a choice was made is to invoke a determinist stance or to request subsequent "reason-giving" behavior. If agency is to be present, there cannot be "true reasons for" a choice.

Finally, choice raises the question of who or what does the choosing (Ellis, 1986; Ricoeur, 1992)). With this question we have turned full circle and are back to identity again. What identity (unity) in what subjectivity do we position as the agent of choosing?

Identity, subjectivity, and agency can effectively illuminate differences among theories. As they search for transcendental claim, behavioral or cognitive theories often emphasize identity (usually a single focal trait) to the exclusion of subjectivity and agency. Most Marxist or structuralist cultural theories focus on subjectivity, deny identity, and discount the effectiveness of agency. Most critical theories focus on identity and agency as the source of emancipation from subjectivity. And finally, social action and structuration theories work all three as dynamic elements of a three-part relationship.

The Second Device:
Material, Biological, and Semiotic Domains

The notion of the individual can also be trisected by the material, biological, and semiotic domains of explanation. The individual is a material object responsive to the explanatory laws of physics and chemistry. He or she is also a life form invested in the explanations of change, individual difference, and the tensions between genetic potentials and materialization in action. Finally, the individual appears as a performative and discursive subject within the semiotic domain. As this subject, the individual is variously constituted within action and discourse.

It would appear vitally important in the project of theory to distinguish the domain or domains in which the individual is being theoretically approached. For example, Burgoon and Le Poire (1992) write (from deep inside their argument):

> According to EV [expectancy violation] theory, communication expectancies are a function of target characteristics, relationship characteristics and context features. Of interest here are target characteristics, which include both general traitlike attributes (such as personality or gender) and statelike attributes (such as giving positive or negative feedback or being in a humorous, entertaining mood). (p. 69)

Interesting questions arise when one attempts to determine the domains in which, say, personality and gender reside, the characteristics which define them as traits, and the manner of their operation within EV theory. Is the gender at issue here a biological or a semiotic trait? Statistical analysis will treat it as a biological trait, but it will be measured semiotically. Similar questions occur when one wonders how an action (as in giving positive feedback) can be the same sort of thing as a state (as in a humorous, entertaining mood).

For theorists who accept multiple domains of explanation, all theories are formulated in and most offer explanation for events in the semiotic domain. Many theorists (both critical and scientific), however, act as if their explanation reached into the biological and the material. And for theorists who accept reductionism as a starting place, all theories must ultimately ground themselves in materialist explanation.[3]

There is a second contrast that is at least partially embedded in the issue of multiple domains: the mind–body contrast (Segal, 1991). This contrast reaches back beyond Cartesian dualism; Popper's transcendental mind is just one of its recent manifestations. Many applications of this contrast return us to the Scholastic essentialist self—one's fully formed, persisting identity—in rejection of materialist explanations (see, particularly, Lewis, 1982). But it is the body that is making its return in places other than communication.

With the exception of feminist writings, the body is notably missing in communication theory (but for the sort of thing that does appear see Meyers & Biocca, 1992; for a more complex analysis, see Bourdieu, 1978). Pain, ecstasy, discipline, carnival, expressions of the body, the body as sign, and the actual "writing on the body" of cultural differences in work, nutrition, decoration, and the like are all topics that have been addressed in feminist thought (Bartky, 1995) but few places elsewhere in the communication literature.

Given the prevalence of material reductionism, this appears to be a strange absence. But, then, many of the confusions that occur in the study of theory cannot be solved by a more careful analysis of the theory itself. The analyst must jump to the community, the paradigm, or the episteme to understand the meanings in place. The meaning of this absence may well be a masculine mark of inquiry.

An equally notable silence is found in the semiotic dimension of self-in-action.[4] When the action self is taken up, it is usually within the rubric that language and other sign systems speak the subject who performs them (e.g., Fiske, 1987) by imbricating the individual user in the rules and structural characteristics of the linguistic. To observe and explain the action aspect of the self from this vantage point is to typically deconstruct individual discourse in order to find the socially charged meanings that motivate the self's thinking. Action is divorced from discourse and treated as a subsequent outcome. What the self says and does, in other words, are separate but related, with action dependent on discourse.

But sign systems provide both the semiotic definition of the self and the sign of the self in performance. Language and action can be seen as necessarily intertwined. Here, the self stands as part of some self-and-other relationship where discourse necessarily takes place in various genres of performance. Linguistic rules and structures certainly infiltrate the collective and coordinated processes by which selves define and get defined, but a more performance-oriented semiotic approach sees it as necessary to account for social customs, traditions, and other prescriptions as guiding factors in managing various indeterminacies created through sign practices (Parsons, 1937; Shotter & Gergen, 1994).

Consequently, what the self says is made additionally understandable by examining what the self does (Harré, 1994). Action does not follow discourse; the two create a collective context of meaning production in which the self brings forth their various forms of behavior that make it knowable as "someone."

MODELS

We now turn to the underlying models of the individual (person, self) that support various forms of inquiry. We can distinguish four separate positions within communication theory: the attribute individual, the conjunctive individual, the situated individual, and the activative individual.

Attribute Model

In the attribute model, the individual is seen as the weighted sum of a finite set of attributes (e.g., sex, intelligence, personality, cognitive structures such as values, attitudes, schemata). Following Hume's injunction, advocates of this model deliberately reject the concept of an "inner self," some coherent entity that is the source or seat of these attributes.[5] Each attribute is viewed as its own "human-defining" unity that transcends its location and expression in the particular person. In hierarchical societies, it would be argued, all members are imprinted with (something like) socioeconomic class, although its value and power will vary across individuals. Socioeconomic class becomes a human-defining trait (at least in hierarchical societies), and the individual is understood by the class value represented. The program of science is the discovery of the attributes and their functions.

The origin of an attribute can be genetic, societal, or cultural, but its point of operation must be the individual. This approach has been called "methodological individualism" (Nagel, 1961), which is the requirement by some epistemologies that explanation find its foundation in the material entity of the individual rather than in social practices or cultural processes.

A typical experiment within the attribute model will use some treatment—let's say different styles of superior–subordinate communication—to test its effects on some criterion measure—let's say job satisfaction. Consider this scenario: At the beginning, our respondent group is a wholly undifferentiated surrogate for all subordinates (superior–subordinate communication is usually seen as governed by the superior of the pair). The single attribute involved at this point is subordinancy which is ordinarily considered a state, that is a set of adjustable determining conditions.

Our initial observations, however, suggest that males will respond to certain communication styles differently from females, as will the higher educated than the less educated. These differences appear to be maintained across different job classifications which is itself the operational definition of levels of subordinancy.

The results of this study intend to tell us nothing about the particular people who participate. (In fact, if the particular people contain the results, the experiment is a failure.) The results intend to tell us what it means to be differentially educated females and males in varying states of subordinancy. The attributes involved are education and gender (again, whether gender or sex depends on whether a semiotic or biological explanation is to be used). What we learn is their operation at various levels of subordinancy. The attribute model appears clearly in the practical advice that might emanate from a study of this sort: "If the subordinate is a highly educated woman in a low job classification, start with style 2."

The attribute model is not limited to science. It also appears in values-based textual analysis (e.g., Trujillo & Ekdom, 1985) and in many of the audience-based critical approaches (e.g., Allen, 1987).

Finally, the psychoanalytic frame of the individual works in much the same way as the attribute model. In the psychoanalytic approach, the individual presents itself as a partitioned subject, the partitions of which—to use popular terminology—are the primal motives of the id, the socially constructed strictures of the superego, and the pragmatic, reality-tested practices of the ego. While psychoanalysis is traditionally a clinical approach, it has been used in a variety of critical approaches (e.g., Silverman, 1983), as well as in the revelation of the politics of desire (e.g., Lacan, 1988).

The attribute model is ahistorical in that it does not locate its explanation in the particular but seeks the more general claim. In our organizational communication example, the advice is meant to cover all highly educated women in low job classifications, although the researcher may be satisfied with a more modest scope. (Other transcendental models would include the 18th-century "good-man-[sic]-thinking-well" we met in our discussion of agency, phenomenology's eidetic consciousness, and the "reasonable person" test of many judicial and statistical decision rules.)

We can expect the attribute model to be in place when words such as "traits," "aptitudes," "states," "stages," "attitudes," "values," "schemata," "scripts," "psychographics," "inculturation," "development," or "socialization" appear, signaling the use of entities locatable in the individual that function as antecedents to behavior. Because of its common use of mentalist antecedents, the attribute model is most often a psychological form. It is a vision of the mind.

It can be contrasted with the conjunctive model, where the antecedents are exterior.

Conjunctive Model

In the conjunctive model the individual is seen as the site of the intersection of material, cultural, and social influences, as, for example, in Durkheim's social penetration. The individual is a collective enterprise and relatively powerless alone, although she or he can participate (or be swept along) in movements of change. The conjunctive model has both a sociological and a cultural form.

Sociological Form

As a sociological form, it was once the expression and is now the legacy of dialectical materialism, continental structuralism, and American functionalism. It emphasizes social, cultural, and ideological institutions and apparati that merge subjectivity and identity and provide the agency of action.

Dialectical Materialism. Dialectical materialism developed out of the writings of Hegel, Engels, and Marx. Although the early writings were less formalized, both Hegel and Marx continued to submerge the individual, leading Kierkegaard to break away from the palatial elegance of Hegel's historical structure to enter the peasant's cabin of existentialism and Marx to reject his own earlier sense of the worker's individual mark. Jeffrey Alexander (1982) quotes Marx to put together the vision of subjugation that colors Marxist arguments today[6]:

> [Marx] stresses that the conditions of capitalism eliminate any possibility for voluntary action or self control: "Free competition brings out the inherent laws of capitalist production, in the shape of external coercive laws having power over every individual capitalist" [Marx, 1876/1962, p. 270]. And once again these competitive laws are just as coercive to the worker as to the owner. "Thanks to the development of capitalist product," Marx writes, the worker "is compelled by social conditions, to sell the whole of his active life, his very capacity for work, for the price of the necessaries of life" [p. 271]. It is no wonder that Marx believes that the exigencies of capitalist production force the relationship between capitalist and laborer to "assume a material character independent of their control and conscious individual action" [p. 97]. (p. 172)

The material determinism of Marxism is nonetheless different from the material determinism of the natural order. The former arises not out of the "Big Bang" but out of our own ideational representations of reality. Capitalism (or any political–economic system) is an ideology—a reality-representing system of ideas—supported by knowledge-producing practices and the means of distribution of the structured discourse that results.[7]

As a dialectic, Marxism stands in opposition as a force for change, a continuing critique exposing the fictive character of representation, the mystification of its methods, and the false consciousness of our acceptance (for a similar analysis, see Mepham, 1979). It is this commitment to the critical review of the dominant which is the key identifying characteristic of arguments to be labeled Marxist in the dialectical tradition.[8] The business of scholarship is emancipation through the change of consciousness (see McLellan, 1986; Russell, 1979).

The individual in Marxism through the 1950s was a product of the dominant ideology and had no recourse in the absence of liberating efforts. There has been a subsequent reclamation of the individual in Hall's (1982) recognition that folks are not "cultural dopes" and de Certeau's (1984) notions of opposition and resistance. As a collectivist, dialectical argument, however, the individual, in Marxist thought, will always appear momentarily in the margins between sets of oppositions, whether those oppositions be class, gender, ethnicity, race, or similar dialectics.

Continental Structuralism. The concepts of the individual as a practical force of history, an initiator of knowledge and action, and a self-defining intelligence disappear within continental structuralism.[9] Their place is taken by a semiconscious expression, the individual "as a living, working, and speaking being who is subject to death, desire and language as law" (Bannet, 1989, p. 158). According to the structuralists, our understanding of the individual will not be found through the examination of people but through the study of the structures that produce the ideological framework in which individuals appear—Bannet's "death, desire and language."[10] Human science in latter-day structuralism is both an empirical and a critical activity that documents structures and their ideological consequences, thereby empowering emancipatory movement or at least temporary refurbishment for those scholars who resist utopianism.

American Functionalism. American functionalism, most readily identified with the latter Talcott Parsons's (1951) structural functionalism[11] and Robert Merton's (1957) less ambitious design, is concerned with a system of interdependent collective variables that define social life. The system is dynamic in that change in one variable effects change throughout. The system emphasizes the collective in that variables appear in (either as a consequence of or within the scope of) collective endeavors.

The individual is defined as a part of a social system beyond his or her personal control. Choice, if it appears at all, is limited to the specific part to be played by the individual within the socially determined alternatives provided. The ontology of the individual is described in a variable-analytic manner through ordained characteristics such as education/occupation/income of father/mother/self; class of birth/attained class; gender; race; religion; dialect;

ethnicity; political and social memberships—all of which converge to answer the question of who I am.

Arising out of a foundational empiricist tradition, American functionalism rejects a critical stance. It has nonetheless been a very optimistic theoretical frame because its adherents believe that science can be put to progressive work to promote social integration (Isajiw, 1968).

Critical Forms

Critical theory and cultural studies are the two most widely cited critical forms of the conjunctive model.[12] Both critical theory and cultural studies are holist and historicist: their proponents believe that it is the unities of actual circumstances that produce the ideologies of practical action. Or in the Marxist phrase, social being produces social consciousness (Thalheimer, 1936). The unreflective individual, given the decline of family-centered life, is necessarily a product of the untempered influences of social institutions: the school, the workplace, and sites of consumption (Wolin, 1992). Subjectivity denies autonomy in this formulation. As Alexander (1992) puts it in his comment on worthy friends and immoral enemies, "Actors are not intrinsically either worthy or moral: They are determined to be so by being placed in certain positions on the grid of civil culture" (p. 291).

Much of the critical form writings of the 1980s and 1990s is concerned with managing the triumvirate of identity, subjectivity, and agency. In the early going, the focus was primarily on the enforcement of subjectivity with its themes of dominance, repression, and subjugation (Grossberg, 1984).

The adoption by cultural studies of Althusser's "ideology is everywhere," and therefore subjectivity is a necessary part of the presentation of self and not a categorical evil, as well as the adoption of Gramsci's concept of hegemony as a loose reality forming a confederation of interrelated ideologies, opened the space of analysis to change and personal expression (Turner, 1990). The individual is still a collective enterprise but now is conceived as one who can exploit the cultural system while yet its subject (Glassner, 1990; Newcomb, 1991). To the themes of dominance, repression, and subjugation have been added the themes of resistance, opposition, and emancipation in the absence of revolution (Morley, 1980).

In the presence of Habermas, critical theory has retained its philosophic character, its critical attack, and its conceptualization of a repressive subjectivity. It maintains its "ideal of an emancipated individual in an emancipated society" (Szahaj, 1990, p. 54) in which the autonomous subject returns.

Cultural studies offers a more modest outcome of a fully contextualized subject who, whether in an enlightened and reflective understanding or more directly through practical knowledge, can work the margins and free-play spaces at least for political gain if not for redemption (de Certeau, 1984).

Summary

The conjunctive model retains its strong statement in current objectivist sociology and in similar sociological expressions in other disciplines. Like the attribute model, it is most effective in variable-analytic approaches that "atomize" the individual into separate independent influences. It is common in so-called quantitative investigations to see the two models combined in studies that make use of "demographic and psychographic," "etic and emic," or "exogenous and indogenous" variables.

The conjunctive model has also been characteristic of traditional critical and cultural analyses. Here the emphasis has been on the effect of cultural "totalities" (as opposed to separate elements) in producing the subject. British and American cultural studies have begun a salvage effort on the concepts of identity and self. This effort, on the American side, has paralleled if not actually connected to a reclamation of Peircean semiotics, pragmatism, and symbolic interactionism in what might be a fin de siècle return to the beginnings of this century (Wexler, 1990). Within cultural studies, at any rate, the working model of the individual has moved noticeably closer to the situated model discussed next.

Situated Model

In the situated model, we change the view from the collective producing the subject to that of the individual finding her or his means of expression in the resources of culture and society. John Hall (1992), for example, proposes a cultural structuralism referencing "diverse configurations of institutionalized meanings, recipes and material objects that may be differently drawn on by various actors within the same social arena or society" (p. 279). It is a significant existential shift that positions the agency of the acting identity in every explanation.[13]

This identity ranges from James's (1908) concept of a moral force whose will creates the circumstances of its success, to Goffman's (1959) unprincipled choice in which the role to be played is the only substance of identity, to Alford's (1991) use of Kohut (1977) and Lacan (1977) to illuminate the incomplete self's closure in the other. In any case, whatever the identity, its material expression is always within the boundaries of meanings supplied by culture and society (Wagner, 1981). The individual is a socially derived presentation. The actualized self is underdetermined and probabilistic but everywhere sociologically addressable. The answer to who I am appears out of a kaleidoscope of social meanings that define the "who" I can be. As Hewitt (1989) remarks, the acting subject "fills the empty container of a role with commitment and energy, making it possible for the situated individual to act with force and direction" (p. 150).

In the situated model, the three components, identity, agency, and subjectivity, are set on more equal footing, although agency is not yet immanent. In the attribute model, the emphasis was on identity as defined by the sum of the traits. In the conjunctive model, the emphasis was on subjectivity and the individual's identity as a cultural production. Here, we have an identity with continuity and a semblance of independence and autonomy that materializes a culturally produced subjectivity in, at least, partial response to personal motives and desires.

Agency while acknowledged remains domesticated under the ready control of global motivations, values, or structures of desire. Motivation, whether organic or conditioned, stands as the determinant of choice. The individual remains comfortably in the hands of the analyst, as choice, deprived of its immanence and local operation, has no epistemological value. We have a "Nintendo" person whose surface variations to the buttons we push belie the fixed code of his or her determination.

Inquiry, within the situated model, concerns the discovery and critical analysis of the symbols and meanings that provide for the subjectivities to be materialized as well as the discovery and operational analysis of the motivations that effect that materialization. Symbols, meanings, and motivations are the explanatory targets for the answers to the questions: What are they? How do they develop? How do they function? What are their consequences? Why do they effect those results? What is the manner of their improvement?

We are finally ready to move to our last model. Just as the relationship between identity and subjectivity separated the situated model from the previous two, the containment of agency we found here will separate the situated from the activative individual in the discussion that follows.

Activative Model

In the activative model, the individual is considered an artful coconspirator who materializes collective resources of action in local and partial performances within the realm of his or her own agency (Anderson & Meyer, 1988). The individual both activates some collection of the social resources of meaning (signs and interpretations) made available by the situation and is activated in turn within the framework of those meanings (Jensen, 1991).

The work site of this model is clearly within the semiotic domain. According to Kerby (1991),

> A person is a being of semiosis, a living body of gestures and articulations that exists in extensive interaction with other acting bodies and the products of semiosis—speech, texts, art works and meaningful action generally. The development of the person will depend on a reflective grasp of, and habitual participation in, this network of social communication and praxis. The human subject must thus be situated within the structures that sustain it rather than posited as transcendent to them; it must be implicated in the production of such structures but need not be taken as foundational. (p. 101)

The activative model positions itself in the center of the tension between the collective and the self. It grants both the necessity and apriority of the collective forms of existence but recognizes that those forms will be improvisationally materialized in local action that will express those forms partially and meta-phorically and can express those forms comically, ironically, or even opposition-ally. Given a way to be, the agent must yet perform *how to be that way* within the contingencies (local circumstances) of that performance. Rather than determi-nants of action, collective symbols and interpretations stand as resources for lives to be lived.

The activative model is a pastiche of existentialism (Kierkegaard, 1958; Sartre, 1956), hermeneutics (e.g., Caputo, 1987), social semiotics (e.g., Hodge & Kress, 1988), American pragmatism (particularly James, 1908, 1912/1922) and the interpretive turn (Taylor, 1991). It returns immanence to agency and fully historicizes the acting agent. But at the same time this model insists that mean-ingfulness is a collective achievement and that each of us is born into and continually contributes to a system of meanings that are the stuff of life. The agent is neither free nor autonomous but rather is altogether implicated (Abou-lafia, 1986; Ricoeur, 1992). The self, according to Wagner (1981), is the "product of human action" (p. 78).

In this model we also see a shift from the self as monad to the self as dyad, accompanied by a shift from monologic action to dialogic participation. The dyadic nature of the self in the activative model suggests that the self exists principally *as* relationship rather than just *in* relationship. In this model, in other words, it is more common to refer to self–other combinations than to self per se. Such a shift raises significant questions about identity and agency, for while the individual is now held accountable for the ways in which he or she interprets and enacts lines of meaningful action, such interpretations and enactments are inexorably linked to actions that have been or might be initiated by others.

The meanings for lines of action emerge within an interplay of the individ-ual actor's understanding of the situation (and the actions that characterize it) and more socially established genres of meaning for various forms of interac-tion. In the activative model, social actors are seen as supervising their own and others' actions in order to bring into being some larger, collective line of activity. What one actor does makes sense principally in relation to the larger line of action—or social routine—that actors attempt to manifest.

Such lines of action are open to continuous negotiation in what they mean. For example, reading a newspaper may be as much a demonstration of social consciousness as it is an act of resistance to a domestic dispute. What the same action can or might mean depends on interpretations of action contexts that are often incomplete, indeterminate, and intermittent.

All action, then, discursive or otherwise, is seen as dialogic in its nature. Actors working together produce themselves and their meanings in various constellations of enacted social forms of behavior (Harré, 1984). Given the constant shifts that can arise, it becomes clearer as to why the activative model necessitates the presence of choice and agency as analytical devices. Each juncture in action can pose social actors with unexpected challenges that cannot be anticipated by social prescriptions for roles and the like. The multiple meanings that can be produced require management and managers. While social forces, institutions, roles, and so on may pose the initial conditions in which actors make themselves known, such prescriptions often do not identify how such actions are to be brought into being.

This latter argument represents a subtle but important shift in the relationship of essence to existence. In the attribute and conjunctive models, essence is in firm control of existence. The priors of genetics, socialization, and inculturation, as well as social practices and cultural forces, define the action of existence. Beginning with the situated model and even more clearly here, action (existence) begins to define the essence of the self. A full existential theory acceptable to current scholarship remains to be developed, but its contours are beginning to appear.

The business of inquiry takes a radical turn under the activative model. It forces the recognition that inquiry is not a method of discovery or a critical analysis but instead a complicitous partner in the meaningful systems in which we live (e.g., McPhail, 1994). Inquiry (science, criticism, journalism, and all forms of discursive claim) is part of the reality producing enterprise. Caputo (1992) offers this argument well in writing:

> Dasein (that is, you and I and in principle everyone else) is always and from the start *in the truth*. Dasein is constantly bringing about the effect of truth, incessantly disclosing the world in this way or that, like it or not. (p. 46)

This stance entails a rejection of innocence and righteousness. The business of inquiry is its contribution to the collective meanings from which individuals arise in action. It is, therefore, as racist, sexist, class-based, and generally exploitive as the system of meaning in which it can be understood.[14] The heros of scholarship are those of our own making.

A COMPARISON OF MODELS

The models that we have been discussing are intended to represent the gathering places of communities from which people write. Their definitions are both elastic and permeable (this is the heuristic escape clause). They are, however, intended to discriminate the various places we have traveled from Descartes's independent and autonomous ego.

Historically, the initiation of conjunctive and attribute arguments began in the writings of Durkheim and Comte, respectively (Alexander, 1982). The conjunctive model had a more rapid development, thanks to the expansion of sociology and the influence of Marxist thought. The turn of the 20th century gave us the foundations of the situated and activative models, the dominant force of positivism as well as of American behaviorism and developmental and cognitive psychology.

In reading the literature of the period, one enters a time of turmoil not unlike our own (and one that may be the "natural" state of the human sciences). That ferment was arrested by the Great Depression, World War II, and fear of World War III. For the first half of the century, positivist-attribute and positivist-Marxist conjunctive arguments gained and held the center and participated in the suppression of their alternatives. From the vantage point of my education, it was methodological individualism or the collective, science or nothing, and the Marxists versus everybody else.

The failures of the positivist project and of classical Marxism, evident by the late 1950s but still not recognized in many intellectual communities, have accelerated the return of the repressed (Hardt, 1989). The postmodern scholarly landscape is excessive, distracting, and contradictory, and my attempts to tidy it up will not prevail, but they might provide a moment's respite.

We will now consider the four models as distinguished across the issues that appear to create their boundaries. Those issues are identity, subjectivity, agency, the body as element of theory, the semiosis of action, the reigning theory of the self, the level of explanation, position regarding the unity of science (with its attendant implications for materialism and reductionism), position concerning the questions of multiple domains of reality, and finally, the purpose of inquiry. Table 4–1 presents a capsule statement for each of the models across these issues; the paragraphs that follow provide additional comment.

Identity

The theoretical recognition of a core identity characterized by continuity and independence occurs in the situated and activative models. In the situated model, identity is the local, materializing force of social forms. That force brings a unique set of conditions and abilities to that expression. The activative model adds an activating component in that the character of social forms must first be activated before they can be acted upon (i.e., they must be brought into play before they can be performed). This component references the improvisational nature of social expression in the relationship between identity and subjectivity. The attribute model deliberately rejects a core identity and substitutes an identity defined by the weighted sum of the set of human-defining traits (Anderson, 1987). The conjunctive model has had little to say about identity, instead concentrating its interest on subjectivity, although identity is finally entering into the discussion.

TABLE 4-1. A Comparison of Models of the Individual

Issue	Models			
	Attribute	Conjuntive	Situated	Activative
Identity	Sum of the traits	Expressed in subjectivity	Acting force	Activating and acting force
Subjectivity	Not usually addressed	Influence intersection	Frame of expression	Frame of expression
Agency	Usually deterministic	Within a given subjectivity	Nonimmanent selection	Constrained immanence
Freedom		Alternatives supplied	Alternatives supplied	Alternatives supplied
Autonomy		Collectively held	Collectively held	Locally attainable
Choice		Collectively constrained	Required but addressable	Required and undetermined
Body	Physical substrate of cognitive traits	Object of desire/ subjugation	Reality check and symbolic object	Present and at issue
Action	Operational variables	Social practices	Agents of social roles	Agency in action routines
Theory of self	No unified entity	Contained in subjectivity	A willing agent	Active and activated agent
Level of claim	Transcendent and foundational	Historical, global, and ideological	Global roles locally produced	Historical, local, and ideological
Unity of science	Generally accepted	Sociological yes; critical no	No	No
Domain of argument	Holds materialism as ideal	Material; semiotic; both	Semiotic	Semiotic
Purpose of inquiry	Discovery and explication	Discovery and explication; illumination and critique	Discovery or illumination and critique	Illumination, critique, and construction

Subjectivity

Subjectivity is the crucial topic of the conjunctive model and is also central to both the situated and the activative forms. Since identity is missing in the former model, subjectivity becomes the only means of referencing the person. Both of the latter models must struggle with the relationship between identity and subjectivity (issues of alienation, deception, conflict, etc.). The attribute model conflates identity and subjectivity into a technical sum, the value of which is objective.

Agency

Agency is ordinarily rejected in the attribute model, a rejection that logically follows from its rejection of identity (no agent is available). With the rejection of agency, the issues of freedom, autonomy, and choice also disappear from this model.

More contemporary forms of the conjunctive model accept the necessity of choice but see that choice making as defined by the subjectivity in place. Once a subjectivity is known, agency disappears as an explanatory element.

Agency is a theoretic necessity for both the situated and the activative models, and is a particularly animated element of the activative model. The difference between them is across the issue of immanence. Most situated forms see agency as explained by global determinants (organic and conditioned motivations). The activative model insists on the existentialist claim that forms are always in the process of becoming in action and that each life expression is a creative act (the idea of a local, uncaused cause) that is subject to influence but not to determination.

Freedom becomes more and more visible as one moves from the conjunctive to the situated to the activative model. In all cases, there is the sense that the alternatives are supplied by and are under the control of the collective.

Autonomy—the power to declare right and wrong—is not a province of the individual in any model (save the Cartesian and the Cartesian-marked). But as the models admit to free-play space—that space locally or temporally outside collective control—the semblance of autonomy becomes locally attainable. With sufficient power or insufficient supervision, the individual may be able to effectively declare right and wrong. In both cases, this autonomy remains a consequence of collective action which may be a deliberate inaction.

Choice is generally not a theoretic concern in conjunctive arguments. It is, however, a concern of the situated and activative models. In situated arguments, choice activity is entirely addressable by theory in that explanation can move to the step behind choice. In activative arguments, genuine choice can be interpreted but not explained. One can speak of consequential understanding but not of antecedents.

The Body

The body appears in the attribute model most effectively as the physical substrate of cognitive traits (sometimes called identity theory), such as in right brain–left brain traits. The body may appear (in rejection of identity theory) as the vessel of the mind or as the socialization object of certain traits (e.g., the "short man" syndrome). The body is much more operative in the other models as object and symbol and often has standing as an agent in its own right. Reality, for example, appears to James (1890/1983) as a "muscle tension."

Action

Forms of action have meaning in all of the models discussed, but the sources of those meanings vary from model to model. In the attribute model, the meanings ascribed to the self's lines of activity are determined by the scientific procedure itself. Action is contained in the operational-defined variables that are the antecedents of separately defined criterion variables that verify or disconfirm scientific hypotheses. Comment is boundaried by the protocol. The significance of action beyond observed outcomes lies outside of the scope of such investigation.

In the conjunctive model, action has been given only the most rudimentary analysis, primarily in the underdefined catchphrase "social practices." Lines of action are treated primarily as evidence of the presence of various social forces at play on the individual. If there is an agency present, such agency is most often attributed to ideological forces or to rudimentary forms of psychological drive theory.

The situated model begins to incorporate action as a necessary component in understanding not only *what* the self is but *how* the self is. Action is a part of the social process by which individuals are able to create and constitute the very conditions in which their selves may thrive. Actions and their meanings become part of the overall mosaic of social meanings with which individuals must grapple in order to know themselves and others.

At the same time, the situated model keeps a firm hand on agency. Roles, their meanings, and their means of enactment are the primary resources of explanation. Where there is the concept of the self-as-role performance, analyses tend not to extend beyond effects produced at monadic and monologic levels of action.

The activative model attempts to rescue action as a viable signifying system that restructures both the nature of the self and the meanings for the lines of action the self enacts. Existence begins to encroach on essence. It is only a "beginning" because lines of action, while often invested with agency, are also required to attend to larger, collective, and coordinated social actions beyond which any one individual participates. The individual self, nonetheless, is given a significant role to play as interpreter and manager of meaning.

In the activative model, the meaning of what any one individual says and does arises more in the relationships between self and other and the ways those utterances or other actions fit together in various patterns of interaction. It is collective action that makes room for the self to emerge in its myriad ways, and it is this same collective action that sustains or alters the self-in-progress.

Theory of Self

The independent and autonomous self is (1) able to engage reality under her own control; (2) able to think her own thoughts about her own experiences and her own ideational activity unmediated by collective accomplishment; (3) able to represent her own experience and ideation in her own knowledge; (4) able to make her own judgments about the value of her experience, ideation, and knowledge; (5) able to literally and entirely declare her own experience, ideation and knowledge; (6) able to direct her own activity from her own engagement and knowledge; and (7) able to enact her own hitherto unknown personage. While we may think of ourselves in that way, no model of theory accepts that formulation.

In each model, each ability is somehow compromised, weakened, or outright rejected. Nonetheless, the presence of the independent and autonomous self will not disappear from the foundation of our theorizing. If nothing else, we need it as a foil for explaining what a genuine theory of the self is. But there is, of course, more: How do we as scholars understand our own observation, representation, and validity of claim in its absence?

Bannet (1989) offers the following to introduce her work on continental dissent:

> It would be impossible to write this or any other book if God and the self were really dead; if the author were really absent from his [sic] work; if language were nothing but an alien circuit which each of us is condemned to repeat; if society were really irredeemable and man irreparably alienated from his world. In the absence of any human form of mind, in the absence of any possibility of truth, meaning or change in the absence of all capacity to say what has not been said before and to add to the stock of our culture, there would be nothing worth saying, no one to say it, and no one to say it to. There would not even be any point in declaring that God and the self are dead. (p. 1)

In the attribute model the independent and autonomous self remains with the "self hyphens" (e.g., self-concept, self-esteem, self-recognition) and in its claims to objectivity as well. The conjunctive model has its uses of objectivity and the stance of the critic (how is the Marxist critique not simply a disguised element of the bourgeois project?). Despite these needs, members of both sets of practitioners have been stern in their repudiation of the independent and autonomous self model.

Scholars associated with either the situated or the activative models by their retention of some form of identity and agency must necessarily have a more relaxed view. The self is an accountable element in their theory and they do not have to view themselves as some kind of "special case."

Level of Claim

Level of claim refers to the location of validity—in history or beyond, global or local, foundational or ideological. Attribute arguments are beyond history (transcendent) and foundational (based on an objective reality). Conjunctive arguments can be historical or not and foundational or not. Most contemporary European conjunctive arguments are historical and ideological. Situated arguments are historical, global in their reach although locally invested, and just beginning to address the issue of ideology. Activative arguments are historical, regional (communities of meaning and interpretation), locally invested, and openly ideological.

Unity of Science

Only the attribute and the sociological form of the conjunctive models would accept the unity-of-science hypothesis. All other arguments specifically reject it.

Domain of Argument

It follows from their position on the unity of science that analysts of the attribute and sociological conjunctive ilks would hold materialism as the ideal and argue for the material reality of their "objects of explanation" (even cognitive states or social forces). Some Marxist conjunctive arguments make use of both semiosis and materialism; others are wholly semiotic. Both situated and activative arguments speak of material practices that are effective semiotically. There are materially real things done but their work is semiotic.

Purpose of Inquiry

Discovery and explication for the purpose of prediction and control are the purposes of attribute arguments and some traditional conjunctive sociology. A critical stances enters other forms of conjunctive sociology and is the heart of the critical forms. Situated arguments often contain an element of critique but may be satisfied with a claim to discovery. Activative arguments work discovery and critique and reflexively recognize their own part in the reality-construction process.

Cognitive and developmental psychology and American functional sociology, as well as those locations that seek to emulate those disciplines, are common disciplinary homes for discovery (as finding what's there) and explication (prediction and control) arguments. Marxist cultural studies, critical theory, and symbolic interactionism make use of discovery (as illumination and interpretation) and critique (reformation and emancipation) arguments. And interpretive sociology, ordinary language theorists, hermeneutics, and hermeneutic ethnography make use of discovery (illumination and interpretation), critique, and construction (knowledge production) arguments.

The conclusion of this review at the point of the purpose of inquiry is also the starting place of our next chapter. The purpose of inquiry is always veridical claim, but how shall validity be defined, particularly in the semiotic domain and in an ideological field?

NOTES

1. Levin (1992), Levine, (1992), Macmurray (1957), Myers (1969), and Wegner and Vallacher (1980) provide overviews. An interesting sign of change across two decades of thought is provided by a comparison of Gergen's 1971 text with his 1991 book.

2. This test was suggested to me by Lawrence Grossberg (1993a) who was quoting O'Hanlon (1988).

3. The fictive devices of mentalist biology can be seen, nonetheless, as undermining the rigor of one's argument, allowing an easy escape into supposedly independent entities which are actually fully under our control.

4. I am grateful to Professor Gerard T. Schoening for offering this comment in a review of a draft of this chapter and for providing some of the language that describes it. His review also prompted the addition of the term "action" in the comparisons of the models in Table 4–1. His contribution is further recognized and traceable in his coauthorship of the article "The Nature of the Individual in Communication Research" (Anderson & Schoening, 1996), which was based on this chapter.

5. Ross (1992) writes, for example, "Strictly speaking there is no such thing as the self—at least not in scientific psychology" (p. 1). A bit later on the same page, he legitimizes the claim: "This insistence that self is not an entity, that it must not be reified, is in line with the usage found in the contemporary research literature on which this book is based."

Part of this conceptualization can be seen as psychology's move to define itself in the face of 19th-century models of the individual that held to an essentialist self.

6. Not all arguments out of dialectical materialism or centered in ideology are necessarily Marxist. But those that do not deliberately work to defend a separate identity quickly fall to this label.

7. Most Marxist argument has held that there can be an authentic (nonideological)

representation which its methods will reveal. In this regard Marxist thought shares the same goal as that of objective empiricism: liberation through truth. My sense of this postmodern, post-Soviet space is that there is a greater acceptance by Marxist and other critical scholarship of an all-encompassing nature of ideology but that some ideologies are less exploitive than others and all can benefit from critique (see, for example, Gurnah & Scott, 1992).

8. The obvious problem of where does a liberated scholarly elite come from, having been exquisitely trained in bourgeois ideology, is the subject of the critiques advanced by Lyotard and Derrida.

9. Continental structuralism is most closely identified with de Saussure (1910/1959), Piaget (1970), and Lévi-Strauss (1967), and culminates in the enigmatic figures of Foucault and Lacan. Structuralist figures can become poststructuralist figures—as did Barthes—and structuralism is often combined with Marxist analysis as in the work of Baudrillard (1981). It is, perhaps, Derrida's attack on logocentrism that marks the beginnings of poststructuralism. The American strain of structuralism is identified with Harrison White (1963) and his students (Mullins, 1973), as well as with linguistic studies of which conversational analysis is communication's most apparent structuralist branch. American structuralism typically lacks the open ideological component common to continental structuralism.

10. The usual line of argument cited here includes Lenin (1960), Lukács (1971), Gramsci (1971), and Althusser (1984).

11. Parsons's early work, *The Structure of Social Action* (1937), was much more in line with the situated individual model described under that heading, but it clearly changed in his later writings (Mennel, 1974). Parsons's work was under regular critique by his student Merton (e.g., Merton, 1948) as well as others. In addition, the tenor of the times was much more in line with the conjunctive model, though Parsons openly resisted behaviorism both theoretically in his writings and politically at Harvard (Mullins, 1973). Perhaps, this was an example of social forces at work.

12. "Critical theory" is the name given to the tradition initiated by the "Frankfurt School" (M. Horkheimer, T. Adorno, H. Marcuse) and most famously continued in the theory of communicative action developed by Habermas. Cultural studies generally refers to the diverse efforts of Richard Hoggart, Raymond Williams, Stuart Hall, and the Birmingham Centre in the field of British cultural studies and its equally diverse American representation found in James Carey, Lawrence Grossberg, and Horace Newcomb, among others.

While an outsider might consider critical theory and cultural studies much the same, they clearly identify themselves as belonging to different intellectual communities. And, indeed, critical theory is much more in the German philosophic tradition while British cultural studies present an ethnological heritage colored by French structuralism and continental Marxism.

Finally, both critical theory and cultural studies, as Marxist enterprises, are deeply influenced by the failure of class conflict as the theoretic engine of Marxism. The road to recovery offered by cultural studies appears to be the more vital one.

13. The model of the situated self draws heavily on American pragmatism, semiotics, symbolic interactionism, and interpretive sociology. The central figures in American pragmatism are C. S. Peirce, W. James, and J. Dewey; in symbolic interaction, they are G. H. Mead, H. Bloomer; in interpretive sociology they are M. Weber, W. Park, C.

Cooley, and W. I. Thomas. It is the use of these scriptures that clearly delineates the situated model from the current movement of cultural studies.

14. Such a claim would include one's own writing. The most severe argument would insist that one does not gain access to authorized claim except in some service of what is meaningful. That service may be the advancement of beliefs in an independent opposition, progressivism, or a value-free science, all of which secure dominant interests. What is intended to be corrective is simply coopted. It is a pessimistic albeit sobering position (e.g., see Dyke, 1993).

CHAPTER 5

THE CHARACTER
OF THE JUSTIFIED ARGUMENT

INTRODUCTION

Our journals and textbooks are replete with arguments, some complementary, some contradictory, but all in some way purporting to be true and making a contribution to our knowledge. They cannot all be true, and therefore authentic contributions, of course, even if we accept the generous mantle of McGuire's (1973) hypothesis that everything is true in some way. What, then, are the criteria by which we decide between the true and the false, the contribution and the distraction? It's a simple question but it is also a gateway to an epistemological swamp.

John Searle, science philosopher and speech act theorist, recently (1994) offered what he considers to be the six foundational premises of the Western rational tradition[1]:

1. Realism: Reality exists independent of human representation. The aim (and criterion of success) of the justified argument is to achieve characterizations of that reality.
2. Representationalism: Language exists in part to exchange meanings and some of those meanings, can provide a literal reference to reality objects.
3. Correspondence: Truth is a matter of accurate representation in literal language.
4. Objectivity: Knowledge is objective content expressed symbolically. That which is known is a true representation and is independent of any normative stance.

5. Methodological autonomy: Logic and rationality are assumed to be formal, contentless methods of truth, validity, and reasonableness.
6. Criterion forms: There are objective—or at least broadly intersubjective—standards for rational argument.

From our analysis to this point we know that these premises presuppose a materialist phenomenal world, empirically accessible through unmediated experience, that is symbolically expressible in meaning-realist language in arguments that correspond to universal forms and standards of logic and rationality.

We also know the objections to these presuppositions: Not everything that is a proper object of analysis meets the materialist criterion—indeed, perhaps most of what is of interest in communication studies does not. Our accessibility to all but the surface of the simplest of objects is never directly empirical but is under the supervision of theory through instrumental observation. Experience itself is not an independent unity but is built up in language and action. The meaning realism of language is a joint discipline of both symbols and the reality they reference. Meaning realism is, therefore, a separate accomplishment addressable in its own right. The content of logic and rationality are their own presuppositions of what makes them true. Further, intersubjectivity is a political, not a veridical, process. There are, necessarily, multiple standards of logic and rationality. It follows, then, that arguments are intentional, rhetorical, and inherently normative products, not the unmanaged outcomes of a universal logic and rational analysis.[2]

These initial arguments position us to consider the variety of replies to the questions of what is true and what is knowledge. Our purpose is not to seek a resolution but to reach a deeper understanding of the complexity of the debate. Equally to the point, any theoretical position can come under attack from any of the several argument frames for what is true. A well-developed theory, in this postmodern age, will be able to mount a spirited defense across a broad field of attack. Finally, this writing itself is enmeshed in these arguments. I do not write from some protected position. Nonetheless, throughout I will be making knowledge claims with no visible embarrassment.

CONSIDERING THE TRUE

This section is concerned with the families of argument that declare the conditions under which members of a scholarly community are justified in holding a claim to be true. These families developed because—our default tradition to the contrary—epistemologists have generally rejected the naive empirical position that we have a direct and incontrovertible connection with the phenomenal world which, in turn, has an isomorphic relationship with a valid theory about it. (The first position is often called "empirical foundationalism" and the second "scientific realism.")

Contemporary empirical positions generally accept the idea that our contact with the phenomenal world is mediated through perceptual signs and theoretical perspectives and that evidence from the phenomenal world underdetermines theories about it (more than one theory can fit all the evidence at any given time).

The question remains: How do we decide when a theory is true? We are not bereft of answers as the list of "isms" below attests. Each argument family offers a separate solution to the question of justified claim, but it is not unusual in the practical arguments appearing in our journals to find elements of several families used to support the validity of a position.

We will consider ever so briefly the following argument families (listed in increasing semiotic order): foundationalism, positivism, correspondence theory, justificationism, verificationism/falsificationism, instrumentalism, conventionalism, programmatic methodism, sociological relativism (paradigms), and hermeneutics.

This list is not complete (e.g., demarcationism with its science elitism could be added), but then it could not be, because argument categories are border tasks not revelations. Further, I am not attempting a review of the philosophy of knowledge, but rather I am selecting those elements that I believe can be profitably mined for our project in the analysis of communication theory. In the sketches of those I do offer, I will do no more than set the boundaries, point the reader to further information, and attempt to draw the appropriate implications for analysis.[3]

Foundationalism

Foundationalists work from the notion that within any justified argument there is a set of prior claims that themselves are unquestioned—and, within a valid argument, unassailable. These prior, unassailable claims form the foundations for the argument above them. Foundational claims must be both true and adequate to the task of supporting their arguments.

Foundational statements are said to be axiomatic. The axioms themselves may be rationally arbitrary (as in the axioms of Euclidean geometry or any other formal system), categorically true (as in Scholastic or legal claims from the "natural law" and Kantian or phenomenological claims of a priori knowledge structures), or empirically true (as in claims from reliable experience; see Alston, 1993)). Foundationalism is itself, therefore, founded on some prior belief in logical rationalism, veridicism, empiricism, or some combination of the same, to which Polanyi (1964) would add the human capacity for insight and commitment. (The technical arguments for empirical foundationalism are well presented in Chisholm, 1982.)

The validity requirement for foundational axioms is that they be grantable, that is, that good reasons can be advanced for their acceptance and no good reason can be offered for their rejection. The "good reasons" of foundationalism, however, are to be rational, true, and/or empirical rather than political, ideological, and/or convenient. Therein, of course, lies another argument, one that distinguishes the Enlightenment from the postmodern world.

If we examine foundationalism writ large, we will be inside Humean, Kantian, phenomenological, or some other great knowledge philosophy. (It is, perhaps, only skepticism that offers a genuine alternative [see Lehrer, 1973].) Foundationalism written somewhat smaller leads us directly to some (any) theory domain. Any domain of theory (and by "theory" I mean any complex of claim, methodology, and membership that produces interrelated statements about the world and not some variable analytic hypothesis or ethnographic insight with pretensions) has a set of irreducibles that cannot be explained within the theory itself. For cognitivism, this set includes the formation and operation of mental structures; for behaviorism it includes the concepts of a stimulus and reinforcement; for semiotics it includes semiosis and significance.

These irreducibles form the single hard-edged boundary of a theory domain. This hard edge is formed because foundational statements mark the point of tautology within a theoretical domain, the point at which explanation can reach no further than its own claim (like a parental "Because! That's why."). It is the point where further questioning cannot be supported. In this regard all theories are foundational. They rest somewhere. Part of the archaeological work in the analysis of theory is to excavate to discover these foundations.

Foundational statements also define the reach of the structure above it. Most work undertaken within a domain is done well above its foundations. The questions and lines of analysis pursued that are foundationally well supported appear with a taken-for-granted naturalness. They are the normal activity of this sort of inquiry. Traditional behaviorism, for example, permits no explanatory retreat to interior mental states. Its foundations deny that line of argument. Cognitivism, on the other hand, inherently directs analysis away from what a semiotician might see as a broad array of cues existing in exterior, collective activity and toward interior scripts or schemata.

Another point of analysis, then, is whether the developing arguments of a theory are true to their foundations. Arguments that overreach their foundations can be marked by disputes that may in turn indicate an operational boundary of the domain.[4] The solution to an unsupported argument is to add something axiomatic or to calve the argument off to go on its own.

Foundational analysis allows us to distinguish between profound and normal (which may themselves be authentic or unauthentic) differences between theoretical explanations. Normal differences take a theory structure in this direction or that, but reveal nothing about the foundations. Differences between forms of attribution theory (Heider, 1944), for example, are all happily part of the cognitive family (see Trenholm's 1991 discussion). A profound difference works all the way down the structure to reveal foundations in conflict in the manner that Parallel Distributed Processing (PDP) arguments appear to do to traditional cognitivism (Boiko, 1990).

Positivism

Positivism has become demonized in current ideological writing. It has come to stand for all resistance (reactionary, of course) to any change (forward-looking, of course) in the way scholars conduct inquiry. Depoliticized, positivism is an effort to combat skepticism with the claim that we can have positive, incontrovertible knowledge about some things. (It is a line of argument associated with Auguste Comte, 1798–1857; the Vienna Circle; and Carl Hempel, 1965; among others [see Phillips, 1987].) The "things" we can know will be empirical (which makes positivism a form of empirical foundationalism) and the method of knowing will be scientific experimentation. It is this demarcation rule and its practical effect of privileging certain knowledge claims and thereby advancing the political value of particular segments of scholarship that has led to the attack on positivism.

Logical positivism was the project of a group of philosophers of science who attempted to develop a scientific language in which observational statements were independent of theoretical statements, but were joined by explicit rules of correspondence. Proper theoretical statements would be fully mathematicized (another source of hermeneutic consternation).

Positivism depends on valid observation being necessarily true and on the independence of theory and observation. Positivism therefore depends on the foundationalist axioms of empiricism. If our observations are necessarily true, then we can have positive knowledge of our observations. Given this positive knowledge, theory can be corrected when it contradicts what is known to be observationally true. If, however, our observations are not directly trustworthy, if they are dependent on language, for example, then the truth of those observations is relative to whatever else is involved—here, the language community.[5]

In the strict formulation of positivism, theoretical statements and observations must be independent. If this independence holds, then the relative value of opposing theories can be compared (Carnap, 1966). If, instead, observations arise out of their theoretical conceptions, then any direct comparison is inhibited. This condition is called "the nontranslatability or incommensurability of theories." It is the conclusion of arguments that hold that there are no common reference points that separate theories can address.

What is the state of positivism today? It is clearly a discredited philosophy of science as a named enterprise. Its principles nonetheless direct most of what would proudly declare itself as science, and its philosophy has been resuscitated in some form of correspondence theory (see Austin, 1961, and as discussed below) or logical empiricism, most notably by Brown (1977), von Fraassen (1980), and Chisholm (1982).

Correspondence Theory

If certain anonymous respondents on the History of the Philosophy of Science Internet list are to be taken at face value, positivism was a noxiously politicized form of correspondence theory. While positivism has passed from the scene, the larger field of correspondence theory that preceded it remains firmly in place today. Correspondence theory holds that a proposition is true to the extent that it corresponds to the facts of the phenomenal world (Goldman, 1986). The work of science is the crafting of propositions about the phenomenal world over which there is nearly universal agreement among members of the scientific community (Quine, 1981; Ziman, 1978).

Contemporary correspondence theory depends on what one of its critics, Feyerabend (1989), calls "the autonomy principle." This principle is a reworking of observational independence. It holds that at least some facts are commonly available to different theories about them, although all facts are made meaningful within some theoretical perspective. Separate theories may attribute different properties to the same thing; it is, however, the same thing to which the attributions are directed. (We might disagree over what the word "attributions" means in the previous sentence, but we would not disagree over the presence of the word in that sentence.)

In this formulation, correspondence theory makes two key concessions unavailable in the doctrine of positivism: (1) observations are not theory-independent (remember van Fraassen's constructive empiricism), and (2) facts can be made meaningful in more than one theory. It remains true, however, that the factual content of the phenomenal world can be violated by a theory and that such a violation can be recognized. Van Fraassen (1980) states that it is the responsibility of a theory to "save the phenomena" and the theory that does it best is to be preferred.[6]

As you might expect, this sort of sloganeering works best when the material criterion of reality can be simply met. Otherwise it raises its own difficulties which Goldman (1986) attempts to assuage with the concept of the "fittingness" of a proposition with its associated "conditions of truth" (p. 154). For Goldman, whatever the process of meaning making is or however that process varies across observers does not negate that it starts and rests upon a factual world (empirical foundationalism).

Theories, then, can be more or less successful in accounting for those facts, even though the facts themselves cannot resolve the differences among successful but competing theories (Warnock, 1962). Those differences, in their historical moment, will be resolved politically, not epistemically. The epistemic solution to "true but competing theories" requires a recasting of the conditions of truth, the range of facts about which the propositions are to be true.

The arguments of contemporary correspondence theory help us to understand both the epistemic condition of latter-day empirical theories and the conflicts that surround them. There is to be a set of facts for which a theory makes an accounting. That set of facts, however, can support more than one theory. In our analysis of empirical theory, we need to seek out (from the theory itself) the facts of the world which that theory purports to explain. These are not the facts of measurement or the results of an experiment but, in our case, the facts of communication.

Finally, I need to point out that there are opponents to correspondence theory. That opposition denies either that autonomous facts exist or that such facts are available in a way so as to provide a foundation for argument (Goodman, 1978; Putnam, 1983). That opposition stands in obvious contradiction to the practice of science. Objective scientists do not consider reality to be dependent on their claims, or doubt their observations in any practical way, or question the goal of accurate representation. It is those foundational beliefs that identify them as objective scientists. That some others may consider foundational empiricism foolish is likely to be of no concern to objective scientists, and certainly, as of this writing, its postmodern death warrant makes it no less dominant in the field of communication science.

Justificationism

Justificationism is the practice of validation of argument based on the structure of the argument per se. An argument is "justified" when it does not contradict what is already known to be true and is structurally sound. The tests of structural soundness appeal to rationality and its expression in logic (Brown, 1988). Proponents of justificationism draw a distinction between what is justified and what is true. One can be both justified in believing something that is false (my belief that an earthquake will not happen in Utah is justified because it preserves my sanity) and not justified in believing something that is true (cold fusion, let's say, is true but we are not yet justified in believing it[7]). Knowledge is both true and justified (Alston, 1989; Audi, 1988).

Statistical decision rules give us an excellent example of a justified argument that allows no comfort of certitude. Statistical decision rules are expressed in quantitative research sentences that contain the words "significant" or "nonsignificant." A finding is judged to be significant or nonsignificant based on the probability that a particular statistic (e.g., Cronbach's alpha, Fisher's F, "student's" t, Pearson's r) will evidence the obtained value if there is no genuine relationship between (among) the variables tested. The decision rule serves a status assignment function. If all other parts of the argument are sound, we are justified in believing that a relationship exists by virtue of the conventionalized rule when the probability of the obtained value given no true relationship is .05 or less and not justified when that probability is .06 or more.

On the other hand, no matter what the probability of a true relationship, there either is or is not a true relationship expressed in the data in hand. The statistical decision rule will tell the researcher how to act in accordance with the relationship, either as if it were true or as if it were false. That action, however, is under the "as if" phrase. The truth of the matter is untouched by the analysis even though we are justified in believing it to be so.

The separation of what is true and what is justified leads us to an immediate problem: How do we get to the true through justified argument? A widely accepted answer is that we don't, for in the end we must rest on some set of foundational claims that are accepted as true (see Quinton, 1973; for the counterargument, see either Will, 1974, or Lehrer, 1974).

This foundationalism returns us to the first element of this test—the noncontradiction of what is known to be true. Science and inquiry in general would appear to move against what is known (the sun revolves around the earth and all that). But inquiry can work on only that which is in doubt.[8] For normal inquiry to proceed not all things are doubtable.

Further, for any study to be accepted as legitimate, the principle issue must be in doubt by a significant portion of the epistemic community. I can doubt that the earth is round, I can advance my doubts through carefully crafted arguments and even scientific experiments, but beyond the Flat Earth Society no one will take those arguments seriously.

The permissibility of doubt establishes the action field of any domain of inquiry. Any domain of inquiry has clearly established problems where doubt about what we know is active. Attempts to answer these problems are what mostly fill our journal pages. Particular problems appear to cycle in our interest, attracting attention for a while and then disappearing for a while but always remaining in doubt.[9] Knowledge claims can also be brought into doubt. The hermeneutic turn in media studies appeared when it became possible to formulate the relationship between text and audience in some way other than in terms of content as a meaning delivery system. While this alternative position is not new, it has been recently authenticated.

But there are also knowledge claims that cannot be doubted except at great risk. Even a radical hermeneuticist cannot doubt (i.e., raise an officially authenticated question) that you can read this sentence with something of my intended effectiveness. For one to argue such would be bracketed as outside the boundaries of the permissible.

And finally, there appear to be taboo topics within domains of inquiry. These topics are taboo because the costs to the normal practice of inquiry are so high as to preclude a significant portion of the taken-for-granted. The topics are recognizable as taboo because it is not the answers that are feared but the questioning itself. It is the questioning that prevents the validation of one's normal labor.

We can find examples of taboo topics in any highly conventionalized practice of inquiry. To return to the statistical decision rule for one example: The probability estimates generated by such tests are dependent on the assumption of a random sample. If the researcher fails to have a random sample, then the estimates are necessarily biased in some unknown way. It is safe to say that no study using human respondents obtains a truly random sample. It is also safe to say that the probability estimates, typically reported in the precision of thousandths, are simply not what are stated.

Nonetheless, no journal editor can turn down a submission merely because its sample is not random. It must be too small, inappropriate, or reveal some other defect but not merely nonrandom alone. We have agreed that this is not an admissible issue because the business of this inquiry collapses if we do admit it. (Lest anyone begin to feel smug, I will repeat my claim that taboo topics exist in *all* lines of inquiry.)

Justificationism, therefore, illuminates an epistemic community as a reasoning enterprise of some coherence in which prior knowledge as well as a developed system of legitimated argument can appear and doubt can be practiced within the limits imposed by both. An approach to theory through justification analysis would lead the analyst to describe the domain of inquiry in which the theory would be located in terms of its foundational beliefs and characteristic arguments.

To return to an earlier example, attribution theory as expressed by, say, Kelley (1973) can rise only from a cognitivist foundation and can be supported only by quantitative justifications. Should we seek to develop a theory to describe the same material condition outside of cognitivism and quantification, we could not develop attribution theory because the foundational beliefs and characteristic justifying arguments that provide the structure of the theory would be different.

I am not yet in epistemic relativism in making this claim (that's a position we explore later in this section), for I can still hold to a common, independent, material condition about which attribution theory and theory X attempt to offer explanation. These two theories will not collapse into one because they are structurally incompatible. (Roth, 1987, after Quine, discusses this as a translation issue and Lenoir, 1993, takes it up as a condition of disciplinary political economy. We cannot combine those arguments either.)

Analysis of this sort helps us to understand why there is such a proliferation of theory (even with an infinitely diverse material world) and the political/ideological character of efforts seeking to resolve this diversity (Plantinga's 1993 final chapter is a good place to get the sense of this). Theory is never disembodied and is always a communal practice. It has to be located within its particular epistemic community. Efforts to declare domination over some corner of the phenomenal world, for example, in physics versus chemistry regarding fusion or in ethnographic versus functionalist explanations regarding media effects, are justly viewed as economic moves.

Can an individual know what there is to be known about some material condition? Only to the extent that the individual can be a competent member of all the epistemic communities that have something to say about it. Now this is clearly an argument in favor of epistemic pluralism (but not relativism), which implies a rejection of a common foundation of epistemic authority espoused by an epistemic reductionism. It is supported by a form of justificationism that holds to a mediate but not ultimate foundation for justified argument. It leads us to a veridical regime of many truths.

Finally, justificationism helps us to understand the normality of normal inquiry. In the normal phase, we are building the structure of knowledge above an undoubtable (if mediate) foundation. But what of those moments of discovery that appear to rock the community? To begin, most moments of discovery are themselves normal moments. What may confuse us is the social practice of attribution of invention or discovery in science and inquiry. The vision in stereotype is one in which all but a handful (or better just one) of scholars dance in their ignorance only to be struck incompetent by the brilliance of some Nobel Prize–winning counterclaim.

The facts appear to be much different. In practice we see a clear front-stage/backstage difference in what are the official texts (e.g., schoolbooks, claims of record, legitimate doubts) of an epistemic community, on the one hand, and its marginal claims, apprenticing arguments, and local disputes, on the other. Every official position has its more-or-less suppressed opposition. A normal discovery is the justified ascendance of one explanation over another within a community that has already provided for both. Attributions of discovery are better seen as post hoc beatifications (a community practice of its own) of particular players.

But what of revolutions? Surely Einsteinian physics has replaced Newtonian physics. And is it not possible that empirically based noetic explanations will replace nomothetic ones to fill our journals with ethnographies rather than surveys? Certainly revolutions happen, but it is their rarity that makes them revolutionary. Further, the revolution is not in the claim but in the change in foundational beliefs and modes of justification. That change preceded even Einstein. The idea of revolutions has much to say about the grand movements of inquiry but little to offer in the analysis of theory, which in the main is much more an ordinary business.

Verificationism/Falsificationism

Verificationism and falsificationism are two separate answers to the question of how actual, historical events can provide evidence for transcendent claims. The question derives from the inductive character of evidence. Briefly stated, any theoretical proposition is a general statement that is to be true for every instance within the scope of the claim. Any experiment (or other actual, historical evidence) is simply a single exemplar of all the possible instances claimed to be covered. If the proposition is true, it must be true for the single instance presented as evidence and it must also be true for all instances not tested. Because there are an indefinite if not an infinite number of instances that are covered by the proposition, the proposition must always be in doubt. As a result, we can never have positive knowledge.

Verificationism attempts to deal with this problem by posing a "weight of the evidence" rule (Giere, 1983). As the number of supporting tests increases, and in the absence of disconfirming evidence, we are justified in holding a proposition to be true by the weight of the evidence. To use the language of justificationism, the proposition passes from active doubt. (A similar line of argument appears in Toulmin, 1961.)

Critics of verificationism are quick to point out that that passage does not confirm the validity of the proposition. Indeed, there can be no "weight of the evidence" because the probability of each fair test is independent of any other fair test. Just as getting a heads in one coin toss does not predict the outcome of the next toss, so finding support in even a thousand tests does not predict support in the next one. Disconfirmation does not get any less likely.

Critics go on to say that not only is it epistemically defective, the practice of verificationism is suspect as well. What is claimed as supporting instances is often a procedurally mixed group of uncertain commonality, perhaps chosen to do the work of support rather than to fairly test the proposition. Further, what appears to be disconfirming evidence is routinely ignored, and in fact often deliberately suppressed. Verification is in the hands of those who benefit from it.

Falsificationism (generally associated with Popper, 1968) accepts all those criticisms of verificationism and states that the positive case can never be proven but the negative case can. If a theoretical proposition must be true for all of the instances within its scope, then the single disconfirming instance proves the proposition false. Positive knowledge is rescued, but it is positive knowledge of what is false.

Critics agree that if a single, authentic instance within the scope of the proposition is false, then the proposition is somehow defective. Duhem (1954) argues that no failure defeats a theory because the evidence is ambiguous. It tells us only that something is not quite right but not what is wrong. That defect, if ever found, may be minor, even trivial, however.

Further, the question of what is an authentic instance covered by the scope of the proposition is not simply answered. The ontological standing of the proposed disconfirmation has to be separately proven, but according to falsification theory itself that proof cannot be given.

The practice of falsificationism is equally suspect. Inquiry doesn't work that way. No one goes to all the trouble of developing a proposition for the purpose of proving it false. Propositions are developed as an accomplishment that provides for other accomplishments. Only the enemies of a claim attempt to falsify it. Falsification too is in the hands of those who benefit from it.

The equal assailability of both verificationism and falsificationism (see Lakatos, 1970, for one such analysis) leaves the door open for the sociological analysis of inquiry. Because there is no apparent epistemic resolution of the question of the validity of a proposition, the ascendence of a particular theory must occur on some basis other than its truth or falsity. Any such basis is sociologically addressable. What follows, then, is a partial listing of the sociological dimensions under which the validity practices of inquiry can be addressed.

Instrumentalism

Instrumentalism is the position that a claim is true because it serves its appointed purpose or false because it does not.[10] Instrumentalism requires that the purpose of the claim be identified, and further that that purpose be of sufficient value to justify attention to the claim (Toulmin, 1953). Though we hear the rustling arousal of the applied versus pure scholarship contentions in the background, instrumentalism is a more generalized position. It would approve of the purpose of truth seeking and then demand answers to how truth was to be sought and known.

Critics of instrumentalism claim that it is not a very demanding test, that it provides no method for selecting among competing theories, and that it allows post hoc justifications and metaphysical flourishes as well. Taking these in order, consider its nondemanding nature: instrumentalism will allow the least desirable of accomplishments to serve as the justifying purpose of the claim. For example, that an analyst succeeds in getting an argument published and thereby gains personal reward is sufficient justification for the claim. Proponents of instrumentalism would agree that scholarship can be justified by its personal economic value and then point out that much scholarship appears to serve no other purpose. It is only under instrumentalist analysis that we can recognize this fact and move toward its correction.

As to the second issue, instrumentalists would agree that the problem of competing theories that adequately serve the same purpose cannot be resolved as stated. They would then attack the problem itself. First they would point out that this is a difficulty common to all approaches to valid claim. It is an incorrigible problem. Their major defense, however, comes in denying the hypothetical. Instrumentalists would claim that theories never serve the same and only the same purpose equally. Theories, like facts, do not read themselves. Rather, for theories to appear to compete, they must have been placed in competition in order to serve the purposes of the competition itself. Again, instrumentalism will allow us to see those other purposes.

The third criticism was its self-fulfilling character in that appointed purposes will appear once it becomes apparent for what a theory is useful. The theory is therefore no more than an extension of some practical activity and does not inform us concerning that activity. Instrumentalists reply that empiricism is the foundation of all practical activity and that for a theory to arise out of experience rather than metaphysics is not all that bad. Further, not all purposes are equally valid and mere restatements of practical knowledge are trivial theories.

Finally, there is instrumentalism's reputed lack of parsimony. Parsimony, which we will meet again in more detail under the heading "Conventionalism," holds that the simplest theory that is true should prevail. Exemplar stories of nonparsimonious theorizing usually involve non-European, so-called primitive practices, although the epicycle solutions of Ptolemaic astronomy are also used. The story that I heard concerns South Sea island yam farmers who guarded their fields after planting lest the yam plants decide to leave.[11] On the belief that yam plants can't travel, critics point out that guarding the fields accomplishes the desired result but serves no real purpose. It is a useless theory that works.

The critics, however, fail to point out that the farmers also plant and cultivate the yams as part of the same "theory of yam farming." Should economy of practice rather than the purposes served by ritualistic guarding become a goal for these farmers, instrumentalist approaches will lead to the elimination of the guarding practices if it serves both the purposes of labor economy and yam production. Parsimony in theorizing is simply another purpose that can be adopted by the theorist.

Instrumentalism is attractive to me because it holds truth to be both an epistemic and a political achievement, requires a direct analysis of the conditions of validity, and motivates an explicit defense of the value of those conditions. It allows us to explore scholarship as a self-justifying, fully politicized human activity rather than as a protected and elitist enterprise (Rouse, 1988). Lines of inquiry can be considered not only for their epistemic value but also for their consequences, both intended and unintended, for the lives we lead.

Conventionalism

Conventionalism holds that valid claim is marked by the characteristics of collectively agreed-upon conventions of validity. A list of those conventions might include simplicity, elegance, reliability, clarity, and reach. Littlejohn, in his third edition (1989), offers scope, appropriateness, fruitfulness, validity and parsimony (adapted from headings, pp. 29–30).

None of these terms is a natural sign of itself or a natural sign of validity. Both what each term signifies and how it demonstrates validity is a collective production of the epistemic community in which it appears. Validity, therefore, is relative to the community of its achievement.

Babbie (1973), for example, tells us what social science is in his listing of logical, deterministic, generalizable, parsimonious, specifiable, empirically verifiable, intersubjective, and progressive (my adaptation from his headings, pp. 28–31). Valid claim, at least in the field of social science, must meet these terms as long as and in the manner that the community enforces them. In 1973, these terms would be barely contestable and within traditional objectivist communities they probably remain so. Elsewhere what terms shall form the conventions of validity and what those terms mean is open to considerable debate.

The debate develops mostly in response to the obvious difficulties in using contestable characteristics as validity definers. To hold that truth is parsimonious is to simply raise the questions: What is parsimony? What group gets to define it? How it can be applied as a criterion. (This sort of conventionalism clearly rejects both meaning realism and literal meaning.)

Given these debates, conventionalism rapidly becomes border patrol and in that activity actually gains value for us in the analysis of theory. Theory analysis can overemphasize surface differences—what one group calls "cognitive maps," another group calls "schemata." Those difference may mask fundamental agreements on what might be called god and devil terms. Cognitive mapping and schemata theory may contest each other for the same explanatory space but they do so within the same conventions of validity. Schemata theory and, say, structuration theory (Giddens, 1984) do not. It's an analytical error not to recognize the difference.

If schemata theory and cognitive mapping are brought into comparison to reduce their arguments, the job will mostly consist of pruning terms to fit. If schemata theory and structuration theory are brought into a comparison for the purpose of reducing the two arguments to one, the task will be accomplished not on the basis of what one or the other claims about behavioral/action structures but on the basis of which conventions of validity will be privileged (Amico, 1993). The reduction will be accomplished not on their truth claims but on what we claim truth is.

We make a similar mistake when we confuse communication science activity with the whole of communication theory. The rectification of this error, an error that fills our textbooks, is a serious and difficult challenge.

Sociological Relativism

This is the current location of Kuhnian paradigm arguments that see forms of scholarship as being communities of understanding. Since validity emanates from that understanding, the answer to what is valid is relative to the community and its larger social presence.

Kuhn's (1963/1970) initial arguments have engendered a widespread response that is well beyond the scope of this summary to discuss. But he accomplished two things that I want to note. He established the legitimacy of the argumcnt that theory revolutions—what he calls "paradigm shifts"—are a sociological rather than an epistemic event. For Agassi (1981), Kuhn argues that science is about solving problems that appear in paradigms that are determined by the scientific elite (p. 247). That argument opened the door to the close sociological scrutiny of science, part of which we have seen and more of which follows.

He also called into question the progressive nature of epistemic change in science. Progressivism in science (or inquiry) holds that authentic change (e.g., from Newtonian to Einsteinian physics) is necessarily change for the better—the better approximation of the phenomenal world (under empirical foundationalism). Kuhn argues that it is merely different. The facts can be equally accounted for before or after the revolution; it is the work that can be done that changes after the paradigm shift.

Acceptance of these two arguments by at least some feminists (Harding, 1986; Keller, 1982), science sociologists (Barnes, 1977; Shapin, 1982), and philosophers of science (Rorty, 1979; Whitley, 1984) started a significant status change for science. Science could no longer be viewed as naturalized epistemology—the single method of genuine knowledge.[12] There had to be other legitimate methods of knowledge production too (Goldman, 1991).

As theory analysts, our acceptance of these arguments means that, first, we have to work to reveal the sociological activity as well as the epistemic value that advances one theory over another. Much of that work is hidden from us. It happens via the appointment of editors and their appointment of review boards, the election of association leaders, who gets chosen for awards and grant funding, how apprentices are trained, through anonymous manuscript reviews, and so on.

It also means that our notion for what we are responsible in the analysis of theory is greatly enlarged. Legitimate theory about the phenomenal world is no longer the sole purview of a singular science. Theory may arise in other domains of epistemic endeavor—for example, literature may speak to the phenomenal world as well as science and there may be more than one form of science itself.

Finally it means that theory associated with a particular epistemic community does not develop entirely within the boundaries of that community. All epistemic communities must be responsive to the activity around them. The social science members of the discipline of communication cannot develop their own paradigm. They are carried along in an endeavor common to the definition of social science. And social science cannot develop except in some response to its opposition. Such are the functions of the paradigm and episteme in which truth claims arise.

Programmatic Methodism

Programmatic methodism is a form of conventionalism in that it holds that a valid domain of knowledge must support a complex, interrelated set of questions and analytical activities—a programmatic set of problems and methods.

Science is therefore a valid domain of knowledge because it supports both a coherent set of claims and the methods by which additional claims can be tested. Candidates for the citizenship of science must demonstrate their ability to incorporate what is known, their affinity for the analytical methods of science (or those closely related), and their unique contribution of new knowledge (Kourany, 1987).

Science may not be the only epistemic domain (mathematics and philosophy or at least logic would undoubtedly be others). Any activity of inquiry, however, that would claim the title must demonstrate an integrated structure of knowledge propositions; a set of methods of similar coherence, convention, and clarity; and the ability to develop new knowledge. (This is a close approximation of Kuhn's paradigm.)

Lakatos (1970) advances programmatic methodism in his arguments that successful theories are not simply propositions but rather research programs. They are a field of inquiry with constituting members, apprenticing programs, a complex of assumptions and stated propositions, and characteristic epistemological practices.

Evidence either positive or negative plays itself against the entire program, not just against a single proposition or hypothesis. It is this force against mass that makes such programs resistant to change. When a theory fails, it is the entire program that fails and its membership disbands.

Lakatos's arguments give us a rigorous standard against which to test the claims made for the theory status of a set of propositions. A few publications or even a narrow membership would not seem to met this test. Robust theories implicate the work of many appearing in several different venues. But therein also lies a problem for analysis. Research programs do not develop under common supervision. In their early stages, major players may work to separate themselves from one another, different theory names may be nominated, and different terms and theory maps may be used before a recognized effort at convergence occurs.

Would I pose a communication theory to meet the Lakatos standard? Well, certainly not accommodation theory, about which I have written (Anderson & Meyer, 1988; Schoening & Anderson, 1995) and named, but did not invent. It is part of the ethnographic actional semiotic interest that infects a small part of the social action field which, in turn, has been connected to the reinvention of American pragmatism, Charles Sanders Peirce, and William James in opposition to behaviorist and cognitivist traditions.

What would it take for accommodation theory to meet the research program standard? Others would have to use it, be disciplined by it, find their facts in it, advance their claims in terms declared in its name. The interpretive ethnographic methods upon which it depends would have to continue along their path to conventionalization and become familiar methods in our publications.

The difficult question with which we have been struggling is whether it has to be true. The answer begins with another question: Under what standard?[13] Certainly it is true enough in that it has been authorized and connected with other legitimated claims. It is in the mix of permitted argument.

The answer to our initial question is that even though accommodation theory has theory in its name it is not—high hopes to the contrary—as of this writing, a true theory. It is in good company.

Sociological Determinism

The strong program in the sociology of science would argue that social forces rather than veridical claim are the determinants of knowledge (Bloor, 1976). Working from arguments that deny the direct engagement of the phenomenal world and that advance an underdetermined relationship between theory and observation, this position holds both validity and the valid to be ever contestable (Richards, 1983). The nature of validity and what shall be deemed valid is a particular social achievement of each epistemic epoch. This achievement involves all of our collective resources: genetics, language, culture, discourse, history, politics, ideologies, and the like.

The strong program has considerable problems of its own (Roth, 1987), not the least of which is the sociological determinants of sociological determinism. Its effectiveness, however, is to remove the protective Enlightenment mask of the true from the face of science. We can see this protectionism in the common claim (e.g., Kerlinger, 1973) that while scientists can be venal, science cannot. Science in its pursuit of the true is self-correcting.

Sociologists of science would necessarily deny that science is somehow a privileged human activity that cannot be corrupted. It is as equally at risk as any other human activity. Further, the claims of science (or any other epistemological field) are never simply true. They may accomplish the true (under some standard) but they always accomplish something else too. For example, they always do the work of promoting science itself.

If truth is plural, if we cannot reduce competing claims on the basis of epistemic value alone, then the character of the other work that is done is crucial to the truth we accept. There is, therefore, a sociological consequence to every truth claim we accept that may itself be corrupt or morally bankrupt.

Hermeneutics

The word *hermeneutics* makes an etymological reference to Hermes, the messenger of the gods. Hermes was required always to tell the truth and only the truth but was not required to volunteer it. The whole truth was available only to those who could ask the right questions.

Hermeneutics, as I use it here, encompasses any scholarship marked by an interpretive turn. The interpretive turn is recognized in any claim of meaning (Bauman, 1978). Hermeneutics, then, moves (with anything from a nudge to a hard push) veridicality from the ontological domain (what is) to the praxeological domain (proper methods of understanding). For the empirically certain, a claim of what is can have an exact solution—a correspondence between the independent object and our claims about it. The interpretive turn rejects this empirical foundationalism and starts its interpretive activity upon an empirical text—an interpretation of an interpretation (Bohman, Hiley, & Shusterman, 1991).

In an explicit recognition of this "double hermeneutics," interpretivists have invoked the figure of the hermeneutic circle or interpretive spiral in which analyst (the reader/critic duality), analysis, and the object of analysis are mutually informing. As a critic, I come to know the analytic object in the progress of my analysis. I understand that analysis as it attains its own object status and consequently some part of subjectivity (the collective stance of comprehension from which I can mount my criticism) in a reflexive understanding of interpretation. There is an ongoing spiral of recognition and awareness. Each interpretive move opens up yet another choice. There is no boundary of the equal sign.

The objects of this interpretive spiral are the texts of practice and discourse by which we constitute human life. This textual declaration of the life world is a celebration of the social construction of reality and a rejection of the material reductionism which would, as Rorty (1991) says, hold us to be "nothing but" something subhuman. We are, instead, the authors and interpreters of the texts by which we live. Those are equally the texts of domination and emancipation, though we are not equally their subjects.

Hermeneutics is founded on the principle that work must be done before some object of analysis can become meaningful. Hermeneutic writing is, therefore, double writing: writing about the object of analysis and writing about the work to make it meaningful. Two elements in hermeneutic theory give it an extremely wide range of expression.

First, hermeneutics, while rejecting the literal meaning of data and the meaning realism of theory, does not require that a factual text, which itself is independent of but necessarily the object of meaning making, be rejected. Depending on one's perspective one can see the empirical under the supervision of the semiotic or the semiotic under the increasingly weakening supervision of the empirical.

Second, the double writing is potentially an infinite recursion, for each effort to fix the work of meaning making is itself an act of double writing, involving the objectification of the effort of analysis and the subsequent analytic effort. Each "fix and analyze" iteration produces the matériel for the next.

Hermeneutics recognizes scholarship as a life to be lived that arises the moment we can act beyond survival (Rose, 1990). When we move from the edge of starvation and predation, we enter into the creative ownership of our motives and the hermeneutic domain. Hermeneutics recognizes truth as a struggle not a status.

Hermeneutics holds theory as the practical effort to establish a point of view by which the world can be revealed (Diefenbeck, 1984). It is not that this theory or that theory is true in its correspondence, but that every theory uses self-presenting but underdetermining events to build consensus facts that can be explained by the theory. The purpose of this explanation is the ideological work it accomplishes. It is the ideological work that makes it true (Boudon, 1989).

Summary

Let me start this summary with a comparison of the conditions under which a sentence can be true within the various definitions of the true we have visited. In foundational (which may include verificationist and falsificationist), positivist, and correspondence arguments, a sentence can be true in and of itself because each word has a fixed or governed referent and the sentence can represent some independently addressable reality. In the more radical parts of justificationism and in ordinary hermeneutics, a sentence is true only in the context of the argument. It is the argument (and not reality) that provides the referents of the words and, therefore, what the sentence can represent. In instrumentalism, a sentence can be true if it provides an effective instruction for acting. In conventionalism, a sentence can be true if it has the attributes of a true sentence, those attributes being set, in Enlightenment terms, by "natural laws" or, in more contemporary terms, by the community of practitioners. In sociological relativism and sociological determinism, a sentence can be true when the community of practitioners as a working element of society maintains it to be true.

We can see that these truth conditions are quite different. Consequently, the truth value of any claim changes as it moves from one epistemological perspective to another. Let me turn now to some additional comment on these perspectives.

This section has been a struggle to write and undoubtedly even more of a struggle to read. The struggle in the writing has been the essentializing work by which each criterion of the true could be positioned to view it in some independence of the others. Analysts in the practical effort to claim something as true will make use of components of all the criteria we have listed and do so in naturalized forms of argument. There are, however, some communalities and distinctions of value.

Both criticism and science are characteristically foundationalist in their arguments. Conventional criticism will ground its arguments in the "undeniables" of the intentional elements of communication: the text, the author, the audience, or the critic. The location of what goes unspoken is a guide, albeit an uncertain one, of what can be true.

Conventional science might begin either with the tenets of material empiricism and determinism and proceed to an analysis of discovery or with facts with pragmatic consequences made meaningful in analysis that has additional pragmatic consequences, but both methods make use of an hard-edged ontological claim of "this not that" somewhere in the beginning. Even when the facts are ideological and not material, the facts nonetheless *are*. One can have, therefore, a rejection of correspondence theory without a rejection of foundationalism.

Because truth claims are embedded in the social practices of different forms of inquiry, there are both justifications and conventions of truth-claiming/making argument. Practical justificationism is much more than Aristotelian logic. It is also dialectic, dialogic, rhetorical, and narrational. The use of a syllogistic form, for example, is as much a rhetorical device as a logical one.

Inquiry is clearly instrumental. It does work. It can build cyclotrons and justified beliefs. As long as we hold that the work of inquiry is the demonstration of the true, then any consequence other than the true is the work of something other than inquiry. The atomic bomb is not a product of atomic theory, so one might claim, belying the historical fact, so critics would answer, that atomic theory developed primarily in the service of the bomb.

The issues of pure versus applied can develop only with truth defined in correspondence theory terms. For the instrumentalist, the truth of any theory is in the technology of its claims. For the conventionalist, it is in the character of its claims.

Do we, then, know better or do we know different? The answer depends on whether there is a knowable location to which our knowledge state is moving. Progressivism in science is dependent on the execution of correspondence theory in ever better approximations of the material. The fact that we can now do different things than in the past is merely a conventionalization of difference as better. Not only can we be a late-20th-century person, we can be no other.[14]

The attraction of correspondence theory is the fate it saves us from. If truth is not what is there, if it is rather what serves our purposes well or meets the marks we hold true, then as scholars we are responsible for its consequences. Such is the hermeneutic difference.

THE NATURE OF KNOWLEDGE

Just as with the true, the nature of knowledge is contested ground. Rather than work through a review of all parties to the dispute, I have chosen to present a middle ground that favors my own interests in instrumentalism and in a semiotic of action. Other positions that could be taken would be the strict application of correspondence theory (Austin, 1950/1964) on the one side and some sort of enduring skepticism on the other (Nelson, 1973).

The principle work of the logical empiricists has been to claim knowledge as a set of nonlinguistic propositions about which we could have certainty (van Fraassen, 1980). The nonlinguistic character of such propositions frees us from the local and historical properties that any expression in a language must necessarily add. Nonlinguistic propositions can be transcendentally true regardless of the semantic character of language and its manner of use. Nonlinguistic propositions solve the problem of meaning realism and the search for literal meaning.

Unfortunately, such nonlinguistic propositions do not exist (Capaldi, 1969). As a result, we must reformulate our notion of knowledge. Knowledge in actual practice is formed in a set of linguistic instructions, the truth value of which is demonstrated in their execution (Strawson, 1964). Because they can be executed in successful and nonsuccessful ways, such instructions can have both true and false expressions.

Consider, for example, a fairly famous nominated knowledge claim: "frustration leads to aggression." As a linguistic expression, its truth content depends in large measure on the manner by which the concept terms "frustration" and "aggression" and the relational term "leads to" are mapped upon mental and action states and the agentry of one to the other. Language use, however, gives us no clear procedure for accomplishing this mapping (D'Amico, 1989). What may have been considered aggression at the time of the writing of our exemplar proposition some four decades ago may have lost that standing now.

Operationalism has been the typical solution to this problem, but it too is no less local and historical than the linguistic expression itself. There are, indeed, an indefinite if not infinite number of operational definitions that can be posed for the terms of this proposition. Some of these definitions will support the proposition and some will not. Both successful and nonsuccessful operational definitions, however, can represent equally authentic attempts to execute the instructions. The claim, then, that "frustration leads to aggression" is both true and false depending on the manner in which its instructions are executed.

Well, we might argue this circumstance is not as difficult as it seems because all we need to do is to refine the original claim through a series of scope-setting statements to include only the successful and exclude the unsuccessful operational definitions. Sorry, both the scope-setting statements and the operational definitions are themselves linguistic statements, and therefore contain both true and false executions (Mayhew, 1976). There is, in fact, no way out of the inherent uncertainty that language introduces (Quine, 1953/1961/1980). The best that we can do is to show that a knowledge claim can have a true historicized expression—that is, be true in a particular time and place. We cannot conclude that all legitimate expressions, even ones that appear to be identical with the true instance, will necessarily be true because time and place must change.

An Electrifying Example

The foregoing is knowledge historicized with a vengeance. But it also appears to be the way in which I understand what it is that I know. I have an apprentice's knowledge of electricity. I can design the electrical service for most households and execute that design in such a way that it will both pass inspection and work (Remarkable, right? A scholar who can do something useful). The pleasure of electricity is its constant character. Electrical devices such as circuit breakers, outlets, switches, wiring, and lighting instruments represent conventional executions of the knowledge claims extracted from the principles of that character.

If something I wire does not work, I do not consider that electricity has changed its character. I assume that there is something defective about the device or my implementation of it. I do not know the character of electricity directly (even though quite a bit of it has flowed through me and I know such formulae as W = VA). I know it in the manner in which the devices work or do not work.

We might wonder, if I had a world-class physicist's knowledge of electricity, would I then know the character of electricity directly? I would not. I would still know it in a set of reality-building executions—most likely classic experiments—that connect, say, Maxwell's equations to that electromagnetic phenomenon. Further, my world-class physicist's knowledge might not include what I already know as an "apprentice electrician." I have no reason to believe that the entire set of world-class physicists would know how to wire a four-way circuit. Maxwell's equations allow for but do not provide those instructions.

I chose the electrical example because I wanted to move the instrumentalist's claim directly into the teeth of what appears to be the transcendent character of scientific knowledge. There is no knowledge inherent in Watts = Volts × Amps. Knowledge is produced in the execution of those instructions.

Managing Another Example

Now let us move the example to the task of the manager in a corporate setting. We might see that task as the coordination of resources, both material and human, in the production of some criterion activity or product. This is not the only vision of this task but it is a common one. Let us assume as an example Alexis Brown, chair of the Department of Communication at Washington Community College, whose responsibility has been defined by her dean as the production of student credit hours (a made-up but mostly true example).

Washington Community College makes its money by selling the opportunity for people to be certified as holding college credit. It collects its money on the basis of units of credit attempted. Units of credit are contained in courses and cannot be sold separately—sorry to belabor the obvious, but it helps to be this crassly specific. Student credit hours (SCH), then, are a function of course enrollment (CE) and course credit hours (CCH). Therefore:

$$SCH = \sum_{n}^{i=1} (CE_i \times CCH_i)$$

where i is a course attributable to the department.[15]

Granting Chair Brown consummate managerial skill, does she now know how to produce student credit hours? She does not, because the manner in which the components of student credit hours—*CE* and *CCH*—are defined, across the variety of conditions under which a definition could be executed, remains unknown. Further, the fact that the definitions can change means that her knowledge state changes according to the political processes by which one definition is replaced by another.

The reason for this uncertainty is that the execution of the terms of our student credit hour equation have a "conferred status" as facts. They are facts only so long as the folks at Washington Community College agree to act as if they are facts. The terms of every linguistic proposition are marked by this conferred status.

In some executions, the collective facts of *SCH* will not correspond to the money coming into the till and the college will either fail or change its collective agreement. But the money flow will clearly accommodate more than one set of definitions under which Alexis Brown will be deemed more or less knowledgeable. Therefore, what is known in the equation is located in the historical moment of the execution of its instructions.

School Daze

A recent article in the *Salt Lake Tribune* (February 5, 1994, section D) reported on a survey conducted by the Park City school district. Over 7,000 questionnaires were sent out; 714 were returned, a number that according to the superintendent, was sufficient to validate the survey. What does the superintendent know? Factually, he has a limited knowledge of check marks on the page. But he and his board members will construct a substantial set of knowledge claims based on those facts as interpreted within the premises of survey methodology. None of these premises were tested in the survey, but their theory provides the instructions concerning the manner in which we are to understand the results. These instructions are invoked in the action of conducting a survey.

It is the action of conducting a survey that is the basis for our knowledge in this case. That basis, however, is not this action as discovery but this action as the interpretive frame for what we have found (Brown, 1977). These statements provide the general principle that knowledge ensues from and is a resource for action (Barnes, 1977).

An Application to Scholarship

From our analysis and these three examples we have learned the following: (1) The resources of knowledge are linguistic propositions that provide instructions for the execution of its terms.[16] (2) Those instructions can accommodate both true and false executions.[17] (3) An execution holds the conferred status of fact according to collective agreement. (4) Knowledge appears in true executions of the instructions contained in linguistic propositions that constitute our resources of knowledge.[18] (5) The truth of any execution appears in the time and place of its performance.[19] (6) Knowledge therefore distributes across collective agreement, time, locale, and action.[20]

We talk of knowledge as action, achievement, state of mind, disposition, ability, and performance (adapted from White, 1982). We find the knowledge of our discipline in the performances and discourses of its members. It is to these, the practical arguments of communication, to which we next turn.

NOTES

1. Searle spoke at a colloquium sponsored by the University of Utah Humanities Center. This listing comes from my notes. My reference acknowledges my indebtedness to his analysis, but I am neither quoting (unless inadvertently) nor working the same purposes (unless inadvertently).

2. I posted my adaptation of Searle's list on one of the philosophy of science Internet lists. It prompted a lively discussion that lasted several weeks and entailed over a hundred major responses. The comments informed my writing in ways not hitherto possible. Special thanks to Tim McGrew, Steve Fuller, C. L. Clark, Lynn Hankinson Nelson, Joe Ragsdale, George Gale, and signatories of ESS.

3. "Ism-izing" is a powerful rhetorical device and potentially a dismissive technique in which all contrary arguments are ismized—nominated for comment—while one's own position remains hidden. An "ism" suffix implies an ideology that from the Western rational position is always suspect. This Western tradition is known in postmodernism as "logocentrism."

4. Using a foundational form of analysis, one looks for these border disputes that reveal the weakness of the foundations below or the working (soft-edged) borders of a theory domain. Inquiry is a human enterprise so not all disputes are foundational nor do all "out of range" arguments get targeted for dispute.

5. We see this argument in the controversy about intelligence tests. Intelligence as it is ordinarily measured is a language-based attribute. Claims about intelligence, therefore, can be held to be culturally contaminated.

6. This position constitutes a rejection of the Duhem (1954) principle that theories can be tested only within themselves as facts arise in theories and are not exportable. The hermeneutic reconciliation between Duhem and van Fraassen comes in the degree of difference that is referenced in the phrase "different theories." Theoretical formulations that rest on the same background assumptions but show surface variations are more alike than different. Such formulations depend on the same constitutive beliefs that produce a common set of facts. This argument is developed further in the section on justificationism.

7. This is the distinction that John Huizenga, author of *Cold Fusion: The Scientific Fiasco of the Century,* fails to make. Huizenga who apparently is the self-designated enforcer for the hot fusion hockey team calls cold fusion "pathological science." Cold fusion may or may not be true, but we are certainly not justified in believing it to be true which, of course, does not mean that we should not be working to produce that justification. Huizenga's arguments would appear to be mostly political rather than mainly epistemic, though that distinction may no longer be possible.

8. By doubt I mean that a principle is assailable. It is quite possible that even a sizeable portion of an epistemic community will believe the principle to be true.

9. My own experience with media literacy and television violence suggests a 10-year cycle. Interest seems to grow over a 3-year period, holds forth for 2–3 years, and then declines for 5 years or so. I have investigated the appearance of media literacy in the journals back to the turn of 20th century and the evidence of its cyclical rise and fall seems worthy of serious study.

10. Suppe (1974) in his encyclopedic effort provides an introduction to instrumentalism (see particularly pp. 29–36) as well as its criticisms.

11. The story is often told with that "thank-God-we're-not-that-foolish" flair. American gardening practices of planting in the light or dark of the moon might also be used. In that case, the contrast would be between *farmers* and scientists rather than between primitive and civilized, though it is the same ignorant and wise comparison.

12. The press for a naturalized epistemology continues, of course. One camp of epistemological realists have left physics as its foundation and now embraces cognitive psychology (Fuller, 1993a, 1993b; Goldman, 1991).

13. I, of course, believe it could ultimately meet all the standards: empirically based, in correspondence with the phenomena it explains, justifiable, both verifiable and falsifiable, conventionalized, paradigmatic, within some current sociological directions of communication inquiry, hermeneutic as well as in development as a research program. I offer this note in a half-serious tone, but it does show that the different criteria could be put together in a common argument and that multiple criteria are probably needed to test theory status.

14. For example, if Darwin was right, then the great advances of medical science in the public works of the 19th century and the procedures and medicines of the 20th are misguided efforts to rescue the individual from a necessary fate of death before procreation and will lead inevitably to the destruction of the species. It is simple human hubris that evolution happens to every species but ours. As I might have been one of the necessary deletions, I would not change medical history. I am pointing out that we don't have any access to the final story.

15. Note the rhetorical force of the equation within this example. More of this discussion is presented in the next chapter.

16. This is similar to the pragmatist position that a proposition is defined by what it speaks the truth of (Rorty, 1982).

17. This claim derives from the underdetermined relationship between any linguistic proposition and its foundation (Roth, 1987). An underdetermined relationship is one where choice inhabits the consequent. The fact that many operational definitions can materialize the factual character of frustration demonstrates the choice involved in the relationship between the term and its phenomenon.

18. This is a necessary move in the understanding of knowledge as a theory of action (Mayhew, 1976).

19. This proposition follows from (or is an expression of) the historicity of knowledge (D'Amico, 1989).

20. I believe that I have been sufficiently forthright that you should not be surprised at the ending of this journey. The fact that our long and arduous review ends in a public place personally endorsed is the purpose of all such reviews (Eagleton, 1980).

CHAPTER 6

THE CHARACTER
OF PRACTICAL ARGUMENT

Theory is not some disembodied state of knowledge but instead is a set of material, heavily discursive (preeminently written) practices that are recognized in some public venue and that may govern other activities. If I am to point to a theory, I will do so in the embodiments of classroom presentations, laboratory exercises, measurement and test designs, conference presentations, journal articles, textbooks, and the like. Theory is a practical effort. To understand theory is to understand this practical effort.

In this chapter we turn to that effort as it is expressed in the practical arguments of objective and hermeneutic empiricism and in a sampling of critical perspectives. There is, of course, the prior question: What should we learn in this analysis? The answer that I hope to develop in what follows will be, perhaps, startling for many of my readers.

First, most theories contain very little in the way of invention, deriving most of their content from the practical requirements of being sensible as theories *of* something. Once the work of meeting those requirements is set aside, what is left are rephrasings, restructurings and, of course, innovations.[1] Our work of understanding theory can be greatly simplified by a prior understanding of the requirements of the domain in which a given theory arises.

Second, the practices of knowledge management—the collective effort to discipline claim—in general mean that theories (1) emanate from predictable sources; (2) are subject to common forms of attack, suppression, and repression as well as to cyclical revival, reemergence, reinvention, and advancement or failure on a mixture of epistemic and political grounds; and (3) are community-based, being both alive and well and dead and gone depending upon the community from which the pronouncement is made.

Third, scholarly arguments are associated with both the tasks of making claim possible and the actual practices of making claims. In crafting their arguments, all scholars must in some way first make claim possible by situating the epistemic ground of their arguments, verifying their community membership, and establishing their credentials and pedigree. These moves authenticate the authority by which they may speak and the voice in which they will speak.

Claim production begins with the establishment of the "quest" (Griemas, 1990). The quest for the claim to be made summons what is not already known to be true[2] into active doubt or nominates it as the unknown, the yet unexamined, or the unconsecrated. This task generates the "calling" to struggle with doubt, face the unknown, discipline the mind, or deny the self, and invokes the "honorable effort" from the author. The success or failure of that effort is reckoned in terms of the reduction of doubt, the claim of discovery, the illumination of the spirit, or the gift of understanding. This is the poetic of epistemic action.

Epistemic communities have developed emblematic ways of speaking and writing this poetics that govern individuals as they seek to distribute news of their work. Claim must ordinarily meet these discursive standards in order to achieve the status of a legitimate argument. Such is the rhetoric of inquiry (Nelson, McGill, & McCloskey, 1987). Our analysis of these discursive practices continues under the following headings: the structure of argument (into the realms of objective empiricism, hermeneutic empiricism, and criticism); the methods of authority, significance, and voice; selected practical issues in knowledge production; and the work that practical arguments do to create the terms by which we understand a given argument to be justified.

THE STRUCTURE OF ARGUMENT

The analysis of the structure of argument covers a three-part range from the sacred to the contested to the mundane. It begins with the axiomatic warrants of argument that provide the connection between evidence and claim. It is here that what counts as evidence, its characterological hierarchy, and its manner of use are discovered. I consider this to be the sacred end of the enterprise because these principles cannot be questioned without an implicit rejection of their axiomatic status (Yearly, 1981). In most cases the sacred is silently incorporated into the argument and one moves to the much more political arena where efforts surrounding the right to speak (authority), the necessity to listen (significance), and the voice of claim (validity) are played out. Finally, one moves this analysis to "bricks and mortar" to examine the components and construction of the actual arguments we read, hear, and practice.

And so we too will do something of the same in the next three sections. We will begin by examining the axiomatic foundations that deliberately or naively permit the argument in the realms of objective empiricism, hermeneutic empiricism, and criticism (this last is admittedly under development).

Foundations: Objective Empiricism[3]

Knowledge claims arising out of objective empiricism will in the main hold axiomatic (unproblematic) the following:

- The validity of observation
- The unity of science and the singularity of explanation
- The independence of theory and observation
- The presence of literal meaning in both the language of measurement and the language of claim
- The logic of mathematics as a representation of the logic of human behavior
- The incorruptibility of conventionalized methods
- The primacy of prediction and the experimental method
- The necessity of generalization

Objective empiricist claims will be characterized (and somewhat problematized) by:

- The necessity of protocol invisibility and response ingenuousness
- The attribute model of the individual
- The absence of agency
- The functional equivalence of respondents either in aggregation or surrogation
- The presence of positivism, conventionalism, or justificationism

Comment on Axioms

- The validity of observation is the axiom of axioms in objective empiricism. To play this role, observation has to have certain characteristics: First and foremost, it is a recognition state that is clearly separate from language, culture, and other learned influences, although such influences may also come into play. Second, it has to be fundamentally trustworthy in its engagement of the phenomenal world. And third, it must be artlessly reliable in its reproduction. In short, there has to be something out there—independent of the observing—that initiates and controls the observation, and whenever "it" is there, the observation can be made.

Observation of this sort is corrective. Good theory can be wrong but good observation cannot be wrong. Theory that does not "save the phenomenon" will not stand because it does not exhibit "empirical adequacy." Obser-

vation can, of course, be biased (systematically changed) or corrupted (erro-
neously performed), but that bias or corruption can be eliminated or controlled.[4] Observation can also be misconstrued. That something happens is not
evidence of why it happens. The proper construction of the "evidence of why"
(erotetic explanation) has been taken over as the right purview of the scientific
method.[5]

• The unity-of-science axiom expresses itself in the willingness of the
analyst to quote any other scientific claim regardless of discipline or explanatory
object. Claims from physics, biology, psychology, sociology, and so on can all be
interwoven at any point in the argument. The unity of science also appears in
the preference of method and the application of mathematics (see below).

If the unity-of-science axiom opens the vistas of argument, the singular-
ity-of-explanation axiom closes them down. The singularity of explanation
(epistemological unity) necessarily rejects claims that make use of so-called[6]
nonempirical tenets (e. g., agency, interpretation, creativity) as central methods
of argument. Weber's *Verstehen* (or special understanding of the human analyst
of human affairs), for example, has been the object of objectivist ridicule. In
general, such interpretations of events are considered post hoc explanations with
limited scientific standing because they fail the foundational test of an objectivist
knowledge claim. None of this is to say that such arguments do not appear.[7] It
is to say that such arguments are vulnerable to rejection and if caught have no
direct defense.

• The independence of theory and observation is a necessary condition
for experience to be corrective of theoretical claims. This separation invokes the
doctrine of scientific realism, which holds that theoretical constructs must
correspond to elements in the phenomenal world. If a quark is proposed, then
a unique, corresponding particle must be found. If aggression is proposed, then
a unique, corresponding state of action must be found.

The claim of independence fails, however, if the element is somehow
constructed in the measurement process or if no direct observational evidence
of the phenomenon can be provided. Intelligence is often read as an example of
the constructionism of this pair. In this reading, intelligence is a conglomerate
of culturally desirable skills. Intelligence, as an entity, does not have a separate
existence.[8] Rather, it is brought into existence in the social decisions regarding
what skills shall and shall not be included.

As an example of the second of the pair, the failure to observe, schema
theory holds to cognitive structures that direct patterns of behavior. The evidence of the structures, however, is the observed patterns that could result from
several sources. No evidence has been provided for the cognitive structures per
se, nor has any method of measurement been proposed (thereby falling into the
"If you can't measure it, you don't know it" category).

The separation of theory and observation allows the hypothetic–deductive
method of testing claim. In this method, a theory statement is given as the

general principle that invokes a particular empirical claim (hypothesis). The empirical claim is then tested through observation.

The connection between the general principle and the particular empirical claim is managed through the application of the logical rules of rational argument as a practice of its own. The connection between the empirical claim and the observations directed by it is managed by the rules of correspondence by which the proper observation is to be made. (Operational definitions are practical examples of these rules.) If observation supports (not proves) the empirical claim, support (not proof) is given to the general principle.[9]

• The doctrine of literal meaning is invoked whenever a meaning attached to a sign is held to be the true meaning that is the natural result of an honest reading of the sign. Literal meaning is the natural consequence of artless semiosis. Literal meaning is a necessary part of any claim that makes use of semiotic resources as agents of outcomes—the typical "content predicts effect" relationship. This protocol claims that the factual characteristics of content are the cause of the behavioral result.

A similar claim is made when measurement makes use of semiotic resources (language, pictures, pictograms, etc.). This use must presume that a literal meaning is in place if the results are to correspond across respondents. Literal meaning is also a necessary part of scientific realism. If claim is understandable only within its theory or within the paradigm of its theory, then its meaning is relative and not literal. Such meaning fails to provide for the separation of observation and theory. (This problem is often temporized by the "close enough" rule.)

• The quantification of observations allows the analyst to bring the powerful logic of mathematics to bear on the analysis of human behavior. This use makes sense only if the logic of human behavior corresponds to the logic of mathematics. This is the singular foundation of a genuine "quantoid/qualtoid" debate. Rarely, however, is it found in such controversies. The presumed value of quantification comes from the success of mathematical models within the material sciences and from the doctrine of logical positivism that holds, in part, that true theory must be expressed mathematically.

• Intersubjectivity has been extended in the practice of conventionalism to the point where the dictum "If we can agree on the rules, then the rules must be true" has gained standing. The use of statistical rules of decision making is a good example. Here a claim is considered true simply because of the outcome of a statistical calculation. That statistical calculation is presumed to confer some special validity characteristic on the result.

In a similar fashion, protocol design that follows the conventions of good practice is a predictor of acceptance independent of the tenability of the claim advanced. That objections can be raised to the findings is not sufficient reason to reject them in the face of internal validity and recognizable qualities of design.[10]

• The primacy of prediction is based on the prior belief in the interconnectedness of the phenomenal world. In this belief, events, conditions, states, and actions have causes that will predict them. Prediction is a powerful knowledge claim because prediction allows us to anticipate and modify outcomes as well as to move to the control and production of outcomes. The evidence for prediction is most clearly stated in experiments where prior states are varied or distinguished to produce different outcomes.

• The final axiom of foundational empiricism is that the purpose of inquiry is to produce generalizable claim across a common domain of the phenomenal world. Generalizability argues that we move toward knowledge when we move from the eternal present. The eternal present is the moment-by-moment presentation of the world as a set of unique, fully random elements, such that knowing one element tells me nothing about any other. In the eternal present, there is no knowledge in this world other than the present moment. Transcendent knowledge is produced when one element has components common with another and even more when one element predicts another. The greatest knowledge is produced with the claims of greatest reduction (and most generalizability): What goes up, must come down; For every action, there is a corresponding reaction. These are statements of immense power. (They are also earth-bound and generally false.)

There is no necessary connection between generalizability and empiricism. (Hermeneutic empiricism, as we shall see, breaks or at least modifies this connection.) Objective empiricists, however, hold strongly to the belief in an interrelated fabric of phenomena. We can observe only the phenomena, but it is the fabric of relationships that constitutes our true knowledge.[11] What justifies the belief in the generalization of claim is its instrumentalism. It is the twins of empiricism and generalization that have given bragging rights to the material sciences.

The practical consequence of these axioms is an argument that is data-based, cross-disciplinary (communication seeks its legitimation in psychology and sociology), is hypothetic–deductive, uses content facts as literal meanings, applies quantification within conventionalize protocols, and moves toward prediction and generalizable results.

Comment on Characteristics

• Protocol invisibility and response ingenuousness refer to the practices of assuming that the conditions of measurement are not themselves explanatory agents or resources of the measured behavior and that each response is a naively truthful representation of what is claimed to be measured. While some comment is occasionally directed to the "potential of contamination" within a protocol or to "unusable responses" in a questionnaire, it is clear that if the particulars of the protocol cannot be ignored and if the measurement is not literal, then generalized claim cannot be offered. As an author, however, I am permitted to admit to these difficulties in the "Limitations" section of the typical report.

• The attribute model of the individual is simply an extension of the principle of an infinitely divisible material world into the doctrine of the self. This extension is motivated by the unity-of-science belief: a principle effective in one area of science must be effective in all areas of science. There can be no monolithic, unified, unique self, although individuals can be unique constellations of attribute values. While the attribute model is at the center of objective empiricism, it is not everywhere accepted. For example, contrary positions would arise in nonfunctionalist sociology.

• The attribute model, of course, implies the rejection of agency, but agency would be problematic at any rate given the traditions of literal meaning and the noncontributing role the respondent plays in explanation. In objective empiricism, the dominating themes of materialism, determinism, and reductionism make agency nearly a taboo topic. When agency is used, it is in a crippled form such as the sum of all determinants of choice which, if we could sort them all out, would obviate the need for agency. True choice demands to be its own cause and its own explanation. This demand has proven unacceptable.

• The attribute model and the absence of agency permit the view of the individual as a functionally equivalent representative as an aggregate under sampling procedures or as a surrogate under most testing situations. The individual as an aggregate or a surrogate offers no unique contribution to the knowledge claim per se. Whatever unique qualities the individual possesses are considered individual differences and are set aside as surface variations that serve to mask the underlying mechanisms in action.

We do complain about the quality of aggregates and surrogates—the use of first-year college students as surrogates for trained managers is an example where complaints might be raised—but these complaints do not imply the rejection of the functional equivalence of *properly* identified elements of a set.

• Finally, as we have seen, there is an affinity between objective empiricism and positivism (experience as positive knowledge), conventionalism (intersubjectivity as objectivity), and justificationism (argument structure—hypothetic-deductive—creates rationality).

Foundations: Hermeneutic Empiricism[12]

Hermeneutic empiricism, coupled though it is with postmodern impulses, is nearly as tractable to a list of conventions. The following principles sit at the core of most of this work:

• The privilege of presence
• A location in the domain of ideology/meaning

- The "constructedness" of reality
- The centrality of communication
- A focus on relationships rather than separate entities
- The acceptance of agency
- An emphasis on historic performances
- The subjectivity of analysis

In addition to the foregoing principles, work in hermeneutic empiricism is characterized (problematically) by:

- The trustworthiness of engagement
- The use of narrative and the codes of narrative
- The assumption and pursuit of understanding
- The management (successful or not) of the tensions in authority and subjectivity as well as those reflecting dominance and subordinance in voice
- A requirement for reflexive analysis

Comment on Principles

- The privilege of presence has two components: (1) the life world as the proper location and object of analysis, and (2) participation as a qualification for interpretation. Phenomenological, existentialist, and ethnological themes are played through the first part of this principle. Phenomenology gives us Husserl's dicta about the primacy of the *Lebenswelt*, existentialism insists on existence being at least an equal partner to essence if not the greater, and ethnology organizes the life world around culture. These themes create a "there" at which it is necessary to be.

It is, then, the participation in the "there" that fulfills a necessary qualification for interpretation. The text of a life must be lived in order to gain access to it as a critical object. Participation achieves this necessary character according to the complexity and duration of engagement. Theories that motivate (legitimate, accommodate) other methods (e.g., long interview forms, protocol analysis) must also account for the loss of being there. Being there authenticates the empiricism of the family name.

- The "there" at which we are to be, while it includes an actual location, is less a physical site than an intersection of significance. For example, I am writing these lines in my office which is an actual place but it is "my office" because lines of meaningful action have been drawn within it. If I were to seek its construction, I would not look for the 2 × 4s (or 50 × 80s in this European flat) within the walls. Rather, I would seek to discover the practices by which it is made meaningful as an office.

Hermeneutic empiricism operates within the semiotic domain, and while all practitioners would not appreciate the escalation of that term to globally encompass their work, all practitioners make use of an ideational rather than a material base for the realities they study. They differ in the character and force of this ideational base as well as in where and how it operates, but it is a domain of significance and meaning rather than one of matter and energy.

• It follows, then, that the reality that is the object of explication is a constructed one, made up of the material made meaningful and of meaningful accomplishments made material. The social construction of reality is quite an unruly character in hermeneutic empiricism. Its guises range from the fantasies of individuals to monolithic ideological forces. There is a tension in hermeneutic theories between reality construction as a collective enterprise and as a set of local practices (not unlike the theorist/empiricist tension in objectivist arguments; see note 11).

As a collective enterprise, reality construction is dispersed, diffused, fractionalized, resulting in the multiple circulations of meaning. To put it another way, reality construction is a dialogue full of dialects, the primary work of which is to keep the conversation going. As a set of local practices, reality construction is the set of observable, material performances by which the conversation is accomplished.

• Whatever the tension between collective meanings and local practices, the construction of reality is essentially a communication enterprise. The peculiar human character appears within this constructed reality through the practices of communication. For the hermeneuticist, our accomplishments arise out of our collectivity, not out of our individuality. Communication makes possible that collectivity. It is managed through the iconic, discursive, and performative practices that are the resources for our communicative efforts. In hermeneutic empiricism, a study of human behavior is a study of communication.

• Hermeneuticists, in the main, reject the monolithic self—as do objective empiricists—but would not embrace the attribute model. Hermeneutic theories generally argue that the self appears in relation to some other, both in identity and subjectivity. There is, therefore, no collection of attributes (there is certainly a material entity) that moves unchanged from one relationship to another. Evidence of the individual is to be given from within the study of the particular, historic, relational practices in which the person emerges.

• There is a strong inclination in hermeneutic empiricism to support the resuscitation of agency (albeit a marked and limited agency, as we have seen). These hermeneutic theories, while emphasizing the collective and the relational, acknowledge the contribution of the particular individual as an active, performing agent of a collective understanding. Evidence and claim within them must preserve that contribution. If nothing more, an acting agent always creates a "possible" to be contrasted with the "actual."

• When the specific agent of action makes a difference, theories must account for the historic character of the claim. *Historic* here does not mean "of the past"; rather, it refers to the study of actual performances of identified, contributing actors. They are "historic" because they are occurring at a specific time and place and are related to other performances within that historical frame.

Many hermeneutic positions hold that it is the analyst's job to detail the performance, the circumstances of its presentation, the action matrix, and the historical frame. The researcher, then, is often directed toward the participant observation methods of ethnography.

• Hermeneutic theories generally hold that human behavior is organized in action signs that are understandable as indicative of what is being done. Human behavior is a symbolic expression that demands interpretation rather than simple observation. The understanding of human behavior is immersed in a double subjectivity—the subjectivity of the actors as agents and the subjectivity of the interpretation—as the objective act has no intrinsic meaning.

The meaning of human behavior is a human accomplishment—as is all meaning—and in this case, an accomplishment of scholarship. A central aim of hermeneutic methods is to reveal the subjectivity of action and to reflect on the accomplishment of the revelation.

• The scientific study of social action is itself social action. Hermeneutic science would hold that truth is a human accomplishment within the semiotic domain. This truth construction accommodates the characteristics of the phenomenal world but is not determined by them, which is to say that the theories of hermeneutic empiricism (as with all empirical theories) must be empirically adequate to the realm of experience.[13] The realm of experience, however, changes its character from one largely independent of the human actor to one that is largely the product of human effort. For the hermeneuticist, we are true to ourselves in truths expressed in local performances by social agents—here nominated as scientists—making politically significant and ethically accountable choices.

Comment on Characteristics

• The "trustworthiness of engagement" operates as a principle in the same manner as the factual character of observation does in objective forums. It is, in the main, an unquestioned given. Clearly its acceptance has practical value for getting the work done. Critically, however, engagement must be as marked as any other meaning making. But problematizing engagement would be a deconstructionist move, calling the whole activity into question. There are, nonetheless, arguments as to whether engagement must be supported by method and conventionalized in technique.

• Narrative is particularly evident in the more ethnographic forms of hermeneutic empiricism, but all forms in some way tell the story of being "there." The use of narrative, which has its own structural demands and well-developed codes (see Propp, 1968), allows us to clearly see the hermeneutic claim that all writing (all discourse) inherently frames the presentational task and denies the possibility of simple representation. Despite scientist hopes of brute facts written plainly, the actual result is another layer of construction.

• The more the impossibility of mere representation becomes apparent in hermeneutic theories, the more the direction of claim is moved to a point of understanding. Understanding appears in hermeneutic theories in two ways. Hermeneutic analysis begins with the premise that there is an understanding in place that makes the practice and discourse sensible. That understanding may be fully submerged from view, but it operates nonetheless.

The first task, then, is the accomplishment of this understanding or member knowledge as an actor, which is generally held to be granted through participation. Once member knowledge is reached, our interrogation, documentation, and description of that understanding by which we can act produces another understanding that irrevocably changes the first. The claimant must necessarily provoke change, even if nowhere else but in the claimant. Hermeneutic empiricism is, consequently, consistently pushed toward the critical.[14]

• The necessity of change, however minor, sets the tension between authority and subjectivity and between the dominant and subordinate voices of argument. The tension between authority and subjectivity arises because, in order to speak, the claimant must first do the work of gaining the authority to speak. But both the authority and the speaking always emanate from some set of ideational and political interests that must be masked if the authority is to appear authentic. The result is that the claimant must manage the performance by stepping in and out of authority and revealing and masking subjectivity.

The tension between dominant and subordinate voices occurs in the potentially exploitive relationship between the claimant and the subjects of the claim. There arises a dominant/subordinate relationship between the claimant and the subjects. The claimant is, in effect, authorized by others—others not the subjects—to speak for the subjects and, in that speaking, to potentially change some aspect of the subjects' world.[15]

• The resolutions of these tensions (which may involve fixing them in place) is presumably to occur in the manner of reflexive analysis, a sort of self-deconstruction or abnegation argument. I qualify with "presumably" because a genuinely reflexive argument involves an infinite recursion. The reflexive argument involves the moments where we see the author and the constructions that provide for the argument, where the words or the actions become transparent and the work being done becomes clear.

The cynical position is, of course, that this unveiling is yet another disguise, but to the extent that it gives the reader a different sort of resource with which to draw judgments, however contained, it is considered to have value.

Foundations: Assaying the Critical

Edward Said (1983), writing about literature, sets the range of activity within the critical along four points: (1) the practical criticism of reviews and analytic journalism, (2) literary and cultural history, (3) cultural appreciation and interpretation, and (4) literary and cultural theory or the contested forms of interpretation. In this section, we turn our attention primarily to the fourth of these, the contested sites of literary and cultural theory.

Stephen Greenblatt and Giles Gunn in their reader *Redrawing the Boundaries* (1992) offer 21 separate sorts of critical theory in their table of contents and apologize in their preface for excluding 12 additional named varieties, an unspecified number of unnamed varieties, as well as the listed numbers of seven cognate areas with a hint of unknown quantities not in the book. So how is a social science naïf doing in this sort of thicket? Probably not well. Nonetheless, I intend to work an argument that emphasizes the similarities of scholarship rather than its differences.

Characteristics of Critical Analysis

The claim of this chapter as it directs this first section is that the variety of theories—increasing as it is—is only in small part a function of separate epistemologies and is in the major part the separate expressions within a particular set of givens. (This is obviously a typical reductionist claim.) Gerald Graff and Bruce Robbins, authors in the same reader (1992) set the claim well when they argue that "literary theory emerges when critics and teachers of literature no longer share agreements on the meaning of terms like literature, meaning, text, author, criticism, reading, aesthetic value, history, teaching, discipline, and department—and, of course, culture" (p. 428). In the larger sense, then, criticism is the debate over these terms, as common grounds for the joust, carried out in the specifics, that is, in the practical arguments of those who can be identified— by choice or not—within the critical project.

The critical project is to transform an object, field, boundary, or whatever from what it appears to be to what it is.[16] That transformation may be sympathetic, as when the critic illuminates the allusions and references to increase the pleasure of the reader; or it may be oppositional, as when meaning is destabilized and the work of the text resisted; or it may a constructive redemption of the text that turns it toward other work.[17] Whatever the form of transformation, criticism depends on the difference between presence and potential. If the text is self-presenting in that it entirely in and of itself fulfills its potential for understanding, no criticism is possible. The text of no potential returns us to "brute sense data"; All other texts, including scientific ones, are implicatory and properly hermeneutic.

Criticism begins by producing the object—be it a fragment, a work, a text, a canon, a field of discourse, a boundary of cultural expression—as amenable to its analysis. It is constructed as a "worthy object" which in combination with its analysis will produce the inevitable claim.[18] This is not to say that criticism cannot fail; it is to say that when it does fail it is not criticism.

The joint work of object and analysis is (1) to simultaneously demonstrate the object as a proper object of analysis and to demonstrate some aspect of its potential hidden in the opacity of its appearance, and (2) to enliven the prior analytic and to demonstrate its power to reveal, provoke, and transform.[19] The critical activity must move itself forward in terms other than that of one more text "baptized," although there is plenty of that too.

The claim of criticism is a claim of what the critical object is, in fact and in some aspect of its potential, but also what that critical object has become, as well as the mastery or subordination of that object (however partial) by the critical analysis in use.

Critical theories will vary, then, across modes of production, frames of analysis, the character of merging ontological and axiological claims, and their criteria of success. Modes of production might include—and equally important, exclude—the use of "natural boundaries" (this book, that film); common readings ("Plato is generally understood to have meant . . . "); competent membership (the cultural scholar as skilled reader of society); canonical agreements (medieval studies include everything published from _____ to _____); categorical definitions (explicit or practiced); and opportunistic poaching (metonymic methods).

Huck (1993) uses natural boundaries and categorical definitions to locate kinds of content in selected issues of *Life* magazine. Taylor (1993) creates a field of nuclear discourse from three exemplars. For Hekman (1990), the method is metonymy or using textual fragments to claim the meaning of the whole.

Frames of analysis are described by their foundations and justifications, which are rarely explicit but can be found in the terms of analysis and their effect (what Said, 1983, calls "precious jargon" and Grossberg, 1993b, defends as "technical language"). For example, logocentric and feminist analysis both use the term "rationality" which is a god term in the former and a devil term in the latter. And again, the various forms of psychoanalytic criticism will necessarily deal with desire and the unconscious within the partitioned subject, but Freudian analysis will move toward the illumination of a mind and Lacanian analysis toward the place of the text (Skura, 1992).

The traditional distinction between science and criticism has been based on the latter's avowed insistence on the open presence of value in claim.[20] For Harrison (1991), criticism is the art of revealing how things can (and, therefore, ought to) stand in relation to one another. Criticism even in its resistant deconstructive forms is the argument of the preferred possible. Said (1983) rings it out: "Criticism must think of itself as life-enhancing and constitutively opposed to every form of tyranny, domination, and abuse; its social goals are noncoercive knowledge produced in the interests of human freedom" (p. 29).

Finally, criticism must set the terms of its own success. These terms are the boundary markers of the community in which such argument can arise. Fish (1994) in his own incessant political action nearly bludgeons us with his claim that what "is fair or meritorious is not determined above the fray but within the fray" (p. 4). The success of criticism is a "political victory" that confirms the superiority of the tradition that makes it possible. The problem of bad argument is not that it might advance something false, but that it undermines the political force of what is true.

Comment and Implications

Criticism, then, is some combination of facts, fact making ("facticity") and interpretation. How the analyst assembles this combination is a sign of membership in various epistemic communities. To pose just three: (1) The traditional (meaning realist) critic would hold the objects of their analysis to be substantially factual and such interpretation that is offered to be well anchored in the factual. (2) Critics practicing more audience-centered criticism still value the facts but must also build factlike texts of the audience and its action upon which to justify the interpretation to be advanced. (3) The most deconstructionist of critics would hold facts to be trivial elements in the analysis (and likely misdirectors at that) and devote their main effort to facticity and the analysis of that fact making.

Each of these positions shows a different vulnerability to attacks on the validity of their claims (which is to say that each has a different validity task to perform). Traditionals are vulnerable to the rejection of the factual as factual. Evidence that shows the factual to be in some part interpretive denies the whole project. The traditional task, then, is to conventionalize the text in the concrete universals of authorial intent and/or in the literalness of meaning realism.

For reception theorists it is the factlike texts of the audience upon which their projects hang. Denying the audience (as does Lacanian analysis) or the evidence of the action claimed denies the whole. The task of this group is to make their factitious descriptions of the audience compelling.

With deconstructionists who move to some emancipatory position, one attacks the unspoken effort to construct the Archimedean point from which the final emancipatory claims are made. Whatever ending is given, the counterargument would go, it is just one point privileged by the author for some reason, on an infinitely extending line of analysis.

With recursive deconstructionists who live off the meaning claims of others (those who John Angus Campbell, 1993, p. 312, characterizes as "de-con artists who 'read' and go free to 'read' again") the fact that their argument is vulnerable to self-immolation simply confirms their position. The effective counterargument to recursive deconstructionism involves the reconstitution of the empirical imperative—a disciplining of the semiotic "float" with empirical constraints.

The validity task of the emancipatory deconstructionist is to make the reader feel both the oppression and the release of the knowledge claim. The task of the recursive deconstructionist is the steady undermining of any factual foundation for a claim of meaning. Their positive program is one of weakness and change, for they believe that power as the constructed dominance of one over the other is inherently dangerous.

The writing of these paragraphs gives ample opportunity to practice the deconstructionist urge. For deconstructionists of any sort, the primary question is what is being accomplished here, the possibility of representation of the field of criticism being mostly a banality. Of particular interest would be the writing in this section where I have taken on a "hidden, objective and omniscient" voice in a seduction of the reader to accept my claims by producing what appears to pass as trustworthy reproduction. You cannot believe me but must believe me because you recognize the legitimized methods of knowledge production that are my acts of repression. But that recognition is also your emancipation. And, of course, my redemption is in this paragraph in which I confess—but whose last sentence is yet another seduction.

Foundations: A Summary

Written in the manner presented in these three sections, it is clear that while the justifications for the effort may change, the work itself is much the same whether in objective empiricism, hermeneutic empiricism, or criticism: in some way or another, the analyst must first constitute the object of analysis. For objective empiricists, this constitution occurs in the processes of measurement whose constitutive effort is most obvious in the operational definition. For hermeneutic empiricists, it is the identification and engagement of the site and actors in the production of the action text. For critics, it is the declared unity of intention, content, oeuvre, genre, age, and so on that sets the horizon of the critical eye.

That object must then be subdued, unmasked, disciplined, and mastered by some superior approach, some set of terms, or a methodology that will discover, reveal, interpret, or constitute the meaning it has for some purpose other than its own. This effort is necessary because the object is opaque, resistant, complex, beyond the view of the ordinary.

The achievement of coherent meaning within an analytical frame is a celebratory occasion. This meaning is the medal of honor of the analytic work. It validates the effort. The achievement of this meaning is the evidence of the object and of the superiority of one's analysis over common sense.[21] It is the instrumentality of the analysis, and, in the best of situations, allows an increasing number of others to pursue their ends.

Following along with what I have just claimed, we can look for this three-jointed backbone in the work of any analysis. What will vary will be the (1) methods of objectification, (2) terms of analysis, and (3) criteria of success.

These three steps will have different surface characteristics as well as being motivated by different foundational assumptions, as we have seen. We move now to the methods by which claim becomes knowledge (Gilbert, 1976) and the prior of these in authority, significance and voice.

MAKING CLAIM POSSIBLE: AUTHORITY, SIGNIFICANCE, AND VOICE

Well before claim can move into the public domain, the work of making it possible must be done. As Charles Bazerman (1988) points out, the writing of science and other forms of scholarship must negotiate the relationship between "reality, literature, audience and self" (p. 47). Part of this work involves establishing the authority of the claimant and the argument, the significance of the issue as a legitimate and as yet unsolved problem, and the accomplishment of the appropriate voice in which the claim can be made. We take them up in that order.

Authority

The venues of claim—our journals, convention slots, and classrooms—are, in the main, zealously guarded by a well-socialized elite of the discipline. Putting principles of blind review to the side (we take them up later), both claimant and argument must demonstrate their authority, their qualifications, to be read.

The necessity of a prior authority of the claimant can be seen negatively as prejudicial or as the operation of some distinctive, closed network. There well may be plenty of both, but the circumstance is not that simple. As recent scandals in big science have shown, the quality of the work that underlies the words of the manuscript is not contained in the argument but in the performance of the research practice. In nearly every case, our single measure of that quality is the training and trustworthiness of the individuals involved. It is therefore not in the least surprising that we make a considerable investment in presence.

Presence, here, means the work of being visible in professional organizations, to gatekeepers, to our elders, in the success of our students, as masters of some content area. We manage that presence by seeking office, volunteering service (say, as reviewers), moving on to a "better" location, recruiting others to our own location, attending and presenting at conferences, developing a consistent program of research, and certainly just by "keeping in touch."

The reward of this work is, first, a greater access to the processes of knowledge production; second, an increased freedom of speech; and third, a deepening control of one's autonomy. Without question, the convention keynoter, guest editor, solicited author, or invited presenter comes primarily from the ranks of authority.

Authority must also be managed within argument. In practical terms, this authority is demonstrated in one's sophistication in positioning one's argument within a content field and in the complexity and mastery of one's methodology. This can certainly translate into "the review of the literature" and (say) "statistics," but it is more than pumping citations and multivariates. It is the confidence that is gained by what is revealed in the author's understanding of both the domain and the terms of its analysis.

This understanding is a necessary prior to the validity of the claim itself. Being true is not enough. A claim must also contribute, have the capacity to become well connected within the discourse and practices of the discipline.

Specific examples of these practices abound. We can look at one already mentioned: the literature review or record of citations. Citation practices are seen as the method by which we locate our membership (Fuller, 1993b), trace the lines of influence (Hickson, Stacks, & Amsbary, 1989, 1993), and even create the terms of oppression (Blair, Brown, & Baxter, 1994).

A literature review ordinarily intends to show the location of the present problem, why it is a problem, how it develops out of the work gone before, and how it follows as a necessary part of the overall picture. Citations are the markers used to show the accomplishments of those intentions.

Part of what seems to drive our understanding of these markers is the naïve belief that the pursuit of any problem creates an objective demand for what must be accomplished—that the markers are genuine memberships, genuine lines of influence, authentic foundations of the present argument.

If we step away from that naïveté, we find citations as part of the rhetorical enterprise that constitues scholarly writing (Nelson, Megill, & McCloskey, 1987). Citations are rhetorical devices (Gilbert, 1977) intending to display membership, claim influence, provide foundations, or even to shift the burden of proof to previous work. Here, citations are hardly the visible markers of the author's dutiful attendance to some underlying logocentric structure. Instead, they are the notations of acts of appropriation, poaching, cooption, and excorporation by which one assembles the resources to advance an authoritative argument (Latour, 1987).

To whichever of these descriptions one subscribes, it is useful to remember that citations are under the control of authors and editors and are deemed successful when they give voice to authority. That success may be described as a careful attention to the independent demands of logical argument or to the ideological preferences of a particular audience. In either case, they are part of the intentional effort to produce authority.

Significance

Unfortunately, it is quite possible to speak authoritatively about trivial things. Despite our chiseled motto that there is no such thing as trivial knowledge, in practice topics get deemed trivial (Meadows, 1974) because they are (constituted to be) undoubtable (testing a truism), easily demonstrated (simple common sense), well rehearsed (another study in . . .), contrary to current thought (crackpot science), touching on the taboo (a nonsense piece, a question that cannot be asked), or unsophisticated (looks like a student's paper).

Significance is implicated in authority. As an editor, I get to tell the author—at least for the moment—what is important. But it also appears in the manner in which we structure the domain of content and the analytic method through which we intend to prevail. Authoritative writing produces the significance of the problem under consideration by showing the necessity of our interest in order to make the domain whole. I write the domain to its limit or to its missing element and then invoke that limit or element as the problem of my argument. Fejes and Petrich (1993) accomplish the task in two sentences: "The impact of mainstream media portrayals of homosexuality on gays and lesbians themselves has likewise received limited attention. One important issue is the role of mainstream media portrayals in the development of gay and lesbian identity" (p. 409).

It can also be demonstrated in the intricacy of the analytic method it provokes or in the sheer magnitude of effort it requires. The cleverness of an experimental design or a complex and detailed engagement of a text testifies to the value of the work. Surveys with thousands of respondents are considered more important than those with only hundreds, although statistical theory does not support that valuation. On the other hand, a small sample of difficult-to-obtain respondents may serve the same purpose, as Stohl's (1993) sample of 20 European managers attests.

Voice

Reviewers of this book have commented on the multiple voices I have employed: the depersonalized voice of expertise, the ironic voice of depreciation, the conspiratorial voice of implication, the redeeming voice of colonization. Some of these voices are under my command, but more often than not I am equally the victim as writer that you may be as reader. The writing to be done correctly invokes its own voice. It is in that level voice of certitude that I tell you that it is certainly true that there are multiple truths, ignoring the obvious contradiction (which Fish, 1994, calls a mere trick of logic, anyway), because the effort would fail if I did not.

Voice is the style of subjectivity. It reflects the place of the author in her or his claim. Weiss, Imrich, and Wilson (1993) use a flat voice to present their professional description of exposing children to potentially disturbing pictures of earthworms:

> Children in the combined exposure condition were exposed both to the live worms and to the three photographs. To control for possible order effects, half of the children were first exposed to the live worms and then to the pictures,

whereas the other half viewed the pictures first and then the live worms. (p. 50)

There is, of course, no emotion in this description, no lived quality. There is no confusion, no pictures dropped, nothing out of order. There is no human response, no smile, no anxious children, no touch of the hand to reassure. The children are merely "things" being done to. This clearly cannot be what happened. The children were talked to, smiled at, comforted by voice and touch, assured, guided through their appointed tasks, praised for their work. But the voice of the scientist, governed as it is by the material criterion, does not speak in these terms.

Contrast the objectivist description with the lived experience of the ethnographer in this bit of description on a remembrance day in Dallas (Trujillo, 1993):

> One of Jean Hill's students, a little black girl, asks him gingerly, "Where did the [shot] come from that hit him in the head?
>
> He points to the same place where Mrs. Hill had pointed earlier. "It came from right behind that fence over there, honey."
>
> The conspiracy professor and his co-"conspirauteur" answer questions for more than one-half hour, including the one about the theory that Oswald had a double and that they buried then exhumed the "wrong" Oswald....
>
> One man in his early twenties laughs and yells out, "They switched bodies?"
>
> But the professor continues seriously. "We are now certain that according to all the testimony of people we talked to, either the body was switched or the head was switched.
>
> Two of Jean Hill's kids groan "oooohh" and crinkle their faces to make an "Oh gross" sort of expression.

It is the task of the hermeneutic ethnographer to demonstrate his (in this case, a man) "been there" authority, to reveal the "what's-it-likeness" of the event which is, nonetheless, written to advance the conclusion. Nick Trujillo's children must live. They hesitate, groan, and crinkle their faces. He cannot submerge their identity in object terms because that voice represents an inappropriate stance toward the episode—disinterested, disengaged, unlived.[22]

Finally, consider Taylor's (1993) critical description of the atomic bomb:

> The Bomb evokes a powerful "siege mentality" of dread, paranoia, and anticipatory grieving. As an element of the apocalyptic imagination, it clarifies our mortality, vulnerability, and—in fundamentalist religious narratives—"fallen" nature. The documented "omnicidal" potential of the Bomb refuses, however, cultural hope for survival and rescue, and subverts the apocalyptic conventions of redemption and renewal. (p. 370)

In the 1950s Taylor had yet to be born and I was a teenager. I practiced "duck and cover" routines and took part in family discussions about fallout shelters.

But I never articulated the bomb in the manner of Professor Taylor. Nonetheless, the description instantly resonates with lived experience. Taylor's description is not ontological; it is a critical contribution to the understandings we can have. His is the powerful voice of a mind in control of its image.

It was the effort of this section to demonstrate that voice represents the subjectivity of the analyst—the socially designed style calculated to immerse the reader in the axiomatic medium that permits the claims made. Voice changes as one changes the basis for claim. The rejection of the writer's voice by a reader is a rejection not of style but of the foundational assumptions of the argument.

PRACTICAL ISSUES
IN KNOWLEDGE PRODUCTION

The production of claim and its transformation into knowledge is never the labor of an individual; it is always a collective enterprise. In this section, we consider some practical elements of the collective forces that shape the character of claim and the production of knowledge. We take them up under the topics of presentational formats, practices of review and audiences, and instrumentality.

Presentational Formats

Presentational formats include all the distribution vehicles currently available and developing, such as the traditional paper-based distribution systems, a developing electronic distribution system, oral presentations, occasional video/film works, and classroom presentations. In "hard copy" forms, one finds the well-established formats and conventions of the comment, article, monograph, yearbook/handbook entry, chapter, and book as well as the somewhat less defined "papers," publications in proceedings, reports, manuals, government publications, and even letters (usually posthumous).

Electronic publishing is developing in somewhat a parallel form. We now have e-mail for letters, fora for comment, electronic journals for articles, hypertext and hypermedia (the latter differs from the former by its inclusion of elements such as graphics, animation, sound, and video) for monographs and books. All these forms are presently of "unknown" professional value (but technically achieve the communication goals of the journal article in a much better fashion).

Oral presentations generally occur at professional meetings, such as conventions, conferences, and colloquia—a list that offers a descending order of topical breadth, presenters, audience, and review. Conventions and often conferences will offer keynote, plenary, panel, paper, and poster presentations. This list is in a decreasing order of importance and in an increasing order of review.

Keynoters and plenary presenters are invited without review of the content they will present to the entire assembly. Poster presenters generally receive two or more reviews on the content they will be allowed only to summarize to passing members.

The few video works that have appeared have been primarily in the area of ethnography/documentary (e.g., Conquergood, 1991).

We have some examples of the classroom serving as the primary mode of public presentation. They come into view when detailed notes are published by a scholar's students (e.g., Mead, de Saussure), usually after the instructor's death (not a recommended career move). But the classroom is an important element in socialization and academic genealogy is tracked in statements like "I was the student of" and "Who did you write your dissertation with/under." Such statements often enter into professional decisions.

In most scholarship, a set of journal articles or a book is the sine qua non of professional success. Whichever one is used in the particular variant of inquiry at hand, it becomes the most conventionalized form within that professional arena. Journal articles and books, therefore, have different professional value in different places and contested value in a common place. In addition, journals themselves are ranked in prestige and books vary along the trade (directed to members of the profession), text (directed to students), and popular (lay readers) dimension in which prestige and royalties are inversely related.

For our purposes, the point of these sometimes subtle differences is that authentic theory—theory taken up and recognized by the scholarly community—has not only content but location. For instance, in general terms, course textbooks present the most conservative form of content, dedicated as they are to hoped-for widespread adoption among the community. Such books are usually well behind the development curve, holding on to theories well after their usefulness has peaked and withholding recognition from the latest efforts in fear of premature ordination.

Journal articles, on the other hand, while quite demanding in the evidentiary realm, are nearly cavalier in their reference to theory. Not only is theory presentation typically limited to a paragraph or two heavily salted with citations, what counts as theory is nearly anything in print. (One critic noted that anyone who can put two words together can claim a theory.)

The most effective theories are those that support one or more programs of research by multiple research teams. These theories will appear in multiple venues and will often be the subject of a retrospective book or yearbook entry. While this is a conservative criterion, it is not a reactionary one in that it recognizes that theory development includes the just born and the stillborn, those growing and those in arrested formation, as well as the robust, the dying, and the dead. It also recognizes that this development does not accrue simply as the result of an inherent heuristic value but because of the political action of the stakeholders in its success (for some discussion of these issues, see Erickson, Fleuriet, & Hosman, 1993).

Our publication venues are the arenas in which this political action shows its face. This action generally works from the entry level on up. For example, the publication of a work—more often than not a book by an established scholar that reaches beyond contemporary arguments (say, Gergen's [1991] *Saturated Self*)—engenders talk in the classroom, electronic references, convention papers, and published reviews. Much of what passes as theory reaches only to this point.

The next step might include articles about the terms and concepts with attempts to work them into the fabric of contemporary scholarship. This is a sort of appropriation move that both distributes the ideas and makes them more accessible and acceptable to the rest of the community. The interpretive turn in communication research has followed this pattern since its recognition in the early 1970s.[23]

What remains is that the theory not only appears as "sign value" in literature reviews but also in the design and decisions of a research program. When that occurs, whatever else its characteristics, we have a fully authenticated theory. To remain such, the research activity must continue or else the theory gradually loses its sign value (dissonance theory may be such an example) and sinks into a dormant or mordant stage to await a reactivation or resurrection.

Practices of Review

We can understand the kind of political action that helps to authenticate a theory by examining the practices of review, those gatekeeping activities that determine the fit and unfit players (Gross, 1990). Practices of review are widely variable across the different formats of distribution. We take them up by format in what follows.

Journals

On the whole, journals show the most consistent and most stringent review process. Most mainline journals use the method of "blind" review. In this method, the author submits a manuscript to the journal editor. The editor then assigns its review to two or three members of the editorial board of review or to "ad hoc" reviewers (for a canonical version of this process, see Garvey, 1979). The manuscript is stripped of all author identification before being sent to the reviewers. (It is often possible to identify the author, nonetheless; see Zimmerman, 1982.)

Credentials for reviewers are their reputation as known by the editor, their arena of work, their compliance with deadlines, and their acceptance of the assignment. Reviewers have a set time limit to return a disposition judgment (publish, revise-and- publish, major-revisions-required-for-resubmittal, reject) as well as a set of comments for the editor and an anonymous set for the author. The editor moderates the process, resolves conflicts (with additional reviews or his or her own decision), and provides the communication link between author and reviewer.

The standard quarterly journal publishes approximately 24 articles per volume and may have several hundred submissions during the year. The review system must function, therefore, to keep most material out (about 90% is rejected; Gans & Shepard, 1994). Reviewers who satisfy this requirement are used more frequently than those who are more liberal in their decisions. The result is a deep conventionalization of the article argument.

Reviews show the same unevenness as manuscripts. Some are well done and some are not. The match between reviewer knowledge and manuscript content is often uncertain (Hammermesh, 1994). Rejection (and acceptance) is sometimes merely the luck of the draw. (It is a slogan that more articles are published through persistence than through insight.) In the end, and in a criterion application of the process, we are talking about a decision made by three people with varying degrees of expertise and attentiveness. Deviations from this criterion application (in either direction) are not uncommon. Publication is no guarantee of high character.

There is, of course, a review that is prior to whatever procedures are in place. That review is the reputation and positioning of the journal (book publisher, etc.) within the field. If the goal is publication, it makes little sense to buck the odds by sending work to an editorial staff that has no history of accepting papers on your topic. Subject matter is simply closed out, or it has to be reconstituted in acceptable ways. Reviewers, editors, and publishers do exercise their authority in easing some and blocking others. The common advice given to novice authors by their established colleagues—Look to what is being accepted and then do likewise—is part of this prior review.

Greg Myers (1990) has called this review process the establishment of the social context of knowledge in which the relationship between "the author, the editor, the referees, and the wider scientific community" manages claim (p. 65). But this review is not a bloodless exercise; indeed, in my opinion, it is part of the politics of exclusion by which certain ideas are advanced and others suppressed. (A powerful statement about this process is made by Blair, Brown, and Baxter, 1994.[24]) If one needs rock-solid evidence of the ideological character of knowledge, one need look no further than these practices of review (for further discussion, see Cole, Rubin, & Cole, 1978; Harnad, 1982).

Conventions and Conferences

Competitive programs at conventions and conferences demonstrate a version of the same review process. The differences are: (1) sometimes abstracts rather than completed manuscripts are permitted in the competition; (2) reviewers are usually given several manuscripts to compare; and (3) the reviewers are ordinarily asked to rank rather than to comment upon (or justify their position on) the papers they examine.

Convention planners have come to recognize that more sessions mean more attendees, and therefore more fees collected. Scholars, in this symbiotic relationship, recognize presenting a paper as an economic value that wins them travel funds and merits pay raises. The result is that the number of traditional sessions has more than doubled in the past 10 years within some professional associations. In addition, poster sessions, a practice in which a paper is not presented but merely made available, have proliferated. Finally, convention planners also offer noncompetitive panels to which speakers are invited or even allowed to volunteer to participate.

Books

There is no consistent system for the review of book manuscripts. Publishers balance their own interests, their reputation in the field, their competitive position, and their economic costs when making decisions to publish. All publishers look to sales as the final confirmation of the value of a work to the discipline. But sales are unpredictable (and an untested measure of worthiness). Much more work is published than is expected to be successful.

Book projects usually start with a prospectus which can be solicited from or initiated by a potential author. The prospectus contains an abstract of the work (a table of contents with extensive description and a sample chapter or chapters) and a schedule outlining the author's plan for completing the project (e.g., date for completing first draft, revision, etc.). If the project is a textbook, an indication of the potential adopters, the present competition, and its relation to the proposed work will be included. This prospectus is evaluated internally and often sent out to reviewers who more often than not are asked to comment on both the quality and the marketability of the work. These reviewers are ordinarily paid a nominal fee. Book publishers need a consistent supply of new material, and a new publisher must build a stable of texts to establish a position in a field. Book manuscripts are in good demand.

As the acknowledgments attest, authors normally have substantial help during the drafting process. Several people will have read the entire draft and specialized help will have been sought for particular sections. Central ideas are often refined or even developed as a result of these reviews.

Once a draft of the book manuscript is completed, it ordinarily goes out for additional review by a subject editor and by a copyeditor. Both are involved in the social practices of claim, but each does different work. The subject editor is concerned about the caliber of argument, factual accuracy, appropriate references and the like. The copyeditor is concerned with the likes of language use, grammar, spelling, and punctuation. The quality level of a publishing house is indicated by the work of these editors.

There are, finally, the issues of multiple editions and copy work. The used-book market wreaks an economic hardship on both publishers and authors. While the price of a used book may be 80% of the original, none of that money goes back to the originators of the work (I am not whining). The publishers' response has been to issue popular books as a series of new editions and to keep the printing of any given edition at a relatively low volume. Ideally, the publisher hopes to sell all its copies of a book just before a new edition is in print. The new edition is intended to undercut the current market for the used copies of the old edition. New editions do not necessarily offer improvements, and more than one instructor has mourned the loss of an older edition.

The legitimizing of the samizdat press run by copy centers everywhere gives us new evidence of what is happening in the classroom. Suits based on copyright law have forced copy centers to return royalties to publishers and authors for the use of their work. A well-recognized linguist (politely unnamed here) remarked to me that he now makes three times the amount on copywork royalties that he makes on the books from which the copies are made.

In media theory, this represents a change from the vertical control of source material in the line down from publishing house to student (the dominant method for hundreds of years) to the horizontal control of material by the end user. In practice, authors have lost most of their ability to control the conditions under which their ideas will be encountered. In ways quite clear, the selection and ordering of copytexts is the work of the final author (the collator of the texts) which may radically change the rhetorical power of the work.

If, as I have argued, we find the knowledge of our discipline in the performances and discourses of its members, then the practices of publication in classrooms, electronic bytes, pixels, and hardcopy implicate our knowing. These practical considerations are mundane but never trivial.

THE RELATIONSHIP BETWEEN JUSTIFIED AND PRACTICAL ARGUMENT

The justified argument is, of course, an ideal form that can never be realized except in some form of a practical argument. The practical argument itself, however, creates the conditions by which justification—or the "right" to believe an argument to be true—can be accomplished. The relationship between the two works form an explicit set of argument components and an implicit set of epistemological elements. The argument components are the product of a theory in action. The epistemological elements are the belief demands required for the argument to be read as true.

In my field of media studies, for example, the theory of what Altheide and Snow (1991) call "phase 3" in media analysis—the social science phase—considered the relationship among three components: content, audiences, and effects, mostly as a linear progression of content through audiences to effects (C → A → E). The theories of this phase (which is still very much with us) varied by the relative presence of the audience, ranging from the rare and vilified "content affects everyone the same way" to the common and generally accepted "content affects different audience segments differentially."

All the writing in that theory set nevertheless positions the researcher as a "discoverer" of what independently is, the claim as an approximation of what preexists, and the reader as the field of confirmation and refutation. In order to accept the typical C → A → E argument, therefore, I must hold (at least during the moment of reading it) beliefs in empirical foundationalism, rationality, determinism, and objectivism.

Social action theories, on the other hand, take the positioned and situated auditor (the audience member) and fashion a downward relationship in which both content and effects are the accomplishment of audience effort. Social action theories, in order to be true to themselves, cannot hold their own arguments to be objective, representational, and referential. Rather, they must be acknowledged as resources in an achieved truth condition. The researcher is identified as an agent in this creation process, the claim as a tool in its achievement, and the reader as the field in which the achievement will be realized.

The problem for us as readers, then, in the theory diversity of this postmodern world, is that each argument we read positions us somewhere epistemologically. For me to address, say, a measurement issue in a direct effects argument requires me to set aside my prior objections to the demanded belief in, say, meaning realism. If I reject the meaning realism required by these studies, the measurement issue (whatever it is) as well as any substantive claim are moot. The consequence, as I move from reader to commentator, is that I either suspend or suppress my disbelief or I do not speak (or speak only in general opposition). I can have no positive presence in that domain of scholarship.

For some—and often for myself—the solution to this problem is to narrow one's focus to the technical issue, be it in logic, methodology, presentation, or whatever and then to address the technicality as it resides within its frame of meaningfulness. This is a "technocrat" solution that addresses only the means and not the ends of argument.

Just as the practice of methods appropriates the practitioner into the field of theory that justifies those methods (the claim I develop in the next chapter), so too does the reading of the books, articles, and papers of the field appropriate us into their epistemological justifications. It is not trivial that we resist reading outside our chosen areas. The practical argument is a powerful rhetorical device—dangerous in that it implicates the reader (Eco, 1992; Harrison, 1991).

THE CHARACTER OF PRACTICAL ARGUMENT: A SUMMARY

We have in this chapter probed into the mystic of theory by considering the methods and practices of its development. Theory of any kind springs from a well-developed generative medium of axioms, principles, assumptions, concepts, and terms. Often major contributions are made by a simple rearrangement of elements. Effective work in theory is not an outside job.

In fact, a good bit of theory work involves establishing the credentials of the theorist and the argument. There is no necessary truth difference in the claims made by a crackpot and the claims made by a scientist. It is the actions we take in reference to crackpot and scientific claims that causes the one to be dismissed and the other to be authenticated.

That authentication is also the subject of material practices in the production of knowledge. Knowledge as a set of instructional propositions and practical actions is a material resource that has location in time and place as well as agents of its production and distribution. As scholars, scientists, and critics, we labor in the field of knowledge. We add, abuse, enhance, degrade, extend, distort, deliver, and deny without guarantee in those labors. Our very ordinary practices matter.

NOTES

1. For example, in the objectivist domain of content → audience → effect, the C → A → E structure generates causal theories based on content characteristics or critical approaches based on intent. Remaining inside the same objective presuppositions, restructuring the arrangement to A → C → E produces reception studies and changing to E → A → C generates functionalist explanations such as uses and gratifications. Uses and gratifications research in media is not a worldview difference from direct effects research. Both are dependent on the same prior assumptions and can reach the same conclusions (effects researchers generate functionalist conclusions when they include audience variables). The primary contribution of uses and gratifications—and it is not trivial—is the proposition of starting with the outcome first.

2. One's epistemic grounds establish what is already known to be true and what can be called into doubt (Dewey, 1938). Several principles are involved: Not everything can be doubted and still remain legitimate scholarship. There will always be the unquestionable and the unspeakable. Not everything doubtable is readily open to doubt; extensive work may be necessary to bring it into doubt. Finally, everything doubtable can be called into doubt but only from some undoubted and unspoken position.

3. As always, I wish to remind the reader that I am not proposing these as essential characteristics of objective research. They are conventional practices expressed as propositions. Within the objective community considerable work is expended to ensure their status as propositions (e.g., codes of research practice, textbooks and handbooks of research, licensure and certification, practices of review, etc.).

4. Controlling bias or corruption is usually done through multiple observations and the application of regression arguments. These arguments make use of central tendency theorems to hold that biases and errors will distribute "normally" (equally on either side of the true value). One need only to take the mean of multiple observations to represent a good approximation of the true value. The tenet that mean scores can represent the true value is one reason why mean scores have high status in objective empiricist arguments to the extent that "taking the mean" is often a substitute for rigorous analysis of bias and error in observation.

5. The scientific method is a (and for some "the") means of knowledge production. It is, therefore, not a particular practice, such as experimentation, but the whole system of purposes, practices, values, and such that characterize the traditional scientific enterprise. That science claims certain forms of explanation as its own raises an obvious ideological question. Science answers that question in its accomplishments. Where material science has failed to demonstrate a rich utility, it has been open to attack. (This footnote moves from objective empiricism to sociological determinism to sociological relativism to instrumentalism to methodological pluralism to deconstructionism, and ends with the unspoken.)

6. The use of "so-called" here is to signal that what is and what is not empirical is open to change. For example, "interpretation" is generally considered to be a non empirical tenet and therefore outside the realm of scientific explanation. PDP or neural network psychology has begun work to ground interpretation in empirical events, however. Interpretation may, consequently, one day cross the demarcation line into objectivist science.

7. The claim that an F-test "approaches significance" is an example of a particular event interpretation dubbed the "close enough" rule.

8. This is a separate argument from the one that indicts intelligence because the test questions are culturally biased by using language specific to experiences some respondents would not have. That argument presumes intelligence exists as a single phenomenon but is improperly measured.

9. The rejection of *proof* in the first case is due to the interposition of correspondence rules between the construct of the hypothesis and the observation per se (and there may be a prior failure in logic as well). Correspondence rules can be false. The rejection of *proof* in the second case is due to the inductive limitation. No general theorem can be proven in the specific case. It can be disproved, however. The support of the positive specific instance, then, is that the general cannot yet be denied (but see also the earlier discussion of verificationism and falsificationism and their difficulties).

10. It should be clear that statistical analysis and design have become ideological in that it is their sign value that is attended to rather than the rigorous demands of statistical theory.

11. The fact that relationships must be recognized and not observed is a source of tension between theorists and empiricists even within common epistemological camps (see Rosengren, 1995, for an example) with counterclaims of the empirical fallacy (making general claims from simple observations) and of empirically empty constructs (using unmeasurable terms).

12. The reader is reminded of earlier caveats about the pitfalls of essentializing a nonconventionalized set of practices. Not all empirical studies motivated by the "interpretive turn" will adhere or even acknowledge all of the principles listed, and undoubtedly

others could be constructed (both limitations clearly follow from any hermeneutic enterprise). The point of the list is both as a heuristic and to fix the object of our analysis. The list is a good example of the double writing required by interpretation: the first participates in the constructed object that provides for the second, the critical analysis.

13. Objective empiricists demand a "correspondence" between the independent facts of experience and the claims about them; denying the independence but not the facts, hermeneutic empiricists require a "resonance" between claims and experience.

14. This change is Harrison's (1991) concept of dangerous knowledge. The moment of understanding irrevocable changes who we are and introduces the uncertainties attendant to change. The implications of this circumstance are substantial. If one's science is no longer simply representational of reality but must necessarily provoke change within that reality, then one has an ethical responsibility for the change so initiated. The scientist has to become the critic with a program of change.

15. I don't want to overly promote the practical power of the analyst here or to underestimate the practical strength of the analyzed's resistance. One cannot, however, simply presume the ethical protection of "an academic exercise" or the ability of the analyzed to resist the force of legitimated agents of knowledge production.

16. I have resisted two alternate endings to this sentence. I could have added "in the mind of the critic" to signal a separate reality from the analysis, but that would be either banal (where else?) or entirely controversial (anywhere else!). I could also have added "or what it could be" to signal the constructionist effort of criticism, but that would suggest that criticism could be something other than constructionist.

17. *Text* and *reader* are, of course, contested terms. I am attempting a nonexclusionary, "Please allow me the convenience of" use.

18. This sentence reads along the traditional subject–object dichotomy, but it contains no necessary vision—although it must permit that vision because some criticism is so practiced—of an independence between the object of analysis and the analyzing subject. The term "produce the object" must include to produce it by pulling it out of one's briefcase and to produce it by creating a unity where none was recognized before.

19. The analytic must necessarily be prior in order to construct the text as a worthy object. It must also be emergent, however, gaining something from its interpenetration of the text. When analytics become rote, they decline.

20. It is now aphoric that science cannot be value-free. That truism to the contrary, the practical arguments of science continue to be structured to exclude value statements. I have argued elsewhere (Anderson, 1992) that every claim of what *is* is also a claim of what *ought to be* (it ought to be because it is necessary for it to be true). Criticism is thus doubly articulated in value for it must first establish what is true about the object of analysis in that it ought to be for the corrective argument that follows. The argument of this footnote, for example, depends on knowledge generating the terms of existence rather than on an independent existence dictating the terms of knowledge. That knowledge-generates-terms claim is true because it is the preferred claim of the argument that provides its demonstration.

21. The failure to achieve this meaning (by which I mean an outcome sensible within the frame of analysis) does not end the work or call the question on the method of analysis. *Time* magazine (May 9, 1994, pp. 69–70) reports a 17-year, multibillion dollar effort to find the vapor trails of the top quark. While I find this obscene, others clearly do not.

22. The "lived" voice is not the only voice of the ethnographer. There are objectivist ethnographies. One can instructively contrast the modern objectivist voice with the early ethnographies, which were also objectivist but clearly in the service of colonizing forces. It is also disconcerting to read those contemporary works that still reflect the "white man's burden" or the view of the "primitive."

23. I can remember more than one call for papers pleading for work that actually does the research instead of just arguing that we ought to.

24. Blair, Brown, and Baxter (1994) intended to offer a feminist read to Hickson, Stacks, and Amsbary (1992), which listed "active, prolific female scholars." Blair, Brown, and Baxter objected to this listing because it pitted women against women, offered one more example of the masculine disciplining the feminine, and held mere production as more important than substance. The rejection of their manuscript provided them the opportunity to comment more widely on the review process itself. In that comment, they provide a reviewer-based description of establishment scholarship as "politically neutral," "respectful toward science," "mainstream," and "politely differential" (p. 398). Their picture is far different from the "how to publish" advice (e.g., Chesebro, 1993) ordinarily offered.

CHAPTER 7

THE RELATIONSHIP BETWEEN
THEORY AND METHOD

My liberal education class had been discussing the issues surrounding the idea of media effects. I had set up a demonstration for them by developing a questionnaire using statements that represented claims made in the NBC "White Paper" on pornography. Some weeks earlier, I had begun the process of "administering the questionnaire" in a pretest, posttest, and delayed posttest design. Such designs are typical when trying to demonstrate short-term and long-term effects in knowledge acquisition and attitude change due to exposure to televised content.

A week after the pretest I showed the video of NBC's program (which, in my reading, tended to support pornography as socially marked, mostly harmless, but with potential negative side effects). I then immediately readministered the same questionnaire as the posttest. Two weeks later I gave the questionnaire again as the delayed posttest.

My class of 24 students—nearly all white, evenly divided across sex, and in their late teens or early 20s—was part of a small denominational liberal arts college. The students were conservative but not reactionary. About a third of the class knew that triple-X videos were available at the convenience store a block from campus. (I knew it too, but that's a different story.)

The class's conservatism showed up on the pretest pretty clearly: explicit sex was pornography, and pornography was thought to be illegal in every case, psychologically damaging, a social problem (though in patriarchal not feminist terms), and its practitioners as well as users touched with a criminal element.

The immediate posttest showed the class believing that not all explicit sexual depictions were obscene; they now understood "obscenity" as the legal term and "pornography" as a political term; they reported that most people had

157

seen pornography without damage to themselves although some were damaged; and they held practitioners and users as "socially marked" but normally not criminal.

The delayed posttest (which was not "delayed" for very long because of the duration of the class) showed the factual items holding their immediate posttest position but the opinion items regressing toward their pretest position.

This is a demonstration that I have used regularly in my classes over the years. I need only to select a television program whose topic is of general interest but not a specialty of college students, whose tone is slightly liberal, and that has factual as well as opinion claims within it—in short, nearly any social report. The results of knowledge acquisition and opinion shift are so reliable that I can commit a good bit of course time to this exercise without concern for its failure.

EMPIRICAL FACT
AND THEORETICAL UNDERSTANDING

To start this chapter, I have returned to the questionnaires that the class filled out. My purpose is to frame an introduction to the relationship between theory and method. In this examination, I have taken up the positivists' project of seeking the independence of observation and theory. I want to know what is empirically undoubtable in these questionnaires and where I must add theory to make the undoubtable meaningful.

The questionnaires are composed of declarative sentences coupled with equal-interval agree/disagree scales. The following is an example:

Pornography has an exact definition in legal proceedings.

Agree Strongly	Agree	Agree Slightly	Neutral	Disagree Slightly	Disagree	Disagree Slightly

Respondents mark the degree of agreement or disagreement they have with each of the statements.

So what are my observations? Because I administered the questionnaires in the open classroom to people I knew by sight, I have observational evidence for my claim that the completed questionnaires are the product of the separate and individual effort of the 24 classmates. Had I sent the questionnaires home or mailed them out, that information would be missing.

All that remains of the separate and individual effort are the marks on the pages of the questionnaire preserved individually by the staple that keeps the questionnaires separate and an ID number known only by the respondent, so that the various administrations can be matched. What I can claim observationally (with no more than trivial amendments) ends here. I can claim the existence of the marks on the page that are the result of separate and individual work performed by particular individuals.

The Assumption of a "Response"

Every claim beyond this point is governed by some commonsense or theoretical assumption. One of the earliest of the common sense assumptions is that the marks are responses regulated by the practical contract of the questionnaire. That contract among other things specifies that the respondent will make an honest effort at reading, be disciplined in his or her interpretation by the intention of the author, and then act in response to that disciplined effort of interpretation.

Well, of course, that's common sense. Ah, but not "of course." I have no reason to expect that this communication contract will be accepted, though I do considerable work in establishing authority and perhaps in trust building to ensure that it is. Analysts show their own doubts when they throw out questionnaires where all the items are marked the same or the markings form some recognizable pattern (like a full-paged X) on the basis that the marks are not responses. Similarly, methodologists argue that the position of a previous mark can influence the placement of a subsequent one and that respondents tend to avoid the end points of the scale. If the marks, for whatever reason, are not responses, then none of what follows as their explanation makes sense.

The contract of a valid response is no small thing. It requires from the respondent an acceptance of the authority of the social practices implicated in the protocol; a skilled, disciplined reading; an honest appraisal of one's own position; a competent evaluation of the difference between that reading and one's own position according to the terms of the scale; and a true report of that difference on the scale itself.

Typically, we have no observational evidence that the marks are or are not responses, as any observable pattern could arise from a true effort. What allows us to move forward is the taken-for-granted assumption that the contract has been fulfilled when the answers "look right." The assumption of fulfillment is untested but effectively validated when we achieve interpretable results.

I call this a commonsense assumption because its character is the same as that which I invoke in writing the lines of this paragraph and because it distributes across all theoretical camps (Else why would they write?). Nearly always, practical assumptions remain uncontested. (If I had to prove all that I assume, I'd never get any work done.) While there are theories that deal with social practices, those theories do not ordinarily direct our choices as researchers-in-action. On occasion, however, the critique of this practical assumption is engaged by the theoretical constructs of signification, meaning realism, and social power.

The Assumptions of Scientific Realism

Scientific realism entails a belief that theoretical concepts have a material counterpart—are "real" (using the materialist criterion). Theoretical concepts must be something more than devices of argument. The theory-in-place of our exercise makes use of constructs that come from the cognitivists. Cognitivist arguments, as we have seen, are centered around the existence of prior mental states that are the agents of subsequent behavior. The agree–disagree response scale makes sense only if there is some basis from which to agree or disagree. There has to be some prior state from which the comparison of agreement or disagreement can emanate. (The neutral or "don't know" point on such scales allows for the inability to compare when no prior state exists.)

Our scales give us no direct evidence of these prior states. I have no independent measure of the existence of such states and I know nothing about the internal cognitive organization of my respondents that would allow me to predict their behavior on the questionnaire. All I have are marks on the page which I then interpret as the consequence of some attitudinal or knowledge state. The argument is the weakest form of the cognitivist position (there are stronger ones) and is entirely circular: marks on the page exist because of the action of prior mental states that we know to exist because there are marks on the page.

All right, then, let's abandon that argument. Let's use some other theoretical assumption for what those marks mean. There certainly are other assumptions to use; we could take them from behaviorism, the historic opponent of cognitivism, or from the newer semiotic positions that are emerging. But we would give up something central to our argument in the process. We would give up the clarity of the effect of media on the individual. Cognitivism is the preeminent position from which to create an argument supporting internal processes of individual change. Behaviorism, for example, makes use of external reinforcement schedules and semiotics makes use of collective understandings. Both of these alternatives substantially reduce the importance of exposure to content as the explanation for what follows.

Given the intent of my classroom exercise, that is a substantial loss. It's a substantial loss for the media researcher too because it denies the view of content as an agent of change. In the traditional applications of cognitive theory, content represents the active elements by which the internal states that control behavior can be manipulated. By varying the content, one can vary the "settings" of the internal states and thereby generate different behavior. That the internal states are different prior and subsequent to exposure allows us to argue for their "change."

The argument for change itself is dependent on presumptions that are untested but accepted in this protocol. Change presumes that the circumstances measured at time 1 (our pretest) are the default conditions: stable, continuing, and of sufficient strength to be predictive of any subsequent measurement. The results of time 1 ought to be what one would expect anytime one measures without intervention.

This conceptualization of change closely follows the idea of change formulated in the laws of motion. Bodies tend to remain in the state they are in unless influenced by some outside force. Material bodies do not instigate change on their own. So too in this conceptualization: cognitive structures tend to remain as they are unless influenced by some outside agent. Cognitive structures, therefore, are seen to behave as material bodies (they do not exhibit agency), which itself is an expression of a materialist position in science.

The argument for change, therefore, depends on a relationship between the results of the pretest and the expectations for the posttest to "tend to be the same unless affected by an outside force." If that relationship does not exist—if the two events are independent and we have no expectations for the posttest—then there can be no argument for change.

Unfortunately, in my demonstration, the evidence for change is exactly the same evidence one would use to argue for independence (the two sets of scores are different). The evidence enters into an argument for change rather than one for independence under the supervision of the theory-in-use and the background assumptions of materialism. One's theory-in-use with its assumptions, then, creates the field of understanding in which empirical events become evidence.

The Assumptions of Normal Science

If we were to elevate my classroom exercise to the level of serious science, it would be considered an example of normal science. "Normal science" (a term we met in the writings of Kuhn, 1970) refers here to the activity of testing one more case of what is already known to be true. In normal science terms, we already know that people change their minds because of televised messages and that the short-term and long-term effects of these messages are different. (These known-to-be-true features justify my research design.) What we are testing is the particular case of the NBC "White Paper" on pornography.

This normal science example allows us to examine the deeply held precedents from which particular theories arise. We can find these by looking at the assumptions of the social practices of our research protocols and the conventionalized methods we employ.

The Assumptions of Social Practices

Research protocols are themselves *social practices* involving power and authority in disciplined relationships. We are often shielded from the vitality of these practices by the language of research design: "The pretest was administered in a classroom setting." "Subjects were 24 students enrolled in an interpersonal

communication course." "Data were collected by means of household interviews." "The researcher completed a schedule of participant observation con-
tacts." In every case, these desiccated phrases cover a myriad of local negotia-
tions and adjustments as people do or don't do what they are told to do, as
another event of scientific research is crafted by both the informed and the
merely clever.

The language and theory of research design depends on the functional
invisibility of the social practices that are invoked by the research protocol.
Because we have no method of testing the effect of one set of social practices
except that of invoking another set, the question is never laid to rest. We can say,
then, that *protocol invisibility* is axiomatic. It is a foundational belief that is
asserted but unprovable.

Axioms such as protocol invisibility declare what must be true if we are to
act in a particular way. These background assumptions do the primary reality-
constructing work that allows particular families of theories to flourish and
restricts the growth of others. (The analogy to a house foundation—unremark-
able, hidden by landscaping, but absolutely necessary for the structure above—is
apt.)

In our example, protocol invisibility means that my students do not recognize their participation in the study or the manipulation of the pretest, posttest,
and delayed posttest design *in such a way that recognition becomes an explanation for the results.* We may want to see this assumption as a naive carryover from
the testing of noninteractive, nonsentient material bodies. Or we may not. In
either case, it is an axiomatic choice to be made but once made it leads to widely
divergent research paths. If, in our example, I dismiss protocol invisibility and
presume instead that my students are knowledgeable coconspirators in the
creation of another social science event, I will say nothing at all about media
effects.

The Assumptions of Conventionalized Methods

My pretest, posttest, delayed posttest design is a toolkit design that requires no
invention on my part but can be read directly from the pages of standard design
textbooks (a classic is Campbell & Stanley, 1963). The selection of this design
imports the assumptions of change into the conclusions that I shall draw about
the effects of exposure. Because pretest/posttest designs are specifically meaningful as devices to demonstrate the consequences of the independent variable—in our case, exposure to the NBC program on pornography—what the
results of the test can mean is a foregone conclusion.

In the normal science application of this design and its implicated use of
statistical decision rules, there can be only three conclusions: the effect of
exposure was found, the effect was not supported, or the results are anomalous.
Any other conclusion crosses the boundary of normal science and cannot be

understood as such. (It can be understood, however, but as something else, such as critique.)

In most cases—and in virtually *all* of the cases we read about—the effect is found. That is the point of running the test and the justification for publishing a report on the test. There is no muckraking in this claim. All normalized fields of inquiry, exact or hermeneutic, work to contain what events can mean and seek to justify that meaning-making work in their claims. We put our beliefs at risk with the test, congratulating ourselves for our courage, but we don't expect to fail. A revolution in understanding doesn't change the events. It changes what the events can mean and the work that is done to make them mean what they mean.

The equal-interval, agree–disagree scales (sometimes called Likert scales) of our example do the same sort of work. These scales are the familiar, conventionalized practices of quantification. They are to be understood under the rubrics of quantitative measurement theory. These scales, in effect, craft a mentalist space defined by three points: agreement, disagreement and neutrality. Positioning in this space is permitted along the line from neutrality to agreement or along the line from neutrality to disagreement. The distance along either of these lines is the same and is divided into three equal segments. The end point of each segment is numbered to indicate the boundary of the segment and quantity of agreement or disagreement.

A number of critiques have been raised about these scales both inside and outside measurement theory. They are not our concern (he said, exercising authorial power). Our concern is the agentry[1] of the selection of these scales for our project. The question is whether by using such scales one's argument also becomes an agent for all the scales imply. Certainly, the practical basis for their selection is that they are an accepted measurement tool that allows one access to statistical methods of public decision making. Their value is that they solve the practical problems of how to measure and how to decide. As a researcher, I can select them for those reasons and none other. My research argument, however, has the higher responsibilities of achieving accuracy and validity. That argument, consequently, is vulnerable to counterclaims that the scales do not represent mental states and/or accurately indicate any agreement or disagreement.

Our conclusion has to be that conventionalized methods, even if used naively or only for their practical value, implicate the claims resulting from their use in all the arguments that make the scales meaningful as conventional methods. The three most important of these are: (1) there is an object to be measured, (2) that object exists independently of the measurement, and (3) there is an isomorphic relationship between the object and the measurement. These are world-defining assumptions. Methods are clearly not neutral tools.

The conclusion of this example is that the relationship between theory and method is a symbiotic one. On the one hand, no theory is complete without a praxeological component and would not come into its fullness without a conventionalized set of methods. These conventionalized methods materialize the evidence that theory warrants. The combination of warrant and evidence provides the justification of claim. It takes both theory and method to produce argument.

THEORY IN PARADIGMATIC METHODISM

In the formal but nonexistent world of inquiry, method is justified by theory; in the actual world of practice, the justifying theory is rarely fully articulated. In fact, in most of the research we read, paradigmatic fragments, implicitly assumed or less frequently explicitly referenced, are the most we get in ad hoc justifications.

The study by Zillmann and Bryant (1982) of the relationship between pornography, sexual callousness, and rape gives us a good working example. In this study, male, underclass college students were differentially exposed to sexually explicit films and then asked to report the prison sentence they would give to an ostensible rapist. Those exposed to several hours of such films during the week of testing reported lower prison sentences. The researchers' conclusion was that massive exposure to pornography trivializes the crime of rape.

Zillmann and Bryant report no specific theory but have rested their method and argument on several generic epistemic building blocks (what social semioticians would call "collective resources of action"). Though no specific theory was advanced to justify either the methods or the conclusion, the paradigmatic elements of empirical foundationalism are fairly clear in what the authors considered not worthy of comment.

A partial listing of those elements would include: that the characteristics of content are self-evident (meaning realism—pornography for the researcher is pornography for the viewer); that content is a meaning delivery system (meaning realism again, as well as determinism—the individual is not an agent of the effect); that the protocol of the experiment is invisible to the respondents and not a social action in which they coconspire (the assumptions of protocol invisibility and the naive respondent); that the effects of content are additive (materialistic cognitivism—cognitive structures are built one piece at a time); that the perspective of the content predisposes the individual to act in particular ways (methodological individualism in support of attitudism); that the cognitive structure (sexual callousness) is the same determinant for all so exposed (material transcendentalism); that the exposure is the agent of the difference in reported behavior (determinism); that the reported behavior is the same category of behavior across all respondents (objectivism); that the operational definition of trivialization (the reported prison sentence) corresponded to the social construct of trivialization (positivism); that the college student responses are functionally equivalent to all human responses to that situation (surrogatism); that the quantification and use of the logic of mathematics is isomorphic to the phenomenon (logical positivism); and, finally, that the researchers are not responsible for the social consequences of their study in turning a bunch of sexually callous, young men loose in Bloomington, Indiana (the primacy of epistemics).

What we clearly see here is that there is no single theory in operation, but rather a nested set of theories, beliefs, and background assumptions (a practical example of the hierarchy introduced in Chapter 1). Nonetheless, this study would be called an example of the "direct effects" theory in media analysis. It would be called such because its design simplifies to "exposure to X leads to consequence Y."

Note that if the researchers had taken a prior history of the respondents' use of pornography and then analyzed the prison sentences for differences across different use histories, the study would be called a "uses and gratifications" study. It is the objectivist paradigm that provides for both, as well as for other cognitive and functionalist theories. It would not, however, provide the basis for a hermeneutic theory.

Zillmann and Bryant's approach to theory is typical across all forms of inquiry: we cannot be explicitly reproducing what we already know to be true in our journal pages. Nonetheless, particular methods implicitly invoke and thereby reproduce their paradigmatic justifications. Problems arise when there is a fracture between what is claimed or appears to be claimed as theory and the methods of analysis.

A good example occurs in G. B. Madison's (1988) *The Hermeneutics of Postmodernity.* Madison first invokes a postmodern hermeneutic position in arguing that to tell another what a text means is an invocation of ideological power, and then proceeds to argue from a meaning realist position that E. D. Hirsch Jr.'s interpretation of Husserl is false and his is better.

Similar fractures would appear in questions about the reliability of an interpretive ethnography (using objectivist assumptions to evaluate a hermeneutic enterprise), in questions about the respondent's interpretation of survey questions (using hermeneutic assumptions to evaluate an objectivist enterprise), in questions about authorial intent in postmodern criticism (accepting author privilege as a natural rather than an effected condition). Such questions can arise only *across* perspectives, but are answerable only *within* perspectives (reliability is not a necessary criterion of hermeneutics but is for objectivism; interpretation is not a requirement of objectivist engagement but is in hermeneutics; authorial intent is always a problematic claim for postmodern criticism but the accepted stance of the logocentric critic). The answers that appear within perspectives are, of course, incommensurably different and contradictory across perspectives.

In the remainder of this chapter, we will examine the typical methodological components for their hierarchical location, their assumptive force, and their naturalized affinities within theory families. We divide once more between objective and hermeneutic empiricism with occasional examples from criticism.

EPISTEMIC JUSTIFICATIONS FOR METHODS TYPICAL OF OBJECTIVE EMPIRICISM

In this section we take up methods of quantification, sampling, surveys, interviews, experiments, statistical analysis, and statistical decision rules to consider the force of such axioms and priors as materialism, determinism, reductionism, empiricism, referentiality, representativeness, precision and accuracy in validity, the trustworthiness of experience, the defense of intersubjectivity, surrogacy, meaning realism, and the unity of science. I will necessarily be minimally descriptive of the procedures and very selective in my comments within the wide range the headings provide. The effort here is to bring to bear the work of the previous chapters to illuminate the underlying enabling propositions and the epistemic consequences of methods.

Methodological Practices

We begin with a rehearsal of the steps by which an objectivist research study is conducted. Research often begins with questions about the characteristics of things, their causes, or their consequences. It begins with the premise that there is something there—beyond the obvious—to investigate and that that something is affected by other things and affects still others as well.

That something or somethings is made available for study in the research protocol, which will include the methods of assessing and engaging the phenomenon. These methods produce the presence of the phenomenon. They will likely include a propositional definition and perhaps an operational definition but certainly some method of measurement.

The method of measurement nearly always provides for the quantification of the phenomenon as, at least, a unique existence and likely as an ordered one too. Quantification both allows and invokes the language of mathematics, the methods of statistical analysis, and the assumptions of both.

If the research question involves cause or consequence, the deductive logic of hypothesis testing and the experimental method may be brought in to play as the analytical frame of the argument.

Because many of the phenomena we study are definitionally and often actually infinite in number, most studies use some sort of selection procedure to produce the analytic samples. Sampling introduces aggregation, surrogacy, and the logic of statistical decision rules.

All of these methods show a great deal of conventionalization. Researchers can appeal to these conventions as justification for the choices that they make and the conclusions that they draw.

We will now consider some perspectives that can be taken, as these steps reside in the epistemological medium that forms both their background assumptions and their foreground of understanding.

Measurement: Materialism, Determinism, and Advocacy in Quantification

The recognition that, at least, some of the mysteries of the material world could be mastered through the logic of mathematics, and that the logic of mathematics could be advanced by careful attention to the regularities of the material, has led to the joint identity of science and mathematics. Quantification is the procedure that provides the linkage between the phenomenal and the mathematical. Quantification applies the formal characteristics of numbers to the empirical characteristics of observations. Once transformed, the empirical drops away and only the formal remains. Thus "purified," observations can enter the logic of mathematics and respond to the demands of this logic.

Quantification, first, makes the reductionist assumption that there is an identity called "a phenomenon." That phenomenon may be a trait such as eye color, an attribute like intelligence, a characteristic like honesty, a behavior like aggression, a judgment like the response to a questionnaire, or whatever. This identity has different appearances in experience. Some folks have blue eyes, some folks have brown eyes. Brown eyes are not a different phenomenon from blue; they are merely a different appearance of the same phenomenon of eye color.

The phenomen assumption is always prior to the operation of quantification. If there is no phenomenon, there is nothing to quantify. If the phenomenon is always as it is (an infinite present unity), there is no need to quantify it. The prior question, then, is what is the unity claimed in the phenomenon and what are its genuine appearances.[2] This is the question of construct validity for which we have no direct solution.

It is the role of theory to provide the argument for the existence of a phenomenon and the character of its genuine appearances. This is its referential function and a test of its empirical adequacy. It does so mostly through nonempirical axiomatic justification. It is the structure and quality, the coherence and resonance of the explanation a theory provides that validates the initial claims of the phenomenon and its characteristics. Empirical study will either support or not support the claims made, but it can offer no resolution of the question of validity.

Once we accept the phenomenal assumption and grant the existence of a unity of different appearances, we can quantify those appearances across four hierarchically ordered concepts: difference, order, change, and equivalence (Stevens, 1951).

Difference

In the simplest form of quantification we are responsive only to difference. We apply different numbers to different appearances and the same numbers to the same appearances. All females are categorized as 1's; all males as 2's. This application involves the operation of sets and problematizes the question of "same and different."

A good example of this problem is the confusion between sex and gender. Practitioners routinely use the sex of the respondent when they actually mean gender. Sex is a genetic formation, but gender is a cultural one. Gender in most theories would not be coequal to sex. But because the sex of a respondent is readily (though *not* always) classifiable, it is used to provide the "same and different" solution the numbers require. Sex, if you will, is the operational definition of gender.

Further, the question of same and different is approached at some level of precision. If, for example, I offer you the observational values of 3.467 and 3.468, I have made the implicit claim that I can distinguish 1,000 categories of whatever it is that I am measuring between the values of 3.000 and 4.000. Further, I would also be claiming that not only can I offer this precision, but that there is value in doing so because there is a genuine difference within the phenomenon under study between its observation at 3.467 and at 3.468.

I would not blame you for being skeptical of this claimed level of precision, on the one hand, or for a gallic shrug, on the other, to eloquently argue the pragmatics of research. This differentiation is what the numbers mean by formal definition but certainly not in practice. As a researcher, I certainly would not be expected to provide the rules of correspondence for those 1,000 categories. Should that difference nonetheless show itself to be significant according to conventionalized statistical decision rules, I would certainly expect to use it.

This point is not an argument for malfeasance. It is that "same and different" are never routine decisions. They are decisions that are put into place through some effort. That work, however, disappears once the numbers are assigned. Objective empiricism deals with the obvious potential for error, not to mention corruption, by an appeal first to the trustworthiness of the experience of same and different and then to the corrective of intersubjectivity.

Order

At the next level of numerical power, my presumption is not only that independent sets of appearance are present, but that these sets can be ordered along a dimension of more or less. I step beyond categorical exclusivity and argue a relationship among the categories. This value (X) represents more androgyny along a dimension of gender, for example.

But how do I know it to be more or less? Again I return to the theory. The theory must be able to express the order of effect of the different values against some criterion (an application of Gale's measure of the real). For example, if intimacy is an ordered index of friendship, then the greater the intimacy the deeper the friendship. But, of course, many theories are exhausted at the point of construct creation. They offer no formally expressed argument for why the phenomenon should order itself in relation to the criterion.

Therein starts the process of "trial and error" theory development under the guise of hypothesis testing. If, as an example, this theory of friendship does indeed use intimacy as its index, then why shouldn't more intimacy have a greater effect on that criterion? Thus one operationalizes both friendship and intimacy in such a way that they can covary to see if they do.

If they do and in whatever way they do, friendship theorists can enlarge their claims. This was a typical bottom-up process that has the appearance of a top-down action. It looks in the presentational argument like theory provided the reasoned basis for the test, whereas the best it did was to hint at a relationship. If the test hadn't worked out, the researcher would have simply gone on to some other way of looking at the relationship—but given the pragmatics of publication, we would not have known. Again, umbrage is not the response I am looking for here, but rather a more sophisticated understanding of the quality of evidence we can provide.

The assumption of order is the naturalized reflex of determinism. The collection of constructs that theorists develop within a domain of study are supposed to relate in some manner. The nature and character of those relationships are often left to methodological practice. Return to Zillmann and Bryant (1982) for a moment. Their article is silent about the theoretical basis that prompted them to choose 36 hours of exposure to pornography for their subjects. Can we assume a conversation that says, "Let's make sure this works by exposing our subjects to a megadose of pornography"? Would a 1-hour exposure have worked as well? Basically we have a finding with no further understanding of why it was obtained. And it is at this point that our theory returns to common sense because we all know how pornography works.

Change

We move up the hierarchy of numerical power when we are able to specify the relative change between observations that are ordered along some dimension of more or less. Such numbers are said to exist on an equal interval scale. Each position on the scale represents the same amount of change in the characteristic being measured. The scales I used in my classroom exercise that opened this chapter were equal interval scales.

Equal interval scales derive from the material criterion of reality and are best referenced against the notion of quantity. The material criterion, we remember, is of the "pick-it-up" quality with intrinsic identity and natural, stable boundaries. Such things can be easily counted; two of them is unproblematically one more than one, and three of them is one more than two.

Returning to the exemplar item, the equal interval scale below the sentence embodies the claim that "Agree Strongly" represents two more units of agreement than what "Agree Slightly" represents. We can clearly see the materialization of agreement as a concept of quantity or perhaps strength, energy, force, attraction—all the well-known words from Newtonian physics.

Notice that, as the researcher in this case, I have not explicitly theorized "agreement" at any place during the exercise or its report, but I have effectively theorized it in the use of my measurement device. My suspicion is that whatever theory of agreement I would actually adopt, it would not envision agreement as divisible into equal units. Nonetheless, my choice of method has placed me inside a particular field of discourse that now invades my thinking and directs what I may say about the results. When I compare the pretest with the posttest, I will be directed to speak of difference in terms of units of change in agreement.

Beyond its character as a tool of quantification, my exemplar scale is also an expression appropriate to cognitive theory. The mentalist structures of cognitivism motivate, influence, or determine behavior. By accepting a conventionalized measurement device of cognitive theory, I have also implicitly adopted the meanings that make it sensible. My work is bordered by this bounded theoretical frame. I can certainly resist and oppose those meanings, but that is specific work that must be performed. Further, the combination of that work of resistance and the presence of those scales can easily form an inherent contradiction within the instrumentality of the report.

My point is that methods, even at the very particular level of item design in a questionnaire, motivate certain theoretical positions. Methods are not neutral and their users do not escape unscathed.

Equivalence

The top of the numerical hierarchy is occupied by numbers that represent unique positions on an ordered scale each a fixed distance from a known (or knowable) starting point. In mathematical terms, such scales are called "ratio scales" and their equivalence to one another can be calculated.

It was a truism of my education, and I know of no contrary claims, that the social sciences have no genuine ratio scales. We nonetheless proceed as if we did (for a discussion of these issues, see Anderson, 1987). The sort of unspoken agreement not to accept this limitation, I believe, comes from the vision of what a science is supposed to be as motivated by a belief in the unity of science. If we are to be a science, we need the same tools as those we deem to be authentic scientists (Rorty, 1987). Many of the practices of the social sciences from instrumentation to typifying discourse appear to be motivated by this identity demand.

Summary

The activities of quantification allow us to recognize the influence of the foundational beliefs of science. Materialism, determinism, empirical trustworthiness, and the unity of science all come into play in the implicit justification for the practices of quantification.

Quantification also allows us to see the epistemic consequences of method. Methods embody their justifications and assumptions. The use of any method is never a neutral act, but always implicates the user in the discourses in which those methods are seen as emblematic.

Aggregates, Surrogates, and Functional Equivalents in Samples

The research of objective empiricism is populated with samples. The quality of samples and of the competence of sampling procedures are significant marks in the evaluation of such work. The theoretical import of samples and sampling can be examined via a short visit to set theory. Any set (or population) is a uniquely defined space that establishes a clear rule for the inclusion and exclusion of its elements (members). Elements in the set must share at least the membership criterion, but they may (or may not) differ in every other regard. Sets are formally infinite; therefore, any actual examination of the elements within a set necessarily involves taking a sample. The use of sampling invokes the considerable constitutive characteristics of set theory in the name of the phenomenon, as we shall see.

Because much of objective empiricism is directed by the attribute model of the individual, the samples that appear in our journals are not actually of people but are rather of the attributes that constitute people. For example, Dean Kazoleas (1993) is interested in cognitive responses. His sample of 188 undergraduates is not intended to represent undergraduates, but rather their cognitive responses. That he uses undergraduates who are vessels of these responses is simply a matter of convenience and is justified by the assumption that members of a set must be functionally equivalent on the definitional criterion—that criterion here being the presence of cognitive response. This functional equivalence permits the 188 cognitive response elements (the undergraduate subjects) to stand as surrogates for all cognitive response elements (humanity). These elements are ahistorical—it does not matter where or when they were selected—and anonymous—it does not matter who they were carried by. It is not the undergraduates who stand as surrogates for us. It is their responses that stand for ours.

Surrogacy is justified by functional equivalence as long as there are no variations across the membership criterion (or the researcher is not interested in those variations). If, on the other hand, one feels that undergraduate cognitive responses might be different from nonundergraduate cognitive responses, the researcher must either limit the surrogacy claim (i.e., redefine the set) or move to a sampling aggregate.

An aggregate is a sample of elements from the set that—according to good practice—intends to represent member variations in the relative proportions in which they occur. The aggregation, however, may not be representative, and one that is cannot be distinguished with certainty from one that is not. This uncertainty of representativeness is resolved by the principle of methodological competence, the reproduction of the normal practices of science. It is the justification called doing one's best.

Representativeness itself and its possibility rest on a separate set of assumptions: the independence of the phenomena (there must be something to represent), the trustworthiness of observation (the observer must be able to access the qualities to be represented), and the representational character of the sign (whatever serves the descriptive function—the sample, a piece of discourse, etc.—must reproduce the phenomena). To the extent that any of these assumptions are not met we begin to speak of error: the theoretical contamination of phenomena, observational biases, measurement error, sampling error, propositional inadequacy, and the like.

Functional equivalence, surrogacy, and representative aggregates provide the solution to the question of the utility of examining some small group of people (such as Kazoleas's 188 undergraduates). They are never "some small group of people." They are the surrogates or representatives of independent, autonomous, anonymous, ahistorical, material, and determinant traits that define humanity. Significant enough, I suspect.

Meaning Realism in Surveys and Interviews

According to a number of surveys (Anderson, 1987; Potter, Cooper, & Dupagne, 1993), the survey is the most common methodological procedure for data collection in our published reports. Such surveys and their interview forms are axiomatically supported by the doctrine of meaning realism. Meaning realism, we may remember, entails the propositions of the trustworthiness and referential character of the sign. Translating these propositions to the discourse of surveys, meaning realism, first, holds that items on a survey are trustworthy purveyors of meanings that are referenced to real objects, states, conditions, and the like. The words can be literally read and then understood from a common experiential base.

Second, the survey items represent a system that delivers the researchers intended meaning in an uncomplicated way. (Certainly, errors occur, but we have ways of testing for and containing the effects of those errors.) Similarly, the replies given, whether to closed or open-ended items, conform to the intent of the researcher and can therefore be read unproblematically by the researcher.

In open-ended items and more extensively in interviews, meaning realism assumes either response ingenuousness or response determinacy. The more common response ingenuousness holds that the evoked responses are ingenuously subordinated to the truth. The responses are under the governance of the intent of the question, and are therefore an extension of the contextual domain (the theory and practice of the research) in which the questions were formulated. The responses are themselves plain speech spoken truthfully.

Response determinacy would discount the respondent's meaning in favor of conceptualizing each response as a particular expression of structural/cultural/social determinants. It doesn't matter what the surface meanings are. It matters that the researcher can extract the characteristic determinants from the aggregated replies. (These are the same practices used by formalist criticism.) In either the assumption of ingenuity or of determinacy, the uncertainty of the respondent action is resolved.

The Argument for Things in the Experimental Method and Statistical Analysis

The purpose of the experimental method is to demonstrate the evidence of cause. The search for causes is motivated by the foundational belief (and its material success) in determinism. The experimental method allows the researcher to confirm the antecedent conditions for a consequence of interest under controlled conditions. The conditions of control are intended to clear away the surface distractions from the underlying structure and to eliminate alternate explanations.

Most applications of the experimental method adopt the material criterion of phenomena by positing variables of separate existence, internal integrity, and natural boundaries. In shorthand, the assumption can be expressed as "X acts on Y to produce condition Z," where X, Y and Z are separate, specifiable phenomena. The result is that variables whose only material existence may be the measurement devices that operationally define them become real in that "hold-it-in-your-hand" sense.

When humans are introduced into the experimental frame, they too are objectified—that is, made into objects that bend compliantly to the researcher's will (we don't call them human subjects unintentionally). As objects, the researcher is not concerned with their individuality, but only with their value as the embodiment of transcendent characteristics. When these objects act as individuals—for example, when they call attention to the protocol, or resist the manipulation or express their opposition to measurement—the researcher categorizes them as "contaminants" and removes them from the analysis. They have failed to become or remain proper objects of study.

Statistics

We can also see the operation of this reification in the "naming" of variables derived from multivariate procedures (e.g., factor, cluster, and discriminant analysis) and the persisting identity of variables modified in partialling procedures (e.g., multiple regression or multiple analysis of variance). In very local terms, both of these sets of procedures involve the calculation of contingent solutions to questions of structure in a particular (in hand), multivariate data set.

In the naming action, the ad hoc solution is escalated into a claim of generalized existence. Factors become the "relaxation function" of television viewing or the intimacy factor of friendship. In the persistence of identity, variables whose initial structural characteristics are reduced in the process of analysis nonetheless retain their full identity (for examples, see Loges, 1994, or Chaudhuri & Buck, 1995).

The implicit arguments are, first, the empirical one that there must be something there that "produces" the observations on which the analyses are conducted. The second involves the rejection of the "contingent solution" nomination in favor of a transcendent surrogacy. This second argument requires some explanation.

Any operational definition, data collection, statistical analysis, or the like is, on the face of it, nothing more than the ad hoc application of a set of conventions. It solves only the problems within that application—that is, it does what it does. But in order to make claims about generalized conditions of the phenomenal world, it must also do something more: it must stand as a representative for all such applications and as a surrogate for the conditions "out there" that it seeks to explain.

It is the action of conventionalism that produces representativeness. Conventionalism sets the standards of competent work. Competent work removes the effect of the subject (those biases of the individual practitioner), which removal renders the work objective, and therefore representative.

Surrogacy returns us to the material. In the material, the argument looks like this: If X is NaCl (table salt), it has the following properties under standard conditions and it always has those properties under those conditions. If, under the appropriate conditions, one finds a substance with those and only those properties, it must be NaCl. Such is the meaning of the independence, integrity, and natural boundaries of things.

The discovery of a set of properties, as in factor analysis, then, is evidence for the existence of a phenomenon that transcends it local conditions (and the fact that factor analysis is designed to produce that evidence and can produce it even in the absence of the presence of true properties). Whereas, in partialling, the fact that a variable is retained, however diminished, is evidence that the true properties (its unique contribution to the solution) have now been found (necessarily ignoring the fact that an additional variable in the equation might remove what is left).

Our understanding of the value of the experimental method and of the interpretation of statistical findings is tightly bound into our understanding of the character of "things." Things have an independence from one another, so that they do not simply disappear in the presence of other things; things have an internal integrity that allows them to persist even under surface changes; and things have natural boundaries that allow us to recognize them unproblematically. The force of reification is to make sense of our statistical analysis and experimentation: we discover things, and things act upon other things.

Statistical Decision Rules: Rationality and the Management of Uncertainty

One tool for rationalizing the course of error with objective empiricism is the use of statistical decision rules. Statistical decision rules are based on the relative frequency of sampling errors (given a random sample) in the representation of a population. Such rules tell the researcher the probability of sampling errors (and only sampling errors—all other forms of error are untested here), but not their occurrence. Because the occurrence of error is not revealed, the fundamental uncertainty of true or false remains.

If we surrender to that uncertainty, our only resource in the face of any question concerning the precision of some population estimate is the reply "I don't know." Because that is an unacceptable answer, we have rationalized the uncertainty by speaking of the rates of error in science as opposed to the occurrence of error in the study at hand. The evidence of that rationalization is in the conventionalization of the ".05 level of significance."

The argument goes something like this: Conventionalizing the rigor of sampling procedures means that competent samples will be drawn in reasonably the same way. It is the responsibility of the peer review process to ensure that only competent samples be permitted publication. Given competent samples, the widespread adoption of the .05 standard will ensure that error in the body of scientific claim will be held close to that level. Thus, in the archive of science, one should expect no more than 5 out of 100 claims to be false. In this manner, error is rationalized in that it has known characteristics and we can reasonably access our risks. Two comments on this rationalizing follow:

First, the argument rests on the ascendancy of rates over critical instances. The argument suggests that science writ large is secure even if some particular instance of science is not. But there are clear circumstances where the critical instance of failure is more important than the rate of success. If a corporate manager selects a course of action from the research literature on management that is wrong, his or her company may go bankrupt. The rate of success in that literature, critical for the science of management, is of no help to this now-bankrupt company; the instance of failure, critical to this company, is expected by the science that produced it.

Second, the demand to rationalize uncertainty has led to abuses within the line of argument. Levels of significance have become talismans of the verdicality of the study reporting them and often stand in place of the careful analysis of the other sources of error possible in the report. Levels of significance report only the expected rate of sampling error. They do not control for or even reveal the occurrence of this error. Further, they are entirely silent on other sources of error such as errors in design, measurement, analysis, or argument.

We have adopted an irrational elevation of a simple decision rule to maintain the vision of the rationality of error because science itself is a rational enterprise. As a scientist, I have a need to know and this method may well be a distorted expression of that need.

Summary: Epistemic Justifications for Objective Empirical Methods

This analysis of a selection of methods has shown that all such methods are deeply embedded in the background assumptions of the objective paradigm. Such assumptions as materialism, determinism, reductionism, transcendentalism, and empiricism are necessary for the methodological practices to make sense. We have also seen that, taken from the other direction, methods necessarily implicate the user in these background assumptions, as well as in those that are associated with the theoretical frameworks of their common use.

EPISTEMIC JUSTIFICATIONS FOR METHODS TYPICAL OF HERMENEUTIC EMPIRICISM

We now pick up some parts of the methods of participation, observation, textual construction, interpretation, writing, and production of critical claim to find their justifications in the prior arguments of hermeneutics, ideology, historicity, existentialism, pragmatism, phenomenology, emancipation, downward causation, and the trustworthiness of engagement. As in the previous section, my intent is to show how methods depend on their priors and implicate their users within them.[3]

Methodological Practices

Studies within hermeneutic empiricism often begin with an interest in how something is done, the social value of an activity or symbolic resource, the meaning of an action or a text, or the requirements of some consequential accomplishment. It is assumed that these interests are best explored in the everyday contexts of actions, texts, and accomplishments or other targets of analysis. There is a resistance to, if not an outright rejection of, formal, decontextualized, or recontextualized approaches to study. The place of analysis is the life world and the first task of hermeneutic methods is to enable the analyst to access meaning-production sites.

For example, Anderson, Chase, and Larson (1990) were interested in the meanings television news programs had for avid news watchers. Given the hermeneutic approach these authors took, they assumed that some of these meanings were called into place in the practices of news watching. In the part of the study outlined below, the researchers were concerned with the manner with which the text of the news was engaged at the point of reception.

Fifty people who identified themselves as avid news viewers were visited at their homes on two or three occasions (some of the separate visits were combined). The researchers explained their study, engaged in extended conversations about the news with their informants, and viewed the news together with the informants while they talked about their viewing practices. This was the method the researchers used to enter the everyday context of engaging with the news.

Once the scene has been entered, the researcher works back and forth between reading and writing the scene. There are different kinds of reading and different kinds of writing. Participation is one method of reading; participation as a member is a privileged form of reading. Conversations about (often called long-form interviews) and walking the analyst through one's practices (sometimes called protocol analysis) are types of interactive reading. Collecting artifacts, member-made photographs, maps, and written materials are forms of noninteractive reading. Taking photographs, making maps, making recordings, doing transcriptions, and writing site notes and field notes are forms of writing down the scene.

This reading and writing produces the research text archived in experience, in collection, and in discursive products of various sorts. This text is read, by means of some method of intimacy, and written up[4] in interpretations that include representational description, referential analysis, meaning attribution, and critique.

With this very short course of introduction, we can now consider the influences that come into play and find their expression in the choices that researchers make as they read and write the texts of hermeneutic empiricism.

Existentialism, Phenomenology, and Empiricism in Participant Observation and Cultural Analysis

If the deep conventionalization of objective empiricism gives the impression of relative methodological calm (while, perhaps, paddling furiously beneath the surface), the methods of hermeneutic empiricism occupy positions along high tension lines of opposition. An example of this tension can be found in the lines strung between the poles of existentialism and phenomenology. These lines of thought position competent claim as either gained in the practice of lived experience or revealed in its formal analysis. These two positions are the central locations of the participant observer and the cultural studies analyst.

The participant observer justifies claim in the primacy of being there in an engagement of the scene. This researcher lives some part of the member life because the understandings that make it all sensible emerge in their enactments. It is a localized, ongoing social construction of reality. In this manner, existence (action) is prior to essence (understanding), a central tenet of existentialism.

For the cultural analyst, ideology as a well-established social construction is prior to both local understanding and action (see White, 1992, for an example). Further, ideology acts through downward causation, and consequently contains all of its memberships (Williams's [1958] "whole idea of society"). In this manner, the academic can comment on the street punk because the governing ideology provides for both. From the particulars of his or her own life, the academic can reach the eidetic principles that govern many lives. This move from present particulars to prior essences is a central tenet of phenomenology.

The cultural analyst works from a "found" text heedlessly made available in society's progress. The participant observer creates the doubly written text as an intentional object of analysis in complicitous interactions with a membership. Their empirical credentials are, therefore, generated in different ways. For the cultural analyst it is the attention to the products of the life world—the everyday expressions of popular culture, consumerism, the media, and so on—that establish these empirical credentials. For the participant observer, it is "being there" immersed in the experience.

In taking on the mantle of these credentials, however, the analyst and the ethnographer are entangled in the nets of phenomenology and existentialism, respectively. Knowingly or not, their claims are colonized by these arguments.

The Trustworthiness of Engagement: Referentiality and Representation

The cultural analyst and the participant observer join hands in the implicit embrace of the trustworthiness of engagement. This embrace may be the first and final requirement for the empirical to remain under the mantle of hermeneutic empiricism. To go through the effort of entering a scene to reveal member knowledge or the close reading of popular culture to reveal its ideological standing can be justified only if the signs of each are not in full Barthesian float (Eagleton, 1990). The texts of action as well as those of the life world must in some authoritative way reference what we intend to reveal.

There seem to be any number of contradictions we could explore at this point. What is referentiality in an existentialist or ideological world? How am I to understand the claim of referentiality that the analyst routinely denies for everyone else? Or perhaps, how do I understand the processes of nomination, ex-nomination, appropriation, and cooption by which a space is made to make a claim in the presence of referentiality? These are certainly dangerous questions to which the reply is often, "It's a struggle."

One move that can be made—and if convention papers and journal submissions are any indication, one that is being increasingly made—is the move to pragmatism. The truth of pragmatism, to paraphrase Rorty (1991b), is whatever it is true of. And the resolution of contradiction and uncertainty of any sort, to paraphrase James (1908), is belief-in-action.

The referential foundation of claim will be demonstrated in the instrumentality of that claim to participate in the ideological or social constructionist processes by which it can be made to be true. For pragmatism, a claim is never propositionally true but becomes true in its interaction with the world. In the language of the 1994 Speech Communication Convention, "Take your claim to the streets."

Representation offers a similar set of difficulties, particularly for the hermeneutic ethnographer. As ethnography has concentrated more and more on the local scene and given up its service to colonialism, what had only been an unquestioned acceptance of representation has been thrown further and further into doubt. Representation is still largely assumed, as the writings of Trujillo (1993) and other ethnographers attest. Representation also motivates such research practices as site notes, recordings, and informant review.

Site notes are those memory aids that the ethnographer produces at the site. They are used as evidence in field notes (which despite their name are actually written in the office) of the empirical character of one's representation. Recordings, whether aural, aural and visual, or transcriptions are also typically used as unmediated and credible representations. Informant review is the practice of taking one's descriptions back to the site to validate their representativeness through informant agreement or correction in some form of serial intersubjectivity.

In these practices, hermeneuticists are attempting to manage uncertainty (or semiotic float) by grounding their interpretations in empirical referentiality, and, as we have seen, in a transcendent ideology, or even in a somewhat localized member knowledge. The force of both of these efforts—grounding in empirical fact and in a persistent if not transcendent collective knowledge—anchors the interpretation and its consequent claim to validity to a foundation outside the interpretive argument itself.

There is no apparent contradiction in these practices as long as we remain firmly in this objective foundationalism. But when we adopt the radical hermeneutic stance and empower an intrusive interpretation, questions appear: What is representation in interpretation that is its own justification? In the hermeneutic conflation of is and ought, how can representation be ethical? How can a scene that varies across subjectivity be managed in representation? Authentic answers to these questions lie in an appropriate reformulation of the concept of representation which the field yet awaits.

Nonetheless, we might get to some edge of an outline in considering the role of reflexivity in representation. Reflexivity is the doubling back of one's argument to entail its own propositions as the objects of analysis. Reflexivity might provide us with a self-conscious representation that recognizes its constructionist efforts—what Van Maanen (1988) might call a "confessional tale." Can representation be referential? I think not, but it can be authentic in that it admits its own legitimating moves—in what the deconstructionists would surely call another act of legitimation. Reflexive or not, one's writing always implicates answers and the writer too.

Agency: The Present, the Particular, and the Critical Instance

On the whole, agency represents a continuing difficulty for all but the more radical hermeneuticists. It limits the scope of claims based on ideology or member knowledge, for the best-laid structures can be disrupted by the single immanent act. It forces the analyst to be mindful of the particular actors and to keep a detailed record of their actions. And it prevents the analyst from generalizing from one improvisational scene to another.

What, for example, is the value of the symbolic interactionist's exportable concept of role if the role can be played with no or nearly no restraint? It becomes a transparent shell, an outline the analyst draws around nominated action.

Agency works directly against the power of traditional science in that it keeps us in the present instead of predicting the future; attends to actual actors instead of attributes or paradigmatic elements like character or role; and shifts our arguments from rates to critical instances.

Analysts work to reinstate that traditional power with terms like "the self as subject" (Lacan, 1968), "overdetermined meanings," "naturalized interpretations," "the political unconscious" (Jameson, 1981), "social roles" (Hewitt, 1989), and even the more timorous "thematic improvisations" (Anderson & Meyer, 1988). All of these terms diminish agency.

Hermeneutic arguments struggle both to reclaim and to contain agency. If human life is, indeed, a present progress of particular critical instances, there is little for the analyst to do beyond the sorting out of the instance at hand. As analysts, we enter Kundera's (1984) "lightness of being." That may be enough, but it is less than many hoped for.

Historicity, Complicity, and Transcendent Claim

Historicity offers many of the same difficulties as agency. Historicity not only locates the action or text to be analyzed in time and place, it also locates the analysis and the analyst in time and place (Rosaldo, 1993). It implicates analysis and analyst in a project (Bhabha, 1994). It substitutes complicity for objectivity. The writing of "*a* story of our time" is also to participate in the creation of "*the* story of our time."

Historicity is the loss of our innocence. Both implicated and complicit, the analyst is another representative of specialized interests, immersed in political action, deprived of transcendent claim. Hermeneuts both acknowledge and resist this conclusion in their writing. Renato Rosaldo (1993) declares that the analyst is "somewhat innocent and somewhat complicit," but admits that even if analysts cannot be "perfectly clean" this does not mean that they "should become as "dirty" as possible" (p. 69).

How do we tell "innocent" from "complicit" for the analyst in the writing, for the analyzed in what is revealed and reviewed, and for the reader in the conclusions that might be drawn? As equally innocent and complicit, where do we stand to witness the difference?

We find at least one source of answers in the management of authority in the arguments produced. The authority of claim can be the holy mission of critical theory (Horkheimer & Adorno, 1944/1972), a philosophical surety (Habermas, 1987a, 1987b), a grand Marxist program (Jameson, 1981), a critical resonance (de Certeau, 1984), the authoritative account of a factual genre (Atkinson, 1990), the decisive but contained claims of the oppressed (Conquergood, 1991; Hekman, 1990), an ironic self-depreciation (Goodall, 1991), a local ethnography (Trujillo, 1993), or the leveling gaze of deconstruction (de Man, 1986).

In each of these, the authority to claim for another is managed in anticipation of the hot breath of the assailants who are never far behind. The representation of one's authority is part of the writing task (see Atkinson's 1990 analysis) and the method used responds to the tensions historicity produces.

Consider the work Wagner (1981) does in commenting on the Daribi's invention of the moral self as he writes in a voice of cultural resonance:

> Learning to dare, to take the moral constraints on invention *just casually enough* to permit the kind of free-wheeling improvisatory action that allows a firm but flexible creation of convention, presents the same necessity in these traditions as the learning of personality does in our own. The moral and

> conventional must be teased, threatened, and cajoled, it must be invented, for this is the only way it can persist at all. (p. 97)

Consider the scope of Wagner's claims in the phrases, "same necessity," "does in our own," "must be teased," "must be invented," "only way," and "persist at all." There is nothing temporizing in this language, no "maybe's," "rather like's," or "appear to be's," which he certainly could have used. In using this extended authorial power, he wants it all. He wants the reader's complete submission to his claim. His method is to write the reader to it.

We do not grant Wagner the authority to make his claim because we have been overwhelmed with detailed evidence, as we might be in an authoritative factual work. We submit because we can see ourselves, on the street, in the office, even at the singles bar working the edge of what's right to show that we are safely dangerous, provocatively conventional, or recklessly domesticated. If he does not tell us what we know to be true, his argument collapses. The historicity of his claim is its authority.

Nick Trujillo (1993) works his authority in much a different way, as these sentences demonstrate:

> Exactly 25 years later, people gather at the place in Dallas where Kennedy was assassinated. (p. 446)

> Some people, especially Dallas residents like the white, married couple in their sixties who have been here since 9:30 A.M., come to this place every year on November 22. (p. 446)

> Others, like Chester Smith, a 30-year-old black male, and Howard Hartog, a 48-year-old white male, drove hundreds of miles from Galveston, Texas, and Edgerton, Minnesota, respectively, to be here for the anniversary. (pp. 446–447)

We are assured by the detail that Trujillo was there. He saw real people with names that ring true from places that we know exist. We are prepared to listen to his voice because his experience makes him trustworthy. But Trujillo's article is double-voiced, for he attempts a "postmodern ideological analysis" that he admits "resists definition." He is forced to teach us what this means.

When the didactic voice wears thin, he returns to the voice of experience to recapture our interest and our confidence. He makes this switch six times in the space of a 20-page article, giving about an equal number of pages to each invocation. Each claim is grounded in a new episode of experience.

In the end, Trujillo uses his experience and our jointly held history to lure us into his project. His final sentence states, "We should encourage our colleagues and students to do field research, because it is in the field, however defined, that the paradoxes of postmodernism may best be understood and experienced" (p. 464). This sentence illuminates the innocence and complicity acknowledged in hermeneutic research. "Do this work," Trujillo says, "and you will be better for it." And we certainly believe him, but slightly off camera we hear, "Do this work and *I* will be better for it."

The Critical Impulse: Utopia, Emancipation, and the Preferred Possible

Historicity insists that researchers are complicit with sectarian and dominant interests by necessity, but the researchers are not without recourse. They may not recover their innocence, but they may directly enter the struggle to do good.

It is an Enlightenment argument that the true is independent of the moral. The idea permitted a science bent on secular goals to flourish. Now deconstructed by the rhetoric of science (Prelli, 1989; Simons, 1989) and by feminist writings too (Belenky et al., 1986; Harding, 1986, 1991; Longino, 1989), the true is seen (in some quarters) as being in the service of some purpose and as being recognizable in the moral space we provide it (Nelson, 1990). The difference, hermeneuticists would claim, between hermeneutic empiricism and objective empiricism on this issue is that the hermeneuticist, no longer unwitting, has the right and duty to choose.[5]

And choose they do, posing utopias of communicative action (Habermas, 1987a, 1987b), frames of emancipation in gender (Goldberger et al., 1987; Sanday, 1981), frames of emancipation in organizations (Deetz & Mumby, 1990) and scholarship (Anderson, 1992), and a mighty host of the preferred possible (Belsey, 1980; Scott, 1990; Sosnoski, 1994), all in a crucible of good intentions and rightful resistance.[6]

The methodological issue is that the critical impulse is not something that is the afterthought of the study: the critical impulse is what the study is about.[7] That choices are made to achieve the conclusion is not self-fulfilling because the argument can fail. The moment of doubt is not the conclusion but whether the argument can be constructed to sustain it. The signs of the phenomenal world are permissive but they cannot mean whatever we want them to mean. They support some explanations and resist others. I may desperately want "trickle-down" economics or the V-chip in television to emancipate the lower classes from the poverty and violence that can mark their lives. But if that emancipation does not show in their application, all but the fanatics move on.

Summary: The Epistemology of Hermeneutic Methods

The creation of the hermeneutic argument as a practical achievement in knowledge claim also does often opportunistic work in positioning the analyst and reader alike across issues such as ideology, historicity, complicity, referentiality, and representation. To write or to read, some position must be taken. The action of writing or of reading denies my innocence on the issues they entail, but not my ignorance.

Methods are made sensible through the entire hierarchy from the episteme to fields, paradigms, communities, frames, and conventions. Each level lays down another layer of instructions for understanding. As an analyst, I can free neither the methods of my choice nor the arguments I create from the implications of these instructions without considerable effort. Methods are not neutral except insofar as neutrality is itself a contrivance.

NOTES

1. I make a distinction between "agency" and "agentry" to mark the two meanings of agent. An agent is both an initiator of action and the representative of some collective understanding that makes the action meaningful. Agency, then, is the "act of willing," the choosing that leads in one direction or the other. Agentry is the representational work that the act of choosing conducts—by choosing to do X, I am understood as representing Y.

2. In the current attention on the differences between women and men there is the argument, at least potentially serious, that there is no species unity across the dimension of sex. There is rather two separate species. The feminist joke along these lines ends with "one human, the other not."

3. In the writing and reading of this section we need to be continually reminded of the absence of the deep conventionalization of method that is present in objective empiricism. There is no "American Hermeneutic Association" style manual to match the one of the American Psychological Association or codes of good research practice like those for sociology, anthropology, and psychology. Furthermore, I would expect the practitioners of hermeneutic empiricism to be fully resistant to efforts to develop such codes, since conventionalization is considered a corrupting process by more than a few of them.

4. The difference between "writing down" and "writing up" is useful for understanding the different writing tasks. Writing down privileges experience; writing up, interpretation. My thanks to Tom Lindlof for pointing out these terms.

5. To illustrate the problem, consider the following scenario: An objective empiricist researcher has an interest in the relationship between violence and happiness in marriage. Her hypothesis is that as violence increases happiness in the marriage will decrease. The problem is that her research locates a small but sturdy group of respondents who not only participate in at least one act of violence against their partner per year but enjoy their marriage as well. What to do with this finding? Publishing the finding, even if thoroughly bracketed in warnings concerning its limitations, will provide a scientific resource for those who argue that domestic violence is the natural consequence of human relations and not part of a patriarchal effort for the subjugation of women. Presuming the researcher has no reason to doubt her findings, objective science demands its publication.

For the hermeneuticist, the problem is not the finding but the original design that established a situation that could be put into the service of the dominant interests. The finding emerged not in discovery, but in the constructions of the background assumptions, the questions asked, the operational definitions used, and the argument frame employed. Moral choices were made at each of those points. What produced this moral conundrum was not the truth or falsity of the finding but the conventional and unreflective morality of the practice of science. The finding appears in the moral choices that made it possible. The finding ought not to have been possible. The researcher, while not culpable, was morally irresponsible.

6. I have written elsewhere that it is the duty of those with more to work for the emancipation of those with less and the right of the less to resist their emancipation. It is the struggle not the solution that liberates. Any solution is just another arrangement of more and less.

7. I am indebted to Janice Radway for her instruction on this topic.

CHAPTER 8

SCHOLARSHIP IN SOCIETY

Scholarship is a public industry whose product is justified knowledge claims. The college professoriate; members of research labs and professional institutes; practitioners such as educators, politicians, and attorneys; and even the occasional amateur—all become working members of this industry when they turn their hands from proprietary interests and seek to influence the commonweal's stock of knowledge.

Scholarship is not the only player in the knowledge industry.[1] But scholarship is the public face of the industry and the place where altruism is supposed to dominate.[2] But even here people gain from what they do; fortunes can be made and most scholars lead very comfortable lives. There is, of course, a rich sociology of analysis from which to study the practices of scholarship, from Mannheim (1940), Scheler (1924/1980), and Merton (1937), who wrote in the first half of the century, to Kuhn (1970), Bloor (1976), Barnes (1977), Longino (1990), and Fuchs (1992) writing in the second half.

One present-day conclusion (Collins, 1975; Crane, 1972; Fuchs, 1992; Whitley, 1984) is that fields of scholarship are organizational domains whose location in society and whose internal practices mark the product of knowledge as surely as General Motors marks automobiles. Scholarship, then, including science scholarship, is a set of human practices with no suprahuman characteristics that set it apart from corporations and governments.[3] It is subject to the same failings and should be subject to the same sort of scrutiny and skepticism. That it attempts to occupy the moral high ground by claiming the true should only intensify our oversight.

THEORY AND CONSEQUENCES

Our oversight here, however, will focus on a topic considerably more narrow than the whole sociology of science. Our special interest is the different societal payoffs that different theory families deliver. We will begin with objectivist theories.

Objectivist Theories

Objectivist theories are those that show a strong affinity for the principles of physical empiricism, materialism, determinism, and objectivity. Objectivist theories are "concerned with a reality that is claimed to exist and act even if it has not yet been observed" (Blaikie, 1993, p. 58). This reality can be observed in a trustworthy and reliable fashion and evidences no volatility in the face of its explanation. Objectivist theories are the traditional theories of science.

If we were to build a collection of objectivist theories, what boundary characteristics would we look for?

1. The first line in the sand would probably be drawn by the use of ahistorical constructs that "stand for" persistent, independent, and autonomous phenomena, states, or conditions (materialism). These constructs populate behaviorist, cognitivist, functionalist, structuralist, and rational choice theories (among others), as well as constitute the variables of objectivist psychology, sociology, and anthropology. These are the "behavioral reinforcement schedules" of meaning acquisition (Osgood, 1963); the "schemata" of cognitive organization (Bloom, 1988); the "teleologies" of uses and gratifications (Swanson, 1979); the "structural stages" that every group must go through in decision making (Fisher, 1970); the "consequences of rational choice" in dyadic interactions (Thibaut & Kelley, 1959); the "strategies of compliance gaining" (Kellermann & Cole, 1994); the "intentions of power and domination" (Cobb, 1994); and the "attributions of negotiated readings" (Liebes & Ribak, 1994)—for just a sampling of the host of subject variables that inhabit our journals.

In each of these examples, the object of study emulates the material in that its study implicates neither the object nor the knowing subject. This material criterion also motivates the atomistic approach of methodological individualism (Little, 1991), which eschews the broad cultural imperatives of cultural, critical, and Marxist studies.

2. The second well-drawn boundary for objectivist theories is the preference for causal explanations (determinism). In their most general form, causal explanations (including conditional and stochastic forms) state that the presence of one phenomenon in some way influences the presence of other phenomena. The explanation of the influenced phenomenon(phenomena) is provided in its relationship with the influencing phenomenon(phenomena).

All effects studies, whether they entail television content in media effects studies, the conditions of intimate relationships, the preconditions of leadership, communicator characteristics of compliance gaining, or the control of stage fright, fall within this boundary. Further, as we discussed in Chapter 7, the presence of experimental protocols or the application of statistical procedures such as path analysis or even correlation, signals an underlying objectivist theory.

The interest in causelike relationships, itself motivated by the scientific goals of prediction and control, will suppress explanations that make use of immanent agency. Choice will always have its explanation.

3. The third boundary involves the trustworthiness of observation. The objects of analysis must present themselves in such a way that the claims about them are independent of the methods of their observation (physical empiricism). Observations must be confirmable and independent of the person doing the observing (objectivity).

Inside this boundary, we find the application of the doctrine of literal meaning. The operational meaning of words, symbols, narratives, objects, and so on must be specifiable independent of their reception. If meaning is locally produced, the researcher cannot predict its consequence in causelike relationships.

4. The fourth line in the sand is one we have not seen before and is the topic of this chapter. This line separates claims of "is" and "ought," fact from value, discovery from implication. This separation (called "Hume's gap") derives from our prior three boundary conditions.[4] The job of the scientist is simply to tell us what is there and how it functions; it is for others—for example, politicians, moralists, or social activists—to argue for what ought to be. Scientists qua scientists do not advocate.

In the ethical realm, scientists provide only the knowledge about the existence of means and their relationship to ends. They do not provide information about the propriety of the means or the rightness of the ends (Snare, 1992). But the argument does not end here, for the obverse conclusion—that no moral statement can be factual—is also drawn. Axiology is fully separated from epistemology. Finally, when epistemology is "naturalized" as science (Quine, 1953/1961/1980), moral knowledge disappears. The moral realm is neither factual nor empirical, and is therefore in an unresolvable domain of human activity.

From the objectivist position, scientists (a) are the only production agents of genuine knowledge (scholarship reduces to science), (b) have no claim to right or wrong, and (c) have no responsibility (as scientists) for the consequences of their knowledge discoveries. That an Oppenheimer provides the equations for an atomic bomb or that the Human Genome Project results in the loss of medical insurance for perhaps hundreds of thousands of people may be regrettable technological applications, but certainly not of issue in the science of these efforts (M. C. Goodall, 1970).

The knowledge gained through the practice of science is both the return and the justification for allocating societal resources to the scientific effort. That knowledge is its own consequence—a good in its own right, but also viewed as a necessary resource for the other work that humankind wants to conduct.

This is a powerful position: nothing can be done without science but science is not responsible for anything that is done in its name. In this formulation, something we call "technology" or "applied science" becomes the political and economic extension of science into the ongoing practices of society. Regulation of technology or applied science and their applications is wholly appropriate. Regulation of science as the autonomous search for knowledge is not.[5]

Cultural Studies and Critical Theories

A very different sort of relationship to society is established in the work of cultural studies and critical theories. Just to review, cultural studies is a melange of interests (Johnson, 1986–1987)—usually with an attachment to the work of Williams and British cultural studies but increasingly identified with continental scholars—that examines the cultural influences, texts, and meaningful relationships of a society with an intent to critically evaluate their consequences (Brantlinger, 1990). (Not every study of culture is a cultural study; cultural studies are the product of that community.) Cultural studies may be identified with materialism and determinism, as is traditional Marxism, but is more likely to adopt some form of constructivism (Mailloux, 1991).

Critical theory is generally identified with the Frankfurt School and the writings of Horkheimer, Adorno, Marcuse, and their colleagues and students. Critical theory has the same explanatory targets as cultural studies, but derives from a German intellectual tradition that centers the place of reason as the basis for societal reform. Cultural studies has never shared this belief; indeed, with its growing dependence on the works of Foucault, Derrida, and Lacan, it now often shows a deep distrust of reason.

Although many guises of cultural studies and nearly all of critical theory could fit inside the first three demarcations of realism, both cultural studies and critical theory reject the objectivist position of the separation of science from society and moral responsibility. Both argue that it is the responsibility of all varieties of scholarship to work for the elimination of oppression (including the oppression of scholarship itself), either through ideas of reform and emancipation on the utopian side or through disruption and the dissipation of power on the deconstructionist side (Dolan, 1991; Pollock & Cox, 1991).

This latter fracture is not a small one. Reformists and emancipationists seek solutions, whether global (Habermas, 1984, 1987a) or local (Williams, 1981); deconstructionists (Lyotard, 1984) stand on continual attack, for they believe that there is no solution but only the struggle (Carmichael, 1991). In both cases, however, the scholar is equally responsible for the critical analysis of what she or he studies and entangled in the political consequences of her or his claims. Scholarship may involve discovery, but that discovery is not its own end. The work is not done until the implications are drawn.

In that critical effort, only the emancipationists can have a positive program. The deep pessimism of deconstruction is its own burden. Nonetheless, both take science out of its sequestered state. Knowledge is never neutral, but aims to achieve certain ends that can be evaluated—rationally by the emancipationists and so as to level it by the deconstructionists.[6]

While the language of the foregoing paragraphs is often grand, the focus of reform or emancipation in actual studies is more life-sized. A recent work by Ted Glasser and James Ettema (1993) offers an example. Writing on irony in journalism, they carefully work their way through the conditions, requirements, and logic of irony to consider its role in journalism. In this journalism setting, they conclude that:

> Irony assumes a moral consensus without defining or defending it. This not only excuses journalists from any obligation to explain or justify their moral claims but it alleviates as well any pressure on readers to acknowledge *in* public or *as* public an issue worthy of their collective attention. (p. 335)

From this conclusion, they draw the implications of the propriety of the use of irony by journalists through a series of statements that describe the positive and negative consequences of its use and end with these thoughts:

> When journalists disclose the truth indirectly or obliquely because they fear official and harsh sanctions against them, irony can be understood as a prudent course of action. But if journalists divulge the truth quietly and cautiously as a matter of convention, or for their own convenience, then irony becomes self-protective and self-indulgent; it is not a sign of prudence but evidence of timidity. (pp. 335–336)

Certainly, this is not a ringing, take-to-the-streets conclusion, but it is well beyond what one would expect to find in a traditional content analysis. But it is not their method that leads them to this difference, it is the difference in the epistemological foregrounding of their argument.

The formulations of scholarship posited by objectivist realism and by the critical approaches of cultural studies and critical theory cannot both be true, although they certainly are both practiced (for a rapprochement, see Livingston, 1988). They represent separate epistemologies (Little, 1991; Roth, 1987). For the objectivists, knowledge is only empirical. For the cultural studies scholar and the critical theorist, knowledge is both empirical *and* critical. Objectivist science may supply the empirical claim, but its work is incomplete, defective in that it refuses to take up its responsibility for the action of its claim in society.

Hermeneutic Theories

Hermeneutic theories offer yet another position on the place of scholarship in society. The main premise of hermeneutics is the rejection of the notion that reality is wholly independent and autonomous of its explanation. Rather, the reality in which we live is formed in a system of cultural meanings that make sense of ourselves and our relationship with the phenomenal world. Equally important, for all but the structuralists, this system of cultural meanings is a product of everyday action, the things you and I do in the daily activity that creates our life.

Hermeneutic theories vary across a number of dimensions, including the size and scope of the system of meanings, its inertia, its coherence and literalness, its extension in time, its variety, and avenues of change. At one end, hermeneutics—which posits reality as embedded in world-defining language with its centuries-long history and genetic forebearing, as well as a singularity of application and reference—is indistinguishable from realism. At the other end, hermeneutics—which posits reality as a polysemic system of meanings that must be centered in improvised performances of both discourse (language in use) and action that themselves are open to rhetorical devices—represents a radically different moral position. It is to this latter reference, this fixing of the hermeneutic position, that I wish to attend.[7]

Hermeneutics of this sort depends on there being multiple domains of reality that require different forms of explanation and represents a field of argument that forsakes the solutions of physical empiricism, materialism, or determinism (Jackson, 1989). The brute sense data of physical empiricism is replaced by the necessity of interpretation. This necessity, in turn, obviates the singular value of the material criterion. Of equal footing is the meanings (interpretations) we have for the object in hand. The fixed relationships of physical causation are replaced by the syntagmatic relationships of semiotics. Syntagmatic relationships provide references but not rules for action.[8] In the semiotic domain, we act analogically rather than deterministically.

All of this suggests that the naturalized performances that we daily observe are the product of a lot of work. This work brings cultural meanings to bear on actual situations to define the agents, declare the means, and enforce the consequences of action (see Mitchell, 1994). The bumper sticker says "Shit happens," but actually it is culturally produced. Scholarship, including science, is part of that system of production.

The ethics of science are embedded in the continuous struggle for meaning that a hermeneutic reality entails. The claims of scholarship stand as a potent resource for subsequent action. Meaningful claims are the platforms of action. That one works to center a claim establishes a line of responsibility for what can be done with it.

The significance of this responsibility can be seen through an analysis of a news report published in the *Salt Lake Tribune* (Monday, February 10, 1992). The story is headlined "Increased Income Doesn't Drop Black Crime Rate," and begins with these observations:

> Rising income and educational levels since World War II were accompanied by a drop in crime rates among whites but not among blacks, said a study released Sunday. The findings challenge "one of the most widely held assumptions of postwar society," namely, that liberal social programs can reduce crime by ameliorating social and economic injustices, said the study's author, Gary Lafree of the University of New Mexico in Albuquerque. (p. A5)

From an objectivist point of view the discovery of a significant correlation between measures of income and education and the FBI uniform crime reports imposes an ethical responsibility to report this finding because it is true. Of course, the truth of the claim can be questioned. But the appropriate method of questioning considers whether the proper method of analysis was competently applied.[9] Given that Lafree did what could be done to preserve the canons of rationality and the rules of good methodology, he discharged his ethical responsibility.

The view from the hermeneutic perspective sees the whole enterprise as a constructionist effort, beginning with the intentions of the scientist as a member of the dominant social group to study race as something independent of the actions and beliefs of the dominant, moving quickly to the ideologically laden measures predisposed to do the work of the dominant, and then examining the considerable efforts by Lafree and his profession to position the claim as true and as a challenge.[10]

A hermeneutic analysis of the use of race as a "scientific variable" would show that this use itself contributes to the reality we hold for the distinction of race. At best, the independent reality of race is a constellation of genetic characteristics. (The fact that the constellation used seems to center on skin color and facial characteristics from a European perspective and not on thumb length or the propensity to develop colon cancer seems to be instructive.) To the best of my knowledge, there is nothing in that constellation that justifies Lafree's claim.

The immediate reply is that race is not a *genetic* reality but a *social* one. In other words, it is created by society. Two questions follow: Who is society? And does society have a choice? If the answers are "Us" and "Yes," then the conclusion may well be that author Lafree is doing the collective's racist work. (This conclusion would be a literal insult to an objectivist and libelous as well.)

It is certainly true that Lafree wrote sentences that can stand as a resource— from legitimate science at that—for a proracist claim. This is also true of the headline that Lafree did not write but did make possible. The strong hermeneutic position would hold Lafree responsible for both outcomes, and since racism is an unwanted outcome, would also hold him duty-bound to contain this value of his claim. This position would hold the Associated Press and the *Salt Lake*

Tribune equally responsible for racisim and would assail me for extending the distribution of the quotation as a racist resource. No one in this list is innocent of practices that can be read as contributing to a racist society.

But does the practice of using race as a demographic variable contribute to racism? To the extent that it reifies social practices as an autonomous reality, it certainly does. To the extent that it suppresses or even stands in the place of other ways of explaining, it reduces our opportunities for understanding in nonracist ways.

Would hermeneutics advise the abandonment of race as a demographic variable? Surprisingly, no. Hermeneutics would advise redesigning the study and its reporting so that racism is less likely to be advanced. One can use race to show that the use of race is not valuable. This, of course, is standpoint scholarship, but remember that hermeneutics holds that all scholarship stands somewhere. Hermeneutics holds that objectivist scholarship simply exnominates (i.e., disguises, renders invisible) its white, masculine, and bourgeois position. In doing so, objectivist realism advances a position as unproblematically true within the semiotic domain and denies its responsibility for the meaningful consequences of the claim.

Hermeneutic claims—that observation is trustworthy only from a perspective and that rationality is itself a form of interpretation—situate the knowing subject—scientist and scholar—as an ethical agent, advancing the conditions by which something can be true and its knowledge produced. Facts are not simply facts, for in their representation they imply action (Mitchell, 1994; Searle, 1975). Part of the action is the construction of the reality to be represented. It is this constructive interplay between phenomena and explanation that forces the ethical question of the instrumentality of scholarship. That topic we turn to next.

AUDIENCES AND INSTRUMENTALITY

An interesting discussion in the rhetoric of science (Gaonkar, 1993, and his respondents) concerns the presence of the audience in scientific and—by extension—all scholarly writing. The antirhetorical position—the claim that science writing has no rhetorical dimension—argues that there is no audience intended in this writing and, hence, no need for a rhetorical effort. Instead, this writing is deliberately directed toward an archive of written discourse rather than a reader. Its entrance into that archive is determined by whether it meets the standards for verdical claim not its persuasability.

This argument cleverly accomplishes two consequences: First it reifies truth in the object of publication, denying the political activity of the publishing act (Tyler, 1987). In doing so it provides the necessity of the work. Second, it renders moot all questions about readability and readers, thereby denying rhetorical and most critical analysis. It is an effective protectionist scheme that shields scholarship from review by lay and expert analysts alike.

If we accept the argument of archival writing, then the audience for a given work need be nothing more than the gatekeepers of the archive itself. It does not matter that a work is unread or has no present force. Its encapsuled truth lies in wait for the moment its value can be shown in the support of yet another addition to the archive. Knowledge production need go no farther and often becomes the overproduction of the routine and the mediocre (Erickson, Fleuriet, & Hosman, 1993). I would also claim that the argument holds the archive as its own end, and it works to preserve the sacred in scholarship.

In practice, however, scholars do not trust in only the truth value of their claims to carry the field and, in fact, embrace very mundane efforts to persuade. Rhetorical analysis, Gaonkar (1993) to the contrary, has begun to break into the persuasive structure of the scientific text (see Bazerman, 1988; Fuller, 1993a; Gross, 1990; Nelson, Megill, & McCloskey, 1987; Prelli, 1989). Other writers (Agger, 1989; Brown, 1987; Edmondson, 1984; Green, 1988) have escalated Geertz's (1988) "blurred genres" claim to equate the texts of science and literature, ethical niceties aside, as common travelers in the same world as tabloids and commercials (Fuchs, 1992).

When one makes the rhetorical move to present science as text, one must insist upon the audience, and therefore make some justification of the work in the response of the audience. When the audience becomes present, one necessarily implicates the instrumentality of the writing. Consequently, there is a necessary relationship between the character of the audience[11] required for the instrumentality to be obtained.

The issue of instrumentality is met the moment public resources are exchanged. Those resources are more than money and matèrièl. They are the resources that allow even the lowest paid instructor among us to live a life of privilege in comparison to those who take on the risks of physical labor. The product we return is the practical argument of our scholarship.

The practical argument of our scholarship, as we have seen, is the set of material practices that constitute the discursive performances recognized as trade books, journal articles, convention presentations, and the like. The practical argument of scholarship therefore comes into being at the moment of its authentication among the membership of an intellectual community. The consequences of that authentication defines the instrumentality of the claims advanced. That instrumentality creates a demand for, and the limits of, the audience appropriate to the work. It is to that combination to which we now turn.

The Audience of Disciplinary Instrumentality

The first level of instrumentality is disciplinary. This instrumentality is defined by sufficient activity to justify the infrastructure of distribution. The audience necessary at this level is that required by the discursive practices of authorship and for the induction of new recruits into scholarship. The discursive practices of authorship do not, of course, require deeply engaged readers but rather some mode of distribution and application (such as citations). This is not to say that there are not deeply engaged readers, but to point out that publications can easily ride on the margins of this low level of instrumentality.

The Audience of Professional Instrumentality

The second level of instrumentality is professional. This level is realized when a discipline's scholarship achieves sufficient recognition to be included in the authorship and training practices of other disciplines. The audience necessary here is the agents of these practices.

The Audiences of Linked Instrumentality

The levels of instrumentality beyond the professional involve a series of linkages in which the activity of scholarship is an agent in the activities of other societal elements. In this process claim is reconstituted at each occurrence of agency into a separate engaged text. Students in a lower division course, for example, do not (ordinarily) engage the texts of advanced scholarship directly. Instead, the claims of such scholarship are reconstituted in the form of classroom textbooks.

Similarly, a "lay public" would engage the claims in the form of journalism or a "popular press" presentation. In each of these instances, we find an audience for the claims of scholarship though not readers of academic journals. Linked instrumentality therefore requires these institutionalized (nonmessianic) agencies of translation.

It is of some concern to note, as Goodall (in Anderson & Goodall, 1994) has pointed out, that as one moves to the higher levels of linked instrumentality, one loses a measure of prestige within the academic community. Work that reaches beyond the professional audience is somehow suspect. This criticism is legitimate when the linkage ends in media play rather than in the utilities of the extended audience.

Linked Instrumentality and Reform:
A Personal View

Fully developed, linked instrumentality involves the development and operation of institutionalized agents of translation that move the claims initially presented in professional scholarship into the practices of some other group. An example of fully linked instrumentality—albeit simplified and romanticized—might be found in the work of plant genetics. Some of this work is the foundation of efforts by plant developers to produce hybrids with desired characteristics. Their work is, in turn, translated by nursery companies into choices for the field. Those choices are advanced and explained by agricultural journals and, in the United States, by local, county-extension officers. The farmer standing in her field holds the claim of the plant geneticist in the seeds in her hand in a more genuine way than if she held a set of academic journals. But those seeds are also her text, and she will produce her own work from them.

There is little question in my mind that the particular success of the material sciences has not been in the validity of their claim but in their ability to make a difference—both good and bad—in the lives of others. It is also my belief that the principal reform of the humanities and the social sciences must be the advancement of the linking institutions by which we can make a difference.

This reform need not be directed by some misguided enthusiasm for redemption. It is the ethical duty of the higher orders of the social hierarchy to work for the meaningful emancipation of the lower orders and of the lower orders to mount meaningful opposition—including resistance to the emancipatory impulses from above. In the absence of "a final solution," we are left with the struggle (Scott, 1990).

The problem with this clarion call for reform is that it can barely be heard above the din of those so busy doing the system's work. But when that work is done—when tenure and reputation are secure—what then? Here, let me impugn no one's motives but my own: it is easy to retire to the fireside of truth when faced with the struggle on the streets.

Social Linkages in Communication

In the 70-plus years of our modern history, the studies of communication—the interests of criticism, rhetoric, public speaking, journalism, broadcasting and all the subdomains, organizational communication, interpersonal communication, and the rest—have accomplished a remarkable growth. We have pushed our way into the academy and claimed a place for ourselves with such vigor that in some places (such as at my own campus) communication has been the most productive in terms of graduates of all undergraduate majors.

This struggle for legitimacy continues; it is not everywhere won. Nonetheless, we are ready for the next step. That step is to prove ourselves outside the academic walls. Not as quaint ethnographers sitting in the comfort of middle-class homes or as consultants doing the work of management or as media groupies, but as people who make a difference in the lives of other people.

My colleague, Irv Altman, internationally known as a social psychologist, has commented that the best that can be said of psychology is that "It has done no harm."

How shall we all do better? I'm glad you asked. In my answer, we must first realize that the scholarly life is a privileged life, taken at cost from the lives of others. As reputable critics, scientists, and scholars of every sort, we cannot allow ourselves to be agents of reality constructions that deflect the legitimate claims to equity that arise from the domain of the less. We must instead work to advance those claims. This responsibility is simply the proper recognition of the price that has been paid by others and of our duty to extend the instrumentality of our scholarship to those who have paid it.

In the end, the ethical choice is clear: we either participate in the meanings that produce the deepening violence, the racial injustice, the sexual harassment, the conditions of homelessness, the inequalities of our society or we actively resist and oppose them at the sites of their production. The course of action is admittedly far from clear, and it is not my intent to question any reasoned course, but I am most suspicious of those scientific claims that begin with, say, the effects of media rather than those of opportunity, education, housing, and a secure life.

The work of normalized scholarship is too often the work of self-service, patriarchy, white racism, and class inequality. There is a moral imperative, therefore, to examine our scholarship for what it accomplishes.

Good scholarship calls on us to consider that instrumentality and to repay the price of privilege by producing scholarship and supporting efforts that strive to make a meaningful difference in the lives of others. That effort will lead us to the emancipatory struggle—a crucible of good intentions and corrective opposition. Emancipation is an ongoing strategy, not a state.

The business of scholarship, quite simply, is to create meanings from which we can act. It is not the discipline of discovery but the participation in the methods of human understanding. Scholarship is a professional practice within the social creation of reality. We have been granted the space, time, and resources (meager though they often are) to practice this craft.

Further, to the extent that the world we study is a product of human accomplishment, the descriptive and the normative must necessarily merge. Hume's gap is not only closed; statements of fact and value are joined at the hip. Because our descriptions participate in the reality they describe, a true description of what *is* is also a claim of what *ought to be*. The implications of these statements are that we must abandon the pretense that our works are objective and neither historicized nor politicized, and we must accept the risk of adopting a moral position (see Bellah et al., 1985, or Jackson, 1989).

We are, if you will, meaning geneticists. Our valid scholarship will produce the strategically engineered seeds of social action by which the occasions of opportunity, education, good housing, and a secure life can grow with vigor and productivity so that all elements of our society can share the harvest.

SCHOLARSHIP AND SOCIETY: A SUMMARY

We have in this brief chapter considered three major frames by which the relationship between scholarship and society can be understood. The first requires the object of our analysis to be independent and autonomous of human accomplishment, accessible to good observation, and amenable to right reason. Given those conditions, the epistemological goal of scholarship is simply a true claim of what is out there and how it functions. In this conception there is a clear distinction between the claims of the true and the consequences of their knowledge.

The second frame finds its main expression in cultural studies and critical theory and involves the true in the service of the good. It may be true that there is a social reality "out there" accessible to observation and tractable to reason, but it is not true that its study must be permitted without anticipating the consequences of our knowledge. Scholarship does not pursue all fronts of knowledge equally. As a human endeavor, it first and foremost considers its own success in what it does. The utilities of knowledge are already entangled before the claim. The claim of knowledge from the beginning entails value. Its critical appraisal is therefore a necessary part of the entire argument.

The third frame takes up the constructivist standard to insist that claim and reality are not separate but, indeed, interact with one another. The meanings we have for the objects of our analysis create the foundations for our actions. Our actions work to make those object meanings true. While race, gender, caste, and similar social distinctions all exist as objects to the individual, they are all human accomplishments that our analysis either advances or impedes. There is no innocence of claim; rather, there is a moral imperative to direct scholarship by its instrumentality.

NOTES

1. From a social action perspective, most of what we know is contained in the day-to-day performances we call "corporate life," "the production line," "a medical practice," or "keeping house."

2. I'm not signaling an intent to muckrake here, although it would be easy enough to do and a number have already done so. (see Bloom, 1987; Kimball, 1990; Wilshire, 1990). I am trying to demystify, however.

3. The contrary argument is that of rationality as a (nearly) perfected method that protects scholarship (science particularly) as an enterprise from irretrievable error and keeps it progressing toward the true. Individual scientists may fail, and indeed entire segments may be misled, but science moves forward. This is the science of our classrooms (Gale, 1979; but see also the essays edited by Wilson, 1970).

4. "Hume's gap" comes from Hume's argument that claims of value cannot be derived from statements of fact. His argument is dependent on facts being independently true of their expression. If facts come into being in their expression, as many interpretive arguments hold, then the gap disappears.

5. An individual identifying himself(?) as a Ph.D. student in physics wrote to the New Yorker, saying that "scientific inquiry is guided by one thing: truth. Its means are the search for truth and its ends are the understanding of it. A by-product of this process is

technology, and it is in the production technology rather than in the practice of science that the ethical and social issues must be considered" (August 1, 1994, p. 7). His letter poses two interesting points: The first reflects on the socialization processes by which scientists are brought into a set of beliefs about their actions. The second considers Mr. Johnson's value as a source in a scholarly work.

6. Further, its pursuit is never autonomous but involves the allocation of societal resources and the inherent trade-offs of a limited supply. The professionalization of science ensures that it cannot be practiced in a harmless way.

7. The argument advanced here and some of the language used appeared in Anderson, 1992.

8. The difference between references and rules is the difference between analogic and propositional knowledge. In reference systems, one works by analogy from a set of particular experiences. In rules systems, one applies a covering proposition. The difference between native competence and traditional grammar is a good example.

9. Two assumptions seem most vulnerable: that measures of income, education, and crime have been consistently applied over the 50-year period and that the reporting methods, reliability, and accuracy across these measures are the same for different socioeconomic and racial groups. If even one of these failed to be true, the comparison would be faulty.

10. The article is unclear about who characterized the finding as a "challenge." The word is not within the quotation marks and therefore may be the reporter's interpretation. But whoever the author, what would the ethical responsibility be for the claim that the findings "challenge 'one of the most widely held assumptions of postwar society?'" Is this a realist claim? Can findings "challenge" (do guns "kill")? In this claim we seem to have stepped into a different domain.

11. This discussion concerns itself with constituted audiences that are real in the sense that we can point to individuals who meet the constituting requirements. Such real audiences, however, are never the actual audiences that engage scholarship. Actual audiences are the ineffable resource from which all constituted audiences are drawn.

CHAPTER 9

COMMUNICATION
THEORY ANALYSIS

Theory must have an object of its explanation, an explanatory form, a method to relate evidence to claim, characteristic explanations within a scope of performance, and a consequence of value. A foundational analysis of any theory will move toward these ends. Such an analysis speaks to the singular, overarching question of "What do I have to believe to be true to live a scholar's life in the fashion of this theory?"

Depending on the definitions used to direct the count, there are now more than a dozen texts on the market that offer an overview of communication theory. Each of these texts is an effort to locate the field in a matrix of nominated ideas. The ideas are nominated by the textbook authors themselves as exemplars of what constitutes a theory in the communication discipline. In order to get some feel for the state of the discipline, I analyzed seven texts, focusing on those that had thrived enough in market competition to at least enjoy a second edition.[1] I reasoned that multiple-edition texts would be more conservative and would have fewer "off-the-wall" inclusions.

My procedure was to list anything that was "named" (whether as a theory or any of its synonyms) and followed by a "centering" citation.[2] Potential entries failed on either side of the test. For example, several authors talked about a "direct effects" theory of mass media but failed to offer a citation to support its existence (although others did), and many citations were presented during discussion that were not grouped under a named theory.

I counted 249 entries, 195 of which were single-entry selections. Eighteen theories were identified by three or more of the authors or author teams. Leon

Festinger's dissonance theory showed the greatest agreement among the authors with five selections.[3] Not surprisingly, the most likely theory to be mentioned in a given text was the theory of the author of that text.

This analysis certainly provides clear evidence of the failure of the positivists' project to regularize and conventionalize the definition of theory. Only 22% of the entries revealed any agreement. Thus today, the questions of what we should recognize as theory in general and what we should recognize as communication theory in particular are unresolved.[4]

It is, however, only by such conscious effort as mine that we can learn about this problematic condition. Individual authors invariably put on a brave face and suggest that they have contained the chaos. Nonetheless, if you learned your communication theory from Stephen Littlejohn, you will have a different matrix in mind than if you learned it from Sara Trenholm.

To compound the confusion, the conclusions that we draw from this analysis will be quite different depending on the epistemological framework in which we place them. Empirical foundationalists might argue that we are a young science, our theory development is at a very low level, and that our theories have not been well tested in the phenomenal world, which is why they have not converged on a set of good explanations. Empirical constructionists might argue that theory constellations will always appear around phenomena and that there is no way epistemologically to reduce their number. The lack of agreement among texts simply reflects the selection of one "star" or another from the constellations. Empirical hermeneuticists might argue that the textbooks themselves are instantiations of authority and power in attempts to define the field. It is the economics of textbook production along with a "reading resistance" to the forced conventionalization that leads to multiple texts and multiple definitions of theory.

Moving along these explanations, we get further away from a validating reality (as well as the complementary expectations of reductionism and the unity of knowledge) that will "solve the problem" and closer to a conception of knowledge as a set of micronarratives assembled within human practices with its complementaries of political action.

In the last position, communication theory, as a singular, is the product of a historicized effort by particular agents to "fix the field." The consequence will always be multiple, excessive, contentious, and disciplined only by the power of its agents. This is what I would expect from my epistemological vantage point. But from that vantage point, I cannot tell you, without good purpose, what communication theory is. There are no generally agreed upon characteristics (and there are certainly no empirical features) that would enable me to declare its boundaries. I can tell you the tests I would apply (and offer the epigraph to this chapter quoted from Chapter 1).

Those tests include (1) the epistemological methods by which the explanatory object is defined, held to be real in some reality domain, and engaged within that domain (Chapters 2–4); (2) the methods of claim production by which an argument is both justified and makes its practical appearance (Chapters 5 and 6); (3) the practices of evidence production within different scholarly methodologies (Chapter 6); and (4) the consequences of living its rubric (Chapters 7 and 8).

What I propose is to investigate briefly the set of 18 theories that were listed in three or more of the theory texts and then to apply my tests to the seminal texts of 10 of these 18[5] And finally, to take this text into more recent theorizing, I will comment on structuration and social action theory.

EIGHTEEN THEORIES

Table 9–1 presents the theory "name," the listing texts (in parentheses by author[s] initials) and the central citations for each of the 18 theories.[6]

Description and Analysis

Looking at these 18 theories we are first struck by what is missing within the boundaries of my selection rule. There is no representation of the Marxist, feminist, or critical theories. Cultural studies, hermeneutics, social action, and structuration are also absent, as is structuralism, existentialism, phenomenology, ideological, and hegemonic theory.

There is a preponderance of cognitivism (9 of the 18 theories would fit some definition of cognitivism) as well as an historical distance (nearly all of the work represents the 1960s and 1970s despite the later dates of publication). It appears that the working definition of theory is best met by the social science model (cognitive science as epistemology naturalized; e.g., Evans, Newstead, & Byrne, 1993). Let us start the analysis of our set of 10 plus 2 by using a theory that meets both of those characteristics, Leon Festinger's cognitive dissonance theory.

Cognitive Dissonance Theory

Festinger's theory (1957) is based on the relationship between cognitive elements that he calls knowledges. The character of the relationship establishes behavior demands within particular frames of activity. He is most concerned with decision making and the methods of dissonance reduction that follow when a decision is made.

His view of reality is that it is multiple, what he calls "physical," "social," and "psychological"—all of which are autonomous of the individual but directly readable by the individual (p. 10), although perceptual errors (recognizable and correctable) may occur. The realities of life are objective and our true knowledges of them are mirrors or maps of their conditions.

TABLE 9-1. Eighteen Theories Nominated by Three or More Theory Texts

Agenda Setting (DMQ; EG; SL, WSJT)*
McCombs, M. E., & Shaw, D. L. (1972). The agenda-setting function of mass media. *Public Opinion Quarterly,, 36,,* 176–187.

Cognitive Dissonance Theory (EG; IRW; SL; ST; WSJT)
Festinger, L. (1957). *A theory of cognitive dissonance.* Stanford, CA: Stanford University Press.

Communication Pragmatics (EG; ST; SL)
Watzlawick, P., Bavelas, J. B., & Jackson, D. D. (1967). *Pragmatics of human communication.* New York: W. W. Norton.

Constructivism (EG; SL; ST)
Delia, J. G., O'Keefe, B. J., & O'Keefe, D. J. (1982). The constructivist approach to communication. In F.E.X. Dance (Ed.), *Human communication theory: Comparative essays* (pp. 147–191). New York: Harper & Row.

Coordinated Management of Meaning (EG; ST; SL)
Pearce, W. B., & Cronen, V. (1980). *Communication, action, and meaning: The creation of social realities.* New York: Praeger.

Cultivation Analysis (DMQ; EG; SL; WSJT)
Gerbner, G., Gross, L., Morgan, M., & Signorielli, N. (1986). Living with television: The dynamics of the cultivation process. In J. Bryant & D. Zillmann (Eds.), *Perspectives on media effects* (pp. 17–40). Hillsdale, NJ: Erlbaum.

Diffusion of Innovations (DMQ; SL; IRW; WSJT)
Rogers, E. M. (1962). *Diffusion of innovations.* New York: Free Press.

Dramatism (EG; SL; ST)
Burke, K. (1968). Dramatism. In D. L. Sills (Ed.), *The international encyclopedia of the social sciences* (Vol. 7, pp. 445–451). New York: Macmillan.

Meaning (EG; SL; WSJT)
Richards, I. A. (1936). *The philosophy of rhetoric.* London: Oxford University Press.
Osgood, C. (1963). On understanding and creating sentences. *American Psychologist, 18,* 735–751.

Narrative Theory (EG; SL; ST)
Fisher, W. R. (1987). *Human communication as narration: Toward a philosophy of reason, value, and action.* Columbia: University of South Carolina Press.

Rhetorical Sensitivity Model (IRW; SL; ST)
Hart, R. P., & Burks, D. M. (1972). Rhetorical sensitivity and social interaction. *Speech Monographs, 39,* 75–91.

Social Judgment Theory (EG; IRW; SL; ST)
Sherif, M., & Hovland, C. I. (1961). *Social judgment.* New Haven, CT: Yale University Press.

Source Credibility (IRW; ST; WSJT)
Andersen, K., & Clevenger, T., Jr. (1963). A summary of experimental research in ethos. *Speech Monographs, 30,* 59–78.

(cont.)

TABLE 9-1. *(cont.)*

Speech Act Theory (IRW; SL; ST)
Searle, J. R. (1969). *Speech acts: An essay in the philosophy of language.* Cambridge, UK: Cambridge University Press.

Spiral of Silence (EG; DMQ; SL; WSJT)
Noelle-Neumann, E. (1991). The theory of public opinion: The concept of the spiral of silence. In J. A. Anderson (Ed.), *Communication yearbook* (Vol. 14, pp. 256–287). Newbury Park, CA: Sage.

Theory of Reasoned Action (IRW; ST; WSJT)
Ajzen, I., & Fishbein, M. (1970). The prediction of behavior from attitudinal and normative variables. *Journal of Experimental Social Psychology, 6,* 466–487.
Fishbein, M., & Ajzen, I. (1975). *Belief, attitude, intention, and behavior: An introduction to theory and research.* Reading, MA: Addison-Wesley.

Uncertainty Reduction Theory (EG; IRW; SL; ST)
Berger, C., & Calabrese, R. (1975). Some explorations in initial interaction and beyond: Toward a developmental theory of interpersonal communication. *Human Communication Research, 1,* 99–112.

Uses and Gratifications (DMQ; SL; WSJT)
Katz, E., Blumler, J., & Gurevitch, M. (1974). Uses of mass communication by the individual. In W. P. Davidson & F. Yu (Eds.), *Mass communication research* (pp. 11–35). New York: Praeger.

---

[*]Initials of authors of the theory texts listed in note 1.

The individual is the sum and the operation of her or his cognitive elements that are themselves the products of their experience with reality. In this attribute model, agency is excluded and the particular person plays no part in the explanation. The cognitive elements function transcendently, not subjectively.

In Festinger's theory, the form of argument is foundational justificationism. As such, it depends on an accessible phenomenal world and the trustworthiness of our experience of that world. That world and its experience is the axiomatic foundation from which all claim proceeds. The quality of the claim will be demonstrated in its rationality, that is, in its justification by means of the canons of logic.

Given the 1957 publication date of Festinger's book (which included work he did in the 1930s), we can expect dissonance theory to show an affinity to mathmaticized language as it appears in its practical form. Indeed, we do find mathematical-like statements such as "The maximum dissonance that can possibly exist between any two elements is equal to the total resistance to change of the less resistant element" (p. 28). Further, we would expect the character of the writing to be under the control of the American Psychological Association style manual, which Bazerman (1988) says "instrumentally realizes" the authority and voice of science (pp. 258–259).

Dissonance theory both derives from and in turn supports survey and experimental methodologies in quantitative research. Cognitive elements are causally related in reliable ways. They in turn are the determinants of observable behavior and provide the explanation for this behavior. Research protocols are invisible (see, e.g., p. 110) and respondents are ingenuous in their actions (see, e.g., p. 221). Cognitive elements are affected by messages from the environment, of which others and the media are a part. Those messages encode their literal meanings and are normatively decoded in the same manner. The "subjects" of Festinger's research were inside a determinant relationship between message and response.

The value component in dissonance theory is located in the true. There is no social program to be advanced (other than science itself). Festinger does offer a few pages of "know thyself" commentary on what dissonance theory means in the lives we lead (see, e.g., pp. 271–275). On the whole, however, he maintains the "science" and "technology" distinction of is and ought.

Dissonance theory is not of the world it describes. We know nothing of how dissonance in Festinger's own thinking influenced the theory of its name. Festinger as a scientist is somehow out of himself, motivated to a different plane of being in the world. Other decision making may be explained by dissonance theory but not his own in the role of scientist.

Uncertainty Reduction Theory

Berger and Calabrese's (1975) uncertainty reduction theory creates a very rational structure to explain interaction behavior between strangers who are entering a relationship by positing a common drive—"uncertainty reduction"—that directs the performances of such relationship members. Moved by the need to reduce uncertainty between them, the relationship members work to develop a predictable pattern of information exchange.

Uncertainty reduction theory falls within the same paradigmatic framework as dissonance theory (although it reports pretensions beyond consistency theories; see, e.g., p. 107). Thus, it is marked by the material criterion and its complement in scientific realism, as well as by determinism, reductionism, the attribute model, the absence of agency, foundational empiricism and formal logic underlying the social science genre of writing, and an expected silence on questions of value.

Rhetorical Sensitivity Model

The same issue of the character of communication in relationships is taken up by Roderick Hart and Don Burks (1972), but here within the symbolic interactionist framework and within rhetorical colorations. Symbolic interactionism and rhetoric drive a contingent, adaptive formulation for relationships and communication, respectively. Uncertainty theory is described in terms of axioms and theorems of causal relationships among variables, while rhetorical sensitivity is posited as a set of rules, maxims, and guidelines for the acting agents of the relationship.

Both uncertainty theory and rhetorical sensitivity theory are true to their respective paradigmatic frames. A side-by-side comparison shows the inherent difficulties of effecting a meaningful reconciliation of their differences. The theories operate within different epistemic frames.

For example, the concept of uncertainty is central to both theories. In uncertainty reduction theory, the presence of uncertainty is a signal for the production of specific behaviors to effect its reduction. In rhetorical sensitivity theory, uncertainty is a necessary condition of multiple selves in relational engagements and is something to be encouraged if appropriate to relational success (see, e.g., p. 87).

Uncertainty reduction theory sees uncertainty as an autonomous determinant of behavior. Rhetorical sensitivity theory sees uncertainty as a condition that can be manipulated by the acting agent.

Even the place of publication of these two works is instructive concerning the differences they entail. The paper on rhetorical sensitivity theory was published in what was then the "science sheet" of the Speech Association of America. The paper on uncertainty reduction theory appeared in the first volume of *Human Communication Research* (*HCR*), a publication of the International Communication Association, a group that broke away from the Speech Communication Association to pursue its members' interests in science and industry. *HCR* is known as a preeminent "social science" journal, and the axiom–theorem style of Berger and Calabrese would be far more attractive to its editorial decision makers than the essay of Hart and Burks.[7] This is not to say that both sets of authors were not perfectly capable of adopting their style to either journal. It is to say that a style, once adopted, participates in the meaningful expression of one's claim.

The symbolic interactionist foundation of rhetorical sensitivity theory leads to a rejection (or at least a diminution) of determinism and the attribute model. Human behavior with its characteristic cognitive determinants becomes social action with its characteristic meanings-in-place. Agency, invention, and even immanence appear.

The acting rhetor of Hart and Burks's argument expects to "make a difference" through the selection of communication strategies in relationships (p. 82). Making a difference through choice entails the evaluation of the difference made under the rubric of ethical choice. The rhetor is responsible for the choice made (i.e., that choice is not determined by some irresistible cognitive state). Rhetorical sensitivity, consequently, must open directly the moral question (which it does only to defer it; see footnote 15 on p. 82).

Neither uncertainty reduction theory nor rhetorical sensitivity theory provide the basis for investigating their background assumptions. It is, however, these very background assumptions that provide for the internal success of the arguments advanced and which make it impossible to reconcile the two positions. These different foundations not only create the bases for necessarily different theories, they also create the bases for different scholarly lives to be lived. Berger and Calabrese have no responsibility for consequences, Hart and Burks do.

Constructivism

The authors of constructivism theory, Delia, O'Keefe, and O'Keefe (1982) hold that humans are first of all biological entities who must engage the phenomenal world through an interpretive process that involves the formation of cognitive constructs (hence the name "contruct*ivism,*" which is not to be confused with "construct*ionism*"). Simultaneously, however, humans are also situated in an ongoing cultural milieu that provides the places and methods of construct formation and strategic use (pp. 151–155).

In practice the multiple realities posited in this theory differ little from the "physical, social, and psychological" realities of Festinger's theory. The cultural and cognitive realities of constructivism are independent and autonomous of the explanations constructivism produces from them. These realities can consequently be objectively studied and described. Strong evidence for my claim comes from the authors' interest in triangulation (p. 181) and the study of "phenomena under diverse conditions" (p. 182).

The engagement of reality is made through the strategic activation of culturally derived constructs. According to the authors, one's science and the study of phenomena are not "wholly independent of the interpretive frameworks employed" (p. 167). But apparently they are independent enough, for the analyst still occupies a place of privilege to speak authoritatively on the constructs and strategies of other people. Delia and the O'Keefes call for a self-awareness "while recognizing the necessity for commitment to particular points of view and methods to learn anything about the empirical world" (p. 167).

The constructivist model of the individual is deeply indebted to the model of the attribute individual. Constructs have a transcendental quality ("as opposed to [being] idiosyncratic"; p. 154) that presumably arises from the stability of socialization practices. But the constructivist model is something more than attributes, for the theory holds itself responsible for explaining the operation of those attributes in common settings. There is no agency present in this model. Strategies are tacit, unconsciously applied. The constructivist model overlaps the border of the conjunctive model and shares some ideas with symbolic interactionism; it can also be linked to the situated model, and even to cultural determinism.

Constructivists are not constructionists. They are solidly on the "essence precedes existence" side of the line, although the essence involved is both biological and cultural. Their explanatory responsibilities are to the categories, contrasts, and strategies that inhabit communication practices. Their formal argument is foundational empiricism and their practical frame is the social science genre.

Their dedication to the requirements of this genre shows itself in what they consider to be radical about themselves (p. 172). They offer a lengthy apology for their use of "free response" measures, pointing out that they also use psychometrics when appropriate. (The purpose of free response data is to ingenuously reveal the natural structures of belief and behavior.) The source of their concern seems to be the epithet of "introspection" (p. 174) and the shades of Wilhelm Wundt. American psychometricians have firmly stood against Wundt's introspective psychology and Weber's *Verstehen*, which they view as violations of the material reality criterion. In the early 1980s, the epithet was a risk of disqualification.

Finally, the reflexivity of constructivism is not meant to advance some social program but rather to improve the practice of social science. The demarcation between ontology and axiology does not appear to be in any way threatened. At least the issue is not addressed in this reference article.

Coordinated Management of Meaning Theory

Barnett Pearce and Vernon Cronen report in *Communication, Action, and Meaning* (1980) that they were raised as scholars in the cognitive tradition of Festinger (p. 9). They go on to say that they have broken with that tradition to embrace the arguments of social action theory.

Specifically, Pearce and Cronen reject the view of an autonomous reality that scholarship seeks to describe to replay (without locating it there) the pragmatic arguments of James. They argue that human reality is the product of the interaction of human activity with the phenomenal world. There is no final truth or any finished facts to be found within this reality (see, e.g., p. 111). Rather, theory will participate in the process of its own construction as both a living and a dead metaphor (see, e.g., p. 116).

Theory is also a product of the process, as are several other structures that concomitantly influence the meaning making of individuals (see, e.g., p. 131). Pearce and Cronen's theory, however, does not "sit above" the "natural" structures of human concourse but is actually one more of them. Theory is *in* the world and must account for its place there.

One's engagement of this reality whether as an elite theorist or as an "innocent civilian" is directed by what one believes to be true. This belief is not without discipline, for the phenomenal world is equally a player in the drama of reality and may "object" to one's actions. At the same time, that discipline is equivocal because it permits more than one reality construction around it. Reality is itself multiple, as is our understanding of it (see, e.g., p. 122).

The coordinated management of meaning (CMM) makes use of the metaphor of "undirected play." Within this metaphor it positions the individual as an element in a system of interpersonal relationships (see, e.g., p. 148). Pearce and Cronen have moved away from the attribute model and toward the situated model of the individual, although they never quite abandon the explanations the attribute model provides them in their focus on systems of rules. They do abandon the position of literal meaning that cognitivism necessitates, arguing instead for an interpretive line.

By granting the phenomenal world the capacity to object to the descriptions we provide, Pearce and Cronen remain true to their scholarly roots as foundational empiricists. They are logocentric in their justifications. Their book is not a play, a poem, or a mystery but instead a reasoned argument of why we should believe what they believe. Given their place in time and the sites they chose in which to advance their argument—mainline journals and major communication conventions—they had little choice.

Pearce and Cronen adopt the principles of programmatic methodism as the means by which they will maintain their status as scientists. They introduce their chapter on their research findings with the purpose of demonstrating "that it is possible to do rigorous research consistent with our theory" (p. 231). The authors go on to present studies that have the obvious "look and feel" of the traditional social science they explicitly reject. The desire to show that they can play in the major leagues produces an interesting counterpoint in argument that submerges the more radical elements of their theory. This is a case in which the conventions of method control the claims that can be advanced. The prior encodings of the hypothetic-deductive methods the authors used remain as resources of contradiction and irony.

Pearce and Cronen are nonetheless true to their theory's demand that knowledge is action and that action entails an ethical stance. Their theory has implications for what ought to be, and the authors do take up their obligation of making these implications explicit. In their final chapter they describe the characteristics of healthy individuals and healthy societies and obviously understand that by providing such descriptions they produce some of the resources by which the reality of those descriptions can be constructed.

Although less than enthusiastic about its situation in spots, CMM is firmly in the world it describes. It is a tool and a product of the realities we construct. Its advocates are politically implicated in advancing its validity and ethically responsible for the consequences of that effort.

Narrative Theory

Walter Fisher (1987) presents his form of narrative theory as a logic of rationality that is not limited to the technical discourse of the logicians. In his theory of knowledge, the well-formed story, marked by coherence and fidelity, is the proper basis for action (see, e.g., p. 90).

Fisher's conception of reality is multiple. We live in domains of objects and agents, phenomena and discourses. Echoing Popper's arguments, Fisher argues that discourse transcends and governs the empirical in our understanding of reality. We engage, transform, and construct our acting reality in the form of stories—narratives developed in the ongoing conversations into which we are all born. There are no stand-alone, meaningful facts per se; instead, facts come into our existence as elements of narrative (see, e.g., p. 108). Facts are not literal but situational. Fisher is a hermeneuticist who recognizes the empirical as one more resource for a good story.

He is also a foundationalist, but his foundation is in the narrative a priori's of intelligence (all intelligence, he suggests), not in the trustworthy engagement of an independent physical reality. Humanity arises in the ability to formulate and recognize narratives that produce the good reasons for action (see, e.g., p. xiii). The individual is a structured intellect situated in a historic field of discourse. There, she is not only the acting agent of her culture but the willing agent of her own intentions.

The "knowledge" of Fisher's theory is a Kantian synthetic, and therefore foundationalist. It is situated on both an innate narrative ability and experience in the world (see, e.g., p. 59). It is also justificationist in that it depends on a particular structure (narrative coherence) for its force. And it appeals to conventionalism as well, imbuing good reasons with relevance, consistency, and consequence (see, e.g., p. 111).

The practical argument that Fisher crafts in his book looks suspiciously like a traditional logocentric one. But then traditional arguments have been redefined as narratives themselves (see, e.g., p. 98). They are now subject to the same rules of judgment as any other form of argument.

Narrative theory presents a preeminently ethical stance. It proposes that knowledge is the production of good reasons for carrying out proper actions. The knowing subject is in command of both the good reasons and the actions to be performed. While narrative is transcendent, knowledge is historical, located in the proper actions in the life world (see, e.g., p. 136). There is no bloodless scholarship.

For Fisher, knowledge and our scholarly pursuit of it should be motivated by love. He states that "love provides the ground of being and is the motive which should inform all others in human decision making and action" (p. 136). Thus knowledge is in the service of the good and the good rests on love.

The scholar who generates facts in the narratives of science plays an important, necessary, but lesser role in the concourse of humanity. That scholar is no less ethically implicated in the narratives he or she produces. The stories of science must motivate proper action. But the present narrative form of science is incomplete (see, e.g., p. 20). It must be incorporated in other stories that recognize their rhetorical character (see, e.g., p. 9).

Cultivation Analysis

George Gerbner has often expressed his belief that whoever controls the stories the world tells, controls the world. It is this belief that is the foundation of cultivation analysis (CA). CA (Gerbner, Gross, Morgan, & Signorielli, 1986) holds that television is an industrialized, central, storytelling system that provides the main socialization processes for a "shared national culture" (p. 18).

The "stories" of cultivation analysis are not the same as the "narratives" of narrative theory, however. Gerbner, et al. pose no overarching logic of narrative. The stories of television are, in fact, a foil, a screen that hides the true face of reality. Cultivation analysis gets its "energy of concern" from its position that the stories of television intercede in our engagement of reality and create a "false picture" of what is real (p. 26).

Cultivation analysis is dependent on an authentic reality addressable by those (whom Gerbner has called the "liberally educated") who can recognize and resist the television ideology. That recognition and resistance is apparently difficult to achieve, so much so that the "research community" is properly "concerned" about television's easy seduction of the masses (p. 17). The proper engagement of reality is an unlikely characteristic of the mass of U.S. citizens. There are strong echoes of critical theory, German rationalism, and Marxist false consciousness in this position.

This position offers the clear view of the conjunctive model of the individual at work. The individual is the site of the materialization of the influence of television's stories. Television is a cultural lever that moves us to a common, albeit distorted, set of beliefs. Resisting television's power to shape reality requires special training and effort.

Cultivation analysis has motivated a long-running research program documenting the components of content (e.g., acts of violence; see p. 26). This research makes its strongest claim via the concepts of encoded meaning and content as the delivery system. The concepts of polysemy and audience interpretation (resistance, opposition) would substantially weaken the value of this content analysis and the power of the analyst.

The argument form is foundational empiricism. Its practical expression makes use of the conventions of content and survey analysis in a standard usage of the social science genre. The practical arguments of cultivation analysis are inextricably bound to the circumstances of the lead author—a powerful dean of a prestigious school who was the editor of an international journal within the field. Those circumstances have been a point of pride (p. 18) for the authors and of envy for others. A sociological appraisal of the presence of cultivation analysis would undoubtedly take those circumstances into account.[8]

The Marxist/critical theory shadings of cultivation analysis detail it as more than an epistemic effort. It offers a double-pronged public policy program to reform both the media and the audience (see, e.g., p. 38). The arguments and the personal testimony of the authors have been used in congressional probes into television violence and government reports (Gerbner, Morgan, & Signorielli, 1982), as well as by the popular press. These efforts have been the manifestation of the "expert in society" (Morgan & Gerbner, 1982) in command of special knowledge arguing for particular actions.

Uses and Gratifications

If cultivation analysis posits the audience as the unwitting materialization of television's stories, uses and gratifications theory (Katz, Blumler, & Gurevitch, 1974) takes the opposite tack, posing the audience as actively engaging content in goal-directed activities (p. 21). Uses and gratifications theory argues for the preexistence of needs and intentions that direct media attendance toward gratifications and uses, respectively.

Socialization processes (of which interaction with the media is one) lead to the formation of needs and intentions (a functionalist form of cognitivism), and the industrial practices of the media (of which feedback from the audience is one) provide utilities within content forms. The uses and gratifications project is to detail the origins and structure of needs and intentions, which implicate media, and the practices and genre of media, which implicate the audience (see, e.g., p. 20).

As with most theories, uses and gratifications owes more to derivation than to invention: it is an intelligent splice of psychological motivations and sociological functions. Uses and gratifications theorists have been mostly silent about their assumptions, but the outlines of objectivism are nonetheless clear. Materialism, reductionism, and determinism, as well as foundational empiricism and the social science genre, are all firmly in place.

While scientific realism remains operational, literal meaning has been undermined. The authors quote Rosengren and Windahl (1972) to note "a growing consensus that almost any type of content may serve practically any type of function" (p. 27). Three pages later this comment is repudiated as an "overgeneralization," and necessarily so. There is no predictive value in an "any–any" relationship and the "science" of uses and gratifications would be endangered if that claim remained in place.

Katz, Blumler, and Gurevitch signal the traditional distinction between knowledge and value while commenting on an "application" of the theory to policy questions. On the other hand, their phrase "producers of junk" (p. 30) and the general difficulty they display regarding the "pleasure" provided by the media world reveal the Calvinistic underpinnings of their argument.

Agenda Setting

Thanks to their well-designed study Maxwell McCombs and Donald Shaw (1972) have garnered the credit for the notion of the agenda-setting function of the media. They trace the formulation back some 20 years[9]; indeed, the phrase most often used to sum up the theory ("The media don't tell people what to think, they tell the people what to think about.") was written by Bernard Cohen in 1963. It is an exemplar case of attribution without invention (albeit not without justification) and another reason for the sociological study of our science.

In the 11-page article, the authors spend less than two pages on the formulation of the theory itself. Consequently, we have very little direct evidence from which to draw our analysis. But what we do have is very interesting.

By using the word "function" in their title, the authors connect their work to the structural-functionalist school of sociology and invoke the "functions of the media" of Lasswell (1927) and Wright (1965), although they reference neither. Given the date of publication, we are nonetheless immediately connected to these writings by the title.

McCombs and Shaw begin their article by warning us about the second-handedness that now characterizes the knowledge of our voting public (p. 176). Their opening sentence captures both a nostalgia for a past that never existed (when "voters-to-a-man"[10] met the candidate in person) and a naturalized expression of the primacy of direct experience. The sentence appears to be part of the intellectual's love–hate relationship with the media.

The other sentence that lays open most of the assumptions of the study occurs in the authors' recommendations for further study, which include "matching individual attitudes with individual use of the mass media" (p. 185). This is a statement of methodological individualism that would hold that sociological functions must be discovered in the actions of the individual rather than in some "in-between" of relationships. It also displays the cognitivism of attitude formation and hints at a direct effect of media use on these attitudes.

Content is treated as literal in that topic classifications of both the media fare and respondents' answers are considered a coding issue rendered unproblematic by high intercoder reliabilities (p. 178). The attribute model of the individual is revealed in the discussion on the "salience of affect" and its consequence—rather than some choice action—on media use (pp. 186–187). And finally, although the article begins with a value-laden warning (used rhetorically to establish the significance of the study), it ends with a call for better science leading to better knowledge as appropriate to the epistemics-only conventions of social science writing.

Spiral of Silence

Elisabeth Noelle-Neumann (1991) offers us a lifetime of work in her formulation of the spiral of silence theory. Noelle-Neumann explicitly focuses on the social character of human life, in ways rejecting (p. 257), but also affirming (p. 260), the methodological individualism of McCombs and Shaw. The spiral of silence seeks to explain the reluctance of the populace to express minority opinions which reinforces the appearance of *a public* opinion on some topic. That reluctance arises, according to the theory, from our social nature, in this case enforced by an inherent fear of isolation (i.e., being severed from the social body).

The theory invests the individual with a "quasi-statistical" sense that allows him or her to evaluate the location of group opinions and to test the risks of opposition. The greater the risks (of isolation), the less likely the individual will be to defy group opinion, and so we spiral into silence. Assuming a group with several factions, the one that can give the appearance of dominance effectively silences all the others, thereby establishing its position as *the* opinion of the group. It is, of course, not the opinion of the group, but it is the *public* opinion of the group. And in democratic societies, it is public opinion that drives decision making.

It is this line of reasoning that establishes the significance of the theory: public opinion is the engine of democracy, and public opinion is formed not through agreement but through fear of the consequences of disagreement.

An analysis of assumptions follows along a cognitivist/objectivist route: Social realities are functionally equivalent to material realities, and our engagement of either is trustworthy. The individual is a social animal governed by the need for social cohesion and the fear of isolation. Proper argument is empirical and explicitly technical (p. 261); common sense is not enough.

The practical expression of this argument in the *Yearbook* article is worth its own comment. That article is garrulous, defensive, didactic, and familiar in tone. It is, in part, written in a feminine, storytelling voice. The commentaries that follow (Csikszentmihalyi, 1991; Moscovici, 1991) are more masculine, granting, nearly patronizing, before moving on to "larger issues" (p. 289; p. 299). That the authors are female and male is less important than the naturalized expression of traditional gender which the articles appear to represent.

Each of the set of articles ends with a more or less ringing affirmation of the importance of the issues before us, but their voices are restrained from telling us how to run our governments or manage our own opinions lest they overstep their authority.

Structuration and Social Theory

Anthony Giddens's rich outpouring of work (Conrad, 1993, counts 14 major works in 15 years) can be seen as part of a worldwide rediscovery of action as the foundation of human life.[11] This rediscovery (see Giddens, 1979) involves a rejiggering of the priorities of existence and essence in theory and the consequent reinvention of agency (the capacity of the individual to do otherwise or to make a difference). Along with structuration, we find radical hermeneutics, the later forms of cultural studies, and social action theory opposing the more or less fixed determinism of Marxism, American functionalism, behaviorism, cognitivism, and the sociobiological approaches—all of which hold to the primacy of essence to existence.

Giddens (1979) sets before him the project of explicating social life, the memberships, organizations, and institution that we recognize as society. He places himself squarely in the semiotic domain by collapsing the distinction between the object of knowledge and the knowing subject (p. 251), by denying the unity of science (p. 258), and by insisting that structural reality is both "medium and product" of human accomplishment (p. 5).

The reality targeted by Giddens is an ongoing achievement originating in the intersection of time (durée), space (locale), and action (practice) (see, e.g., p. 54). The engagement of this reality is within both "the practical consciousness" of action and the "discursive consciousness" of language, which coupled with a Lacanian unconscious constitutes the subject (see, e.g., p. 25).

This subject is more than a conjunctive site, however, being an active agent in the social systems in which it resides. The individual is both situated within structure and is an activator of structure. There is a mutual dependence between structure and agency (see, e.g., p. 69) that echoes the interactionist argument of reality as the interrelationship between deterministic forms and practical action (James, 1912/1943).

Giddens argument is a resonance, what Banks and Riley (1993) call a *grande idée*. He offers no empirical evidence but instead uses an eclectic set of premises to set aside the arguments of others to offer hope to the disaffective. His is a powerful, rhetorical effort.

In his 1979 argument Giddens fails to make the move that both radical hermeneutics and social action theory make in placing science as a player in the knowledge game. Instead, Giddens opts for a special status, called "mutual knowledge," which is separate from an authentic but nonetheless a lesser common sense (p. 251). Further, science can still deliver "objectively valid knowledge" independent of the ideology in which it may be entangled (p. 181). Science in some way stands outside his own theory.

The ethical stance of Giddens's foundational writing is in at least two different places. In one location, we find a theory of social change that insists on choice by positing "avoidable possible worlds" (p. 230). And in another location we have a strangely disembodied science recording the scene. This fracture does not survive in Giddens's theory (see Giddens, 1990), but it is a good example of the limits of the practical argument as structuration theory would describe it.

Social Action Theory

The final theory of our 10 plus 2 review takes us to the conclusion of the social construction of reality where action is the basis of essence and science is a privileged but in-no-way unique player in the knowledge-production game.

Observation is oblique, at the margins of perception. Claim, comment, and critique come from authorized and exnominated positions.

Social action theory has roots and affinities with pragmatism, existentialism, Peircean semiotics, symbolic interactionism, and language philosophy, as well as with nearly any line of thought that documents the struggle of human life. Gerard Schoening (1992) has formulated six principles (here adapted from Schoening & Anderson, 1995) that speak fairly well to the tests of our analysis. They are:

1. The "meaningful world" (i.e., "reality") must both be produced and maintained in consciousness. Correspondingly, the *meaning* of reality has no autonomous existence and must be brought into being in deliberate ways.

2. The engagement of this reality emerges through the performance of identifiable lines of action that signify "what is being done." As such, any material fact will always be made "real" in conjunction with some known and knowable activity.

3. All lines of action are dialogic and improvisationally enacted by local agents as partial expressions of a collectively held semiotic of action.

4. The "decoding activities" produced by signifying lines of action shift as those lines are reinterpreted and performed in different routines (in the same way that a sentence changes its interpretive power by its position within a paragraph). As such, the meaning potentials for both content and interpretive practices remain open-ended.

5. "Knowledge" is made concrete in signifying practices and is thus necessarily relative to, and contingent upon, the here-and-now performance characteristics of a given social collective's routine. Any domain of knowledge is a cultural production, reproduced in local settings.

6. The social scientist has an ethical obligation to contribute understanding about social practices to the social worlds investigated. The social action researcher is therefore obligated to inform social groups about the potentials and consequences of their reality-construction practices.

The first four principles of social action theory follow closely the line of argument developed in structuration theory. There are separate domains of reality. Human life is made meaningful in the semiotic domain through collective accomplishment. The human individual is activated by and an activator of meaning. Structuration makes use of a reconstituted structuralism to deal with the extension of action into essentializing frameworks. Social action works a solution to the same problem through a semiotics of action.

Both structuration and social action theory emphasize the local nature of human action. They would appear to be most congenial with empirical methodologies that are locale-sensitive, such as the various ethnographic methodologies.

There is a necessary break in the justified argument from foundational empiricism. Facts are no longer verifications but necessary resources of knowledge production. Justified arguments cannot be produced without them, but there is no final resolution of them. Practical argument forms for both structuration and social action theory are evolving (see Banks & Riley, 1993, and Anderson, in press, for respective discussion and examples).

It is with the issues of knowledge onward that the substantial differences between structuration and social action theory can be seen. Social action theory places science clearly inside the practices it wishes to explain. Knowledge is produced in instrumental action and is the intentional reproduction of that action. To say that $E = MC^2$ is knowledge is to invoke the social action practices by which $E = MC^2$ is made meaningful as knowledge.

Finally, social action theory confronts the ethical question directly and accepts the burden of the responsibilities for creating knowledge about ourselves and for the consequences of that knowledge.

Conclusions

In this analysis, we have looked at twenty (18 from the theory books plus 2 new ones) different theories that have a distinctive presence in communication. These theories appear to distribute themselves over three centers: cognitive/functional, actional, and discursive.

Cognitivist/functionalist theories hold to some prior state, need, motive, or mental structure that initiates and directs behavior. Essence therefore precedes existence. Both forms of theory tend toward methodological individualism. The distinction between them is that the former is more psychological in orientation and the latter is more sociological.

Actional theories find essence in existence and the motives of action in the action itself. They may be directed by methodological individualism—as are most forms of symbolic interactionism—or they may find their explanations in collective relationships—as do structuration and social action theory.

Discursive theories are centered on the texts and discourses of society. They are directed by the reality principle of language. They are much more oriented toward the cultural collective than the individual.

Figure 9–1 places our 20 theories plus an amalgam called cultural studies (21 theories in all) in relation to these centers and each other. The table treats cognitivism/functionalism as ground zero, the point from which all others are seen, which I think accurately describes the state of communication theory. The coordinates that follow the theory names indicate the distance from ground zero (if any), first in the actional direction and then in the discursive direction.

Those coordinates represent increasing values of incommensurability. The

	0	1	2	3
0	Agenda setting 0,0 Dissonance theory 0,0 Social judgment theory 0,0 Source credibility 0,0 Uncertainty reduction theory 0,0	Diffusion of innovations +1, 0 Theory of reasoned action +1, 0 Uses and gratifications +1,0		
1	Cultivation analysis 0, +1 Meaning 0, +1	Communication pragmatics +1, +1 Spiral of silence +1, +1	Constructivism +1.5, +1	Social action +3, +1 Structuration +3, +1
2			Coordinated management of meaning +2, +1.5 Dramatism +2, +2 Rhetorical sensitivity +2, +2	
3	Narrative theory 0, +3			

Cultural studies 0, +3; +1, +3; +2, +3

The first coordinate values describes the left-to-right position (cognitive [0] to actional [+3]); the second the top-to-bottom position (cognitive/actional [0] to discursive [+3]). The center lines are drawn in at the midpoint (1.5,1.5) of this space.

FIGURE 9–1. A relational analysis of 21 theories.

greater the difference of these values between theories, the less capable we are of providing a comparison across the terms internal to the theories. For example, we can certainly debate whether the drive for the reduction of dissonance and the drive for the reduction of uncertainty are one and the same motive for cognitive consistency. Both theories spring from the same background assumptions and both reside within the same epistemic domain. Therefore, they are axiomatically similar and share the same factual field to which they are both responsible.

On the other hand, to debate the dimensions of ethos from source credibility against the power dimensions of the authorization resources of structuration is to argue across both axiomatic domains and factual fields. The only way that comparison can be made is to establish covertly one set of background assumptions and epistemic standards, which necessarily privileges one of the theories, as the comparative foundation. That covert action is not unusual. The common practice of theory texts to provide some paragraphs of criticism and critique covering widely disparate frames of theory is an example. That sort of writing is the unrevealed author speaking to us from some sacred location.

The comparison of theories that spring from different epistemic domains cannot be honestly done on a propositional basis, sentence by sentence. That comparison has to be conducted at the level of the community of practice. What is the program of research that is supported by this theory? What do the advocates of a given theory do? What life do they live? What consequences redound?

BEYOND THIS TEXT

The criticism and critique of theories from different epistemic domains cannot be carried on at the level of claim and terms. It has to be carried on at the level of priors. It has been the effort of this book to provide a framework for that analysis and the work of this chapter to provide some examples.

What remains is for the reader to draw the implications for action. What might I as the author hope? I would hope for an end to the epistemic provincialism to which we condemn our apprentices through techniques of curriculum and training. An early emancipation from the canonical textbooks that do the work of induction and a speedy enlightenment into the political processes by which forms of knowledge gain ascendance would seem to be the first orders of business.

One part of the sociopolitical processes of graduate education that should be thoroughly disclosed is the apprentice economy that characterizes many programs. Students are often programmed to accept a particular way of thinking by a system of assignments and then systematically discouraged from examining other viewpoints or competing epistemologies. The payoff is a collection of junior colleagues compliantly enthusiastic about the same ideas.

It certainly seems true that in this postmodern era of difference we need to know the difference the differences make. Taking a stance and making a commitment are no less necessary now to have something to profess, but the taking and making ought not to be the naturalized consequences of our training. These decisions are the resolutions of individual resources to the common good and should be widely informed.

Lynn Nelson concludes her fine book *Who Knows*, by declaring that the Cartesian covenant is dead. That covenant granted a veil of protectionism to the domain of science by proclaiming the separation of the true and the good, knowledge and value. Such a Humean separation can stand only if knowledge has no consequence, has no implication for action. This sort of knowledge can exist only as an object completely independent of the knowing subject.

No analytical system now makes that claim. It is generally accepted that all scholarship—including science—is implicated in action, and therefore in questions of value.[12] For good reasons, we scientists have nonetheless been reluctant to give up the privilege of remaining beyond political scrutiny. The growing critique of scholarship, including the sacred of science, as well as the continued legislative and endowment pressures on the academy, suggest that the artifice is apparent. We need to face up to our persistent and necessary advocacy and turn that advocacy to face its questioners.

There will be a mutual benefit in this move. There is no question that our scholarship can inform the values that circulate in society. Similarly, scholarship is enhanced by the careful, reflexive study of its own multilayered value structure.

Finally, the recognition that the truth value of any claim is in its character as a platform for action centers the instrumentality of scholarship as its evaluative criterion. Some care must be taken in drawing the implications of this claim. To begin with, knowledge disappears when it is not performed. And, too, the value of that performance is not always immediately apparent. Consequently, the argument that we should not do this or that scholarship or that we have too much of this or that kind of work has a powerful potential.

Nonetheless, we cannot avoid the issue by lofty appeals, the pretense of the "archive," or misapplication of collegiality. We need to carefully and consistently consider what we are about and those about us. The ultimate question in the evaluation of any theory is What can I do with it? The answer of advancement in the academy or the pleasure of an elite should not be enough.

NOTES

1. The texts were:
    Griffin, E. (1994). *A first look at communication theory* (2nd ed.). New York: McGraw-Hill.
    Infante, D. A., Rancer, A. S., & Womack, D. F. (1990). *Building communication theory.* Prospect Heights, IL: Waveland Press.
    Jablin, F. M., Putnam, L. L., Roberts, K. H., & Porter, L. W. (1987). *Handbook of organizational communication.* Newbury Park, CA: Sage.
    Littlejohn, S. W. (1992). *Theories of human communication* (4th ed.). Belmont, CA: Wadsworth.
    McQuail, D. (1987). *Mass communication theory* (2nd ed.). Newbury Park, CA: Sage.
    Severin, W. J., & Tankard, J. W., Jr. (1992). *Communication theories: Origins, methods, and uses in the mass media.* (3rd ed.). New York: Longman.
    Trenholm, S. (1991). *Human communication theory.* (2nd ed.). Englewood Cliffs, NJ: Prentice-Hall.

2. I don't exclude the possibility of some "effect of the subject" here. As with all textual materials, judgments had to be made to apply even this simple interpretive rule. While I have no doubt that a team of raters would come to (create) the same principle facts, the numbers might be different.

3. The large number is interesting given Berger's (1991) claim of the paucity of theories in communication.

4. This is not unusual to communication and is not one more reason for doubt about our own worthiness. My experience with psychology, sociology, and anthropology would suggest that we would find much the same there. Although "theory books" have been in production for a longer time in psychology and sociology—leading to a greater expectation of conventionalization—there are more of them—allowing for more diversity. Further, the lack of agreement within the field of communication theory is precisely what the sociological conditions of the human sciences would predict, and what a hermeneuticist would expect.

5. The 10 selected cover the range of differences rather nicely without repetition. For reasons of textual economy, I will analyze only the work cited rather than the community of work that a theory should imply. This choice can motivate two misconception which I have directed this footnote to resist: first, that a theory belongs to its nominal inventor, and second, that a theory is consistent with a single set of arguments. I continue to argue that a theory is an epistemic community of action, not a text or set of propositions, and that such a community while able to distinguish itself from others need not show high internal consistency.

6. Some disclaimers are in order: Fields of study or domains of theory development such as semiotics or ethnography or cognitivism or symbolic interactionism are not included as separate theories. There was no agreement on many of the names used for the nominated theories. I used the citation as the basis of similarity and either used one of the text names or constructed one from those used by the texts. There is more than one citation when it was clear that the authors were talking about the same "theory" but referenced it differently. Finally, the recognition by three of more authors attaches no special epistemological status to these 18 theories.

7. *Speech Monographs* has traditionally been known as the science journal of SCA, but it never held to the tight focus that is used to describe *HCR*.

8. The difficulty in these sentences is that they imply more than what is wanted to be said. The myth of science is that ideas rise or fail on their epistemic merits. It is this myth that the sociology of science expressly denies. No idea survives without sociopolitical work on its behalf. Gerbner's circumstances are simply public knowledge and others are not.

9. Rogers and Dearing (1988) trace it back to the early 1920s in the works of Lippmann and Park.

10. This past was undoubtedly before women's suffrage.

11. Steven Banks and Patricia Riley (1993), whose review informs my own, recommend the reading of Giddens, 1979, 1981, 1984, 1985, 1987, 1989, and 1990 for a thorough presentation of the theory. Following my preference, I will stick to the foundational 1979 work.

12. This sentence is a good example of Latour's (1987) "5th step in the creation of knowledge where the claim is made as fact absent any signalling modalities."

Glossary

Accuracy: in traditional empiricism, the measure of fit between an entity and its representation

Agency: the character of acting/doing that invests choice in the action

Agent: one who acts or is the determinant of a result

Agentry: the notion that action always represents some ideological interest; the actor is an agent of those interests

Aggregates: collections of elements in a study

Ahistoricity: the requirement that argument must transcend time and place

Appropriation: the use of any theory or concept from one domain to advance a particular claim in another

Archimedean Point: the true, objective point form which all other arguments can be addressed

Authentication: conferring legitimacy, declaring the real, granting significance

Authorial Intent: a privileged point in interpretation against which the proposed interpretation must be measured

Autonomy: independence of judgment

Authority: the collectively granted right of an author to advance claim credibly

Axiology: the study of value

Behaviorism: an approach to the social sciences that stresses the empirical analysis of the behavior of individuals

Berkeleyism: the doctrine developed by Irish philosopher George Berkeley (1685–1753) that holds that physical objects exist only through mental perception

Bounded Theoretical Frames: knowledge frameworks which support conventionalized theories

Brute Sense Data: that of the phenomenal world which directly impresses itself upon us

Causality: both a relationship and a form of explanation in which the character or

223

course of one phenomenon is held to be the result of the character or course of another phenomenon

Choice: the ability to do otherwise

Cognitivism: the mainstream of modernist psychology emphasizing the analysis of the individual's mental structures, as the repository of culture and society and as the determinants of behavior

Conferred Status: a truth-value or definition given by the collective

Contemporary Empiricism: a form of empiricism that "relaxes" the rule of independence between theory and observation

Conventionalism: the theory that a claim is judged on the basis of conventions of validity that have been determined collectively

Conventionalized Methods: the methods in any given knowledge community that are taken to be the standard and proper approaches to research and analysis

Correspondence Theory: the theory that a proposition is true only to the extent that it corresponds to the facts of the phenomenal world

Deconstructionism: an approach to knowledge that rejects notions of material realism and literal meaning and holds that there is no privileged point from which to advance claim

Demarcationism: the effort to define a line separating genuine science (thought of in terms of evidence and experiment) from other realms of inquiry

Determinacy: the state or quality of being determinant

Determinant: a thing or factor that determines

Determinism: the doctrine that any phenomenon exists in causal relationships that provide their form, structure, and action; the belief that al phenomena are both the result of some agent and the agent of some result

Determinist: having the character of determinism

Dialectical Materialism: a philosophy developed from the writings of Hegel, Engels, and Marx, combining a notion of material determinism with the concept of dialectic as a historical force that drives events toward a resolution of the contradictions that characterize each historical epoch

Dialogic: signification structured as dialogue; the continuous, interactive, generative process of language

Disciplinary Communities: a knowledge community in which scholarship is materialized; a community bound by common institutions, discourses, beliefs, and practices

Discursive Practice: characteristic language use that serves to distinguish and locate meaning

Downward Causation: a semiotic approach that holds that the upper levels of an argument constrains its foundations

Emancipatory Deconstructionist: a critic who holds that there exist emancipatory points from which better arguments can be advanced

Emancipatory: liberating as from a deterministic relationship

Empirical Adequacy: the attainment of theory when it preserves the phenomenon

Empiricism: the ideological belief in the primacy of empirical arguments; the search for knowledge through observation and experimentation

Episteme: a coherent knowledge system on the grandest scale

Epistemology: the study of the origin, nature, methods, and limits of knowledge

Essentializing: a constructionist effort in the creation of an ahistorical object of analysis

Excorporation: the act of stripping a term from its collectively held meaning and using it to further different ends

Existentialism: the philosophy that existence precedes essence and that human beings have no predetermined nature or range of choices but always are required to choose

Exnomination: the naturalization of the position from which claim is advanced thereby rendering the location invisible

Fact: that which is considered to contain a set, unquestioned meaning

Facticity: the construction of a particular claim to act as fact

Falsificationism: the theory of scientific knowledge developed by Karl Popper that holds that theories can never be proven to be true, but incorrect theories can be proven to be false

Foundationalism: an epistemic approach that holds that knowledge must be built upon certain irreducible claims

Freedom: the presence and recognition of genuine alternatives

Functional Equivalence: any of a set of practical methods by which elements are considered sufficiently comparable to be considered equal

Functionalism: an approach to the social sciences that views a society as an integrated whole, in which each part functions to maintain social order

Generalization: the development of universal principles from specific empirical claims

Hegelian Relationship: a relationship in which the subordinated is more knowledgeable than the dominant; a master/slave relationship because the slave must know the master better than the master must know the slave

Hermeneutic Empiricism: an interpretive approach to knowledge that assumes the world is comprised of multiple domains of phenomena with no common foundation and that human engagement of the phenomenal world occurs across these multiple domains

Hermeneutics: an interpretive approach to the study of texts, both written and social, that stresses the inherent subjectivity of the interpreter

Historicity: a requirement that argument account for time and place

Hypothesis: a testable statement expressing a relationship between phenomena

Iconic Practices: the material products of action that convey and establish meaning

Idealism: the belief that reality is fundamentally mental in nature

Identity: a sense of the unified self that exists across time and situation, as well as the constellation of characteristics and performances that manifest the self in meaningful action

Ideology: any wide-ranging system of beliefs, ways of thought, and categories that provide the foundation for political and social action

Idiosyncrasy: the mental constitution peculiar to a person; a claim wholly dependent on that constitution

Immanence: a self-presenting event requiring (and allowing) no further explanation

Improvisation: a recognizable action attributable to the contingencies of time, place, and actor

Incommensurability: when different theories share no neutral standpoint from which to objectively assess the merits of the one versus that of the other

Incorporation: the assimilation of concepts or symbols of another for one's own ends

Independence: freedom from determination

Indetermination: a relationship in which the cause of some phenomenon cannot be resolved

Instrumentalism: the theory that a claim can be considered true if it succeeds in serving its appointed purpose, or false if it does not

Intercoder Reliability: a measure of agreement between observers used to advance validity claims

Interpretation: the assigning of meaning or semantic value

Intersubjectivity: the empirical measure of objectivity; a shared subjectivity

Isomorphic Transduction: exact reproduction from one field to another

Justificationism: the practice of validating an argument based on the structure of the argument per se; justification depends on the argument's rationality and expression in logic

Kantianism: the doctrine developed by German philosopher Immanuel Kant (1724–1804) that holds that the content of knowledge is developed through perception, but its form is determined by a priori categories of the mind

Knowledge Production: the act of transforming particular claim into collectively held knowledge

Legitimation: giving authority to

Local and Partial Knowledge: explanations that hold true in one domain, but have no transcendent value

Logical Positivism: an epistemic approach associated with the Vienna Circle of the 30s; an approach that asserts the independence of observation and theory, but seeks to join the two by explicit rules of correspondence

Logocentrism: the critical position that the meaning of a text is in its correspondence to something external to it (reality, the intent of the author, etc.)

Methodological Individualism: the epistemic requirement held by many within the social sciences that places the explanation for collective action within the individual

Naive Empiricism: an epistemic tradition that holds that the phenomenal world is directly accessible through observation

Natural Sign: a sign factually connected to its object; an idea of naive empiricism

Nominalism: the belief that all universal or abstract terms have no general realities corresponding to them and exist in name only

Nonutopian: the belief that there are no final solutions to human inequity

Normal Science: a term popularized by Thomas Kuhn that refers to a mature state of a knowledge paradigm in which the major innovations have been completed and the work is in the resolution anomalies and minor problems

Object of Analysis: that which is the focus of, and is produced by, claim

Objective Empiricism: an approach to knowledge that assumes phenomena are perceivable but autonomous of perception and exist in a stable, deterministic network of relationships

Objectivism: a philosophy that holds that there exists a truly objective point from which to conduct analysis across all domains of experience

Ontology: the study of the nature of reality and being

Operationalism: a science realism solution that holds that concepts and terms can and must be defined in terms of identifiable and repeatable operations

Overdetermination: a term from critical studies that describes the relationship between a cultural text and its preferred reading

Paradigm: the notion developed by Thomas Kuhn that scientific work is both the product of, and serves to reify, a framework of concepts, results, and procedures that dictate what is considered to be knowledge

Parsimony: the belief that the simplest theory that is true is the best theory

Performative Practice: the methods of performance that convey and establish meaning

Phenomenal World: the material foundation of experience

Phenomenology: a philosophy which is characterized by an emphasis on everyday life and the intentional analysis of its eidetic character

Phenomenon: something that is shown, revealed, or manifest in experience

Positivism: a philosophy of knowledge that holds that the only form of positive knowledge is the description of sensory phenomena

Poststructuralism: a variety of postmodernism defined by its reaction against French structuralism and associated with writers such as Derrida and Foucault; a theoretical approach which holds that meaning is formulated intertextually and rejects a logocentric foundation

Pragmatism: the philosophy of meaning which holds that the meaning of a theory is contained in the practical effects of adopting it

Praxeology: the study of practices, performances, actions; the manner of knowing

Preferred Possible: a justification of constructionist or critical analysis that holds that analysis can advance the interests of human freedom and opposes those of tyranny

Programmatic Methodism: a theory that defines a valid domain of knowledge as one that supports a complex, interrelated set of questions and methods of inquiry

Progressivism: the belief that scientific inquiry is progressing over time, reaching a better approximation of the physical world

Protocol Invisibility: the assumption that the governing protocol plays no part in the explanation

Protocol: a set of rules of observation, measurement, and analysis, whether implicit or explicit

Quantification: the transformation of observation into mathematic form

Realism: the belief in a reality that exists objectively and is revealed through representational devices

Recursive Deconstructionist: critic who holds that meaning is never fixed and that no claim can be supported by a factual foundation

Reductionism: the belief that the universe is explained by a finite set of statements;

any explanatory move that offers the same explanation for more than one phenomenon

Referential Character of Signs: the belief that every sign refers to a single ideational object

Referentiality: the state of referring to an object, concept, event

Reflexivity: the ability of analysis to reveal its own constructedness

Representation: the claim that language can describe without deletion or addition

Response Ingenuousness: the practice of assuming that response to scientific measurement is a naively truthful representation of what is claimed to be measured

Scholarship Fields: broad academic communities that produce and export specific paradigms

Science Realism: the belief that scientific concepts must have concomitant elements in reality

Scientism: the belief that the methods and terms of natural science are the only proper elements of inquiry

Semiosis: the moment of semiotic understanding; when the sign develops meaning

Semiotic Excess: use of the character of the sign to signify more than its referent

Semiotics: the study of the significance and meaning from sign systems

Significance: in semiotics, having the potential for meaning; in ordinary language, having importance, relevance, consequence

Singularity of Explanation: paradigmatic explanation

Social Construction of Reality: the belief that meaning is constructed through human accomplishment and does not exist essentially

Social Practices: collective human action made meaningful within a social/cultural framework

Social Action: a philosophy that holds that knowledge is defined through human action

Sociological Relativism: the theory that knowledge is produced within communities of understanding; truth or falsity is therefore relative to the community and its larger social presence

Statistical Decision Rule: the use of probability of events to determine the veridical character of given event

Structuralism: a group of theories that hold that a priori structures mediate our understanding of the phenomenal world and limit human agency

Subjectivity: the doctrine that all discourse (and, therefore, all propositional knowledge) is marked rhetorically and politically; entails the rejection of an Archimedean point

Surrogates: substitutes that have the same character and consequence and serve the same function as the original

Tautology: the point at which explanation can reach no further than its own claim; when further questioning cannot be supported

Trustworthiness of Engagement: an underlying assumption of hermeneutic theories that engagement with the object of analysis provides a credible basis for claim

Trustworthiness of the Sign: the belief in a transcendental relationship between sign and meaning
Underdetermination: a relationship in which the agent does not fully contain the consequent; when multiple theories can explain the same phenomenon
Undetermination: the condition of a self-presenting phenomenon
Unity of Science: the hypothesis that all scientific observation and claim are transportable across all knowledge fields and ultimately reduce to a single knowledge
Utopian: the claim of a final solution for human inequity
Validity: the truth-value of a claim
Verificationism: the theory that a claim can be considered true if it can be verified through scientific tests; claims that cannot be verified, such as those of metaphysics or theology, cannot be considered to be true or false
Voice: a discursive tool which represents the subjectivity of the author; a socially designed style which reflects the basis for claim

REFERENCES

Aboulafia, M. (1986). *The mediating self: Mead, Sartre and self-determination*. New Haven, CT: Yale University Press.

Agassi, J. (1981). *Science and society*. Dordrecht, The Netherlands: D. Reidel.

Agger, B. (1989). *Socio(onto)logy: A disciplinary reading*. London: Routledge & Kegan Paul.

Agger, B. (1992a). *Cultural studies as cultural theory*. London: Falmar Press

Agger, B. (1992b). *The discourse of domination: From the Frankfurt School to postmodernism*. Evanston, IL: Northwestern University Press.

Ajzen, I., & Fishbein, M. (1970). The prediction of behavior from attitudinal and normative variables. *Journal of Experimental Social Psychology, 6,* 466–487.

Alexander, J. C. (1982). *Theoretical logic in sociology: The antinomies of classical thought: Marx and Durkheim* (Vol. 2). Berkeley and Los Angeles: University of California Press.

Alexander, J. C. (1992). Citizen and enemy in symbolic classification: On the polarizing discourse of civil society. In M. Lamont & M. Fournier (Eds.), *Cultivating differences: Symbolic boundaries and the making of inequality* (pp. 289–308). Chicago: University of Chicago Press.

Alford, C. F. (1991). *The self in social theory*. New Haven, CT: Yale University Press.

Allen, R. C. (1987). Reader-oriented criticism and television. In R. C. Allen (Ed.), *Channels of discourse: Television and contemporary criticism* (pp. 74–112). Chapel Hill: University of North Carolina Press.

Alston, W. P. (1989). *Epistemic justification: Essays in the theory of knowledge*. Ithaca, NY: Cornell University Press.

Alston, W. P. (1993). *The reliability of sense perception.* Ithaca, NY: Cornell University Press.

Altheide, D. L., & Snow, R. P. (1991). *Media worlds in the postjournalism era.* New York: Aldine de Gruyter.

Althusser, L. (1984). *Essays on ideology.* London: Verso.

Amico, R. P. (1993). *The problem of the criterion.* Lanham, MD: Rowman & Littlefield.

Andersen, K., & Clevenger, T., Jr. (1963). A summary of experimental research in ethos. *Speech Monographs, 30,* 59–78.

Anderson, J. A. (1980). The theoretical lineages of critical viewing curricula. *Journal of Communication, 30,* 64–71.

Anderson, J. A. (1981). Research on children and television: A critique. *Journal of Broadcasting, 25,* 395–400.

Anderson, J. A. (1987). *Communication research: Issues and Methods.* New York: McGraw-Hill.

Anderson, J. A. (1992). On the ethics of research in a socially constructed reality. *Journal of Broadcasting and Electronic Media, 36,* 353–357.

Anderson, J. A. (1994). The role of interpretation in communication theory. In N. Metalinos (Ed.), *Verbo-visual literacy: Understanding and applying new education communication media technologies* (pp. 211–222). Quebec: Concordia University Press.

Anderson, J. A. (In press). Thinking qualitatively: Hermeneutics in science. In M. Salwen & D. W. Stacks, (Eds.), *An integrated approach to communication theory and research.* Hillsdale, NJ: Erlbaum.

Anderson, J. A., & Avery, R. K. (1988). The concept of effects: Recognizing our personal judgments. *Journal of Broadcasting and Electronic Media, 32,* 359–366.

Anderson, J. A., Chase, R., & Larson, T. (1990, June). *Patterns of viewing and descriptions of use for broadcast television news.* Paper presented at the meeting of the International Communication Association, Dublin, Ireland.

Anderson, J. A., & Goodall, H. L., Jr. (1994). Probing the body ethnographic: From an anatomy of inquiry to a poetics of expression. In F. L. Casmir (Ed.), *Building communication theories* (pp. 87–129). Hillsdale, NJ: Erlbaum.

Anderson, J. A., & Meyer, T. P. (1988). *Mediated communication: A social action perspective.* Newbury Park, CA: Sage.

Anderson, J. A., & Schoening, G. T. (1996). The nature of the individual in communication research. In D. Grodin & T. R. Lindlof (Eds.), *Constructing the self in a mediated world.* Newbury Park, CA: Sage.

Apel, K.-O. (1980). *Toward a transformation of philosophy.* London: Routledge & Kegan Paul.

Armstrong, P. B. (1990). *Conflicting readings: Variety and validity in interpretation.* Chapel Hill: University of North Carolina Press.

Assiter, A. (1990). *Althusser and feminism.* London: Pluto Press.

Atkinson, P. (1990). *The ethnographic imagination: Textual constructions of reality.* London: Routledge.

Audi, R. (1988). *Belief, justificationism and knowledge.* Belmont, CA: Wadsworth.

Austin, J. L. (1950/1964). Truth. In G. Pitcher (Ed.), *Truth* (pp. 1–31). Englewood Cliffs, NJ: Prentice-Hall.

Austin, J. L. (1961). *Philosophical papers.* Oxford: Oxford University Press.

Avramides, A. (1989). *Meaning and the mind.* Cambridge, MA: MIT Press.

Babbie, E. R. (1973). *Survey research methods*. Belmont, CA: Wadsworth.

Badzinski, D. M. (1991). Children's cognitive representations of discourse: Effects of vocal cues on text comprehension. *Communication Research, 18,* 715–736.

Bakhtin, M. M. (1986). *Speech genres and other late essays*. Austin: University of Texas Press.

Bales, R. (1951). *Interaction process analysis*. Reading, MA: Addison-Wesley.

Bandura, A., Ross, D., & Ross, S. A. (1961). Transmission of aggression through imitation of aggressive models. *Journal of Abnormal and Social Psychology, 63,* 575–582.

Bandura, A., Ross, D., & Ross, S. A. (1963). Imitation of film-mediated aggressive models. *Journal of Abnormal and Social Psychology, 66,* 3–11.

Banks, S. P., & Riley, P. (1993). Structuration theory as an ontology for communication research. In S. Deetz (Ed.), *Communication yearbook* (Vol. 16, pp. 167–196). Newbury Park, CA: Sage.

Bannet, E. T. (1989). *Structuralism and the logic of dissent*. Chicago: University of Illinois Press.

Barker, M., & Beezer, A. (Eds.). (1992). *Reading into cultural studies*. London: Routledge.

Barnes, A. (1988). *On interpretation*. Oxford: Basil Blackwell.

Barnes, B. (1977). *Interests and the growth of knowledge*. London: Routledge & Kegan Paul.

Barthes, R. (1974). *S/Z*. New York: Hill & Wang.

Barthes, R. (1975). *Pleasure of the text* (R. Miller, Trans.). New York: Hill & Wang.

Barthes, R. (1986). *The rustle of language*. New York: Hill & Wang.

Bartky, S. (1995). Foucault, femininity, and the modernization of patriarchal power. In J. P. Sterba (Ed.), *Social and political philosophy* (pp. 453–467). Belmont, CA: Wadsworth.

Baudrillard, J. (1981). *For a critique of the political economy of the sign* (C. Levin, Trans.). St. Louis, MO: Telos Press.

Bauman, Z. (1978). *Hermeneutics and social science*. London: Hutchinson.

Bazerman, C. (1988). *Shaping written knowledge*. Madison: University of Wisconsin Press.

Beach, W. A. (1990). Orienting to the phenomenon. In J. A. Anderson (Ed.), *Communication yearbook* (Vol. 13, pp. 216–244). Newbury Park, CA: Sage.

Becker, H. S., & McCall, M. (Eds.). (1990). *Symbolic interaction and cultual studies*. Chicago: University of Chicago Press.

Belenky, M. F., Clinchy, B. M., Goldberger, N. R., & Tarule, J. M. (1986). *Women's way of knowing: The development of self, voice, and mind*. New York: Basic Books.

Bellah, R. N., Madsen, R., Sullivan, W. M., Swindler, A., & Tipton, S. M. (1985). *Habits of the heart: Individualism and commitment in American life*. Berkeley and Los Angeles: University of California Press.

Belsey, C. (1980). *Critical practice*. London: Routledge.

Berger, C. (1991). Communication theories and other curios. *Communication Monographs, 58,* 101–113.

Berger, C., & Calabrese, R. (1975). Some explorations in initial interaction and beyond: Toward a developmental theory of interpersonal communication. *Human Communication Research, 1,* 99–112.

Berkeley, G. (1710/1974). *A treatise concerning the principles of human knowledge*. New York: Doubleday.

Berkowitz, L., & Rawlings, E. (1963). Effects of film violence on inhibitions against subsequent aggression. *Journal of Abnormal and Social Psychology, 66,* 405–412.

Berman, A. (1988). *From the new criticism to deconstruction: The reception of structuralism and post-structuralism.* Chicago: University of Illinois Press.

Bernstein, R. J. (1983). *Beyond objectivism and relativism: Science, hermeneutics, and praxis.* Philadelphia: University of Pennsylvania Press.

Bhabha, H. K. (1994). *The location of culture.* London: Routledge.

Blaikie, N. (1993). *Approaches to social enquiry.* Cambridge, UK: Polity Press.

Blair, C., Brown, J. R., & Baxter, L. A. (1994). Disciplining the feminine. *Quarterly Journal of Speech, 80,* 383–409.

Bleicher, J. (1982). *The hermeneutic imagination: Outline of a positive critique of scientism and sociology.* London: Routledge & Kegan Paul.

Bloom, A. D. (1987). *The closing of the American mind.* New York: Simon and Schuster.

Bloom, C. P. (1988). The roles of schemata in memory for text. *Discourse Processes, 11,* 305–318.

Bloomfield, L. (1933). *Language.* New York: Holt and Company.

Bloor, D. (1976). *Knowledge and social imagery.* London: Routledge & Kegan Paul.

Bohman, J. F. (1991). *New philosophy of social science: Problems of indeterminacy.* Cambridge, MA: MIT Press.

Bohman, J. F., Hiley, D. R., & Shusterman, R. (1991). Introduction: The interpretive turn. In D. R. Hiley, J. F. Bohman, & R. Shusterman (Eds.), *The interpretive turn: Philosophy, science, culture* (pp. 1–14). Ithaca, NY: Cornell University Press.

Boiko, R. B. (1990). *Toward a neurohermeneutic theory of interpretation and mind/body relationship.* Unpublished master's thesis, University of Utah, Salt Lake City.

Bolles, E. B. (1991). *A second way of knowing.* New York: Prentice-Hall.

Boudan, R. (1989). *The analysis of ideology* (M. Slater, Trans.). Chicago: University of Chicago Press.

Bourdieu, P. (1978). Sport and social class. *Social Science Information, 17,* 819–840.

Brantlinger, P. (1990). *Crusoe's footprints: Cultural studies in Britain and America.* New York: Routledge.

Bridgeman, P. W. (1927). *The logic of modern physics.* New York: Macmillan.

Brown, H. I. (1977). *Perception, theory, and commitment: The new philosophy of science.* Chicago: University of Chicago Press.

Brown, H. I. (1987). *Observation and objectivity.* New York: Oxford University Press.

Brown, H. I. (1988). *Rationality.* London: Routledge.

Brown, R. H. (1987). *Society as text.* Chicago: University of Chicago Press.

Browning, L. D., & Henderson, S. C. (1989). One-way communication transfers in loosely coupled systems. In J. A. Anderson (Ed.), *Communication yearbook* (Vol. 12, pp. 638–669). Newbury Park, CA: Sage.

Buchowski, M. (1989). Ethnocentrism, eurocentrism, scientocentrism. In J. Kmita & Z. Krystyna (Eds.), *Visions of culture and the models of cultural sciences* (pp. 199–214). Amsterdam: Rodopi.

Buller, D. B., LePoire, B. A., Aune, R. K., & Eloy, S. V. (1992). Social perceptions as mediators of the effect of speech rate similarity on compliance. *Human Communication Research, 19,* 286–311.

Burgoon, J. K., & Le Poire, B. A. (1992). Effects of communication expectancies, actual communication, and expectancy disconfirmation on evaluations of communicators and their communication behaviors. *Human Communication Research, 20,* 67–96.

Burke, K. (1968). Dramatism. In D. L. Sills (Ed.), *The international encyclopedia of the social sciences* (Vol. 7, pp. 445–451). New York: Macmillan.

Campbell, D. T., & Stanley, J. C. (1963). *Experimental and quasi-experimental designs for research.* Chicago: Rand McNally.

Campbell, J. A. (1993). Reply to Gaonkar and Fuller. *Southern Communication Journal, 58,* 312–318.

Canfield, J. V. (1990). *The looking-glass self: An examination of self-awareness.* New York: Praeger.

Capaldi, N. (1969). *Human knowledge.* New York: Pegasus.

Caputo, J. D. (1987). *Radical hermeneutics: Repetition, deconstruction, and the hermeneutic project.* Bloomington: Indiana University Press.

Caputo, J. D. (1992). On being inside/outside truth. In J. L. Marsh, J. D Caputo, & M. Westphal (Eds.), *Modernity and its discontents* (pp. 45–64). New York: Fordham University Press.

Carey, J. W. (1989). *Communication as culture: Essays on media and society.* Boston: Unwin Hyman.

Carmichael, T. (1991). Postmodernism, symbolicity, and the rhetoric of the hyperreal: Kenneth Burke, Fredric Jameson, and Jean Baudrillard. *Text and Performance Quarterly, 11,* 319–324.

Carnap, R. (1928/1969). *The logical structure of the world.* Berkeley and Los Angeles: University of California Press.

Carnap, R. (1966). *Philosophical foundations of physics.* New York: Basic Books.

Carruthers, P. (1992). *Human knowledge and human nature.* Oxford: Oxford University Press.

Casmir, F. (Ed.). (1994). *Building communication theories.* Hillsdale, NJ: Erlbaum.

Chaudhuri, A., & Buck, R. (1995). Affect, reason, and persuasion: Advertising strategies that predict affective and analytic-cognitive responses. *Human Communication Research, 21,* 422–441.

Cheney, G., & Tompkins, P. K. (1988). On the facts of the text as the basis of human communication research. In J. A. Anderson (Ed.), *Communication yearbook* (Vol. 11, pp. 455–481). Newbury Park, CA: Sage.

Chesebro, J. W. (1993). How to get published. *Communication Quarterly, 41,* 373–382.

Chisholm, R. M. (1982). *The foundations of knowing.* Minneapolis: University of Minnesota Press.

Cobb, S. (1994). A critique of critical discourse analysis: Deconstructing and reconstructing the role of intention. *Communication Theory, 4,* 132–152.

Cohen, B. C. (1963). *The press and foreign policy.* Princeton, NJ: Princeton University Press.

Cole, S., Rubin, L., & Cole, J. (1978). *Peer review in the National Science Foundation.* Washington, DC: National Academy of Sciences.

Collins, R. (1975). *Conflict sociology: Toward an explanatory science.* New York: Academic Press.

Connolly, J. M., & Keutner, T. (1988). Introduction: Interpretation, decidability, and meaning. In J. M. Connolly & T. Keutner (Eds.), *Hermeneutics versus science: Three German views* (pp. 1–67). Notre Dame, IN: University of Notre Dame Press.

Conrad, C. (1993). Rhetorical/communication theory as an ontology for structuration research. In S. Deetz (Ed.), *Communication yearbook* (Vol. 16, pp. 197–208). Newbury Park, CA: Sage.

Conquergood, D. (1991). Rethinking ethnography: Towards a critical cultural politics. *Communication Monographs, 58,* 179–194.

Coulter, J. (1998). *Mind in action.* Atlantic Highlands, NJ: Humanities Press.

Crane, D. (1972). *Invisible colleges.* Chicago: University of Chicago Press.

Crapanzano, V. (1992). *Hermes' dilemma and Hamlet's desire.* Cambridge, MA: Harvard University Press.

Cronin, B. (1982). Progress in documentation: Invisible colleges and information transfer. *Journal of Documentation, 38,* 212–236.

Csikszentmihalyi, M. (1991). Reflections on the "spiral of silence." In J. A. Anderson (Ed.), *Communication yearbook* (Vol. 14, pp. 288–297). Newbury Park, CA: Sage.

Culler, J. (1979). Jacques Derrida. In J. Sturrock (Ed.), *Structuralism and since* (pp. 154–179). Oxford: Oxford University Press.

Cummins, R. (1989). *Meaning and mental representation.* Cambridge, MA: The MIT Press.

D'Amico, R. (1989). *Historicism and knowledge.* New York: Routledge.

David, P. (1992). Accuracy of visual perception of quantitative graphics. *Journalism Quarterly, 69,* 273–292.

Davidson, D. (1980). *Essays on actions and events.* Oxford: Clarendon Press.

Davidson, D. (1984). *Inquiries into truth and interpretation.* Oxford: Clarendon Press.

de Certeau, M. (1984). *The practice of everyday life* (S. F. Rendell, Trans.). Berkeley and Los Angeles: University of California Press.

Deetz, S., & Mumby, D. K. (1990). Power, discourse, and the workplace: Reclaiming the critical tradition. In J. A. Anderson (Ed.), *Communication yearbook* (Vol. 13, pp. 18–47). Newbury Park, CA: Sage.

DeFleur, M. L., & Ball-Rokeach, S. (1989). *Theories of mass communication* (5th ed.). New York: Longman.

Delia, J. G. (1977). Constructivism and the study of human communication. *Quarterly Journal of Speech, 63,* 66–83.

Delia, J. G., O'Keefe, B. J., & O'Keefe, D. J. (1982). The constructivist approach to communication. In F. E. X. Dance (Ed.)., *Human communication theory: Comparative essays* (pp. 147–191). New York: Harper & Row.

de Man, P. (1986). *The resistance to theory.* Minneapolis: University of Minnesota Press.

Derrida, J. (1972). *Speech and phenomena* (D. Allison, Trans.). Evanston, IL: Northwestern University Press.

Derrida, J. (1982). *Margins of philosophy* (A. Bass, Trans.). Chicago: University of Chicago Press.

Dewell, J. (1938). *Logic: The theory of enquiry.* New York: Holt, Rinehart and Winston.

Diefenbeck, J. A. (1984). *A celebration of subjective thought.* Carbondale: Southern Illinois University Press.

Diesing, P. (1971). *Patterns of discovery in the social sciences.* New York: Aldine.

Dolan, F. M. (1991). Deconstruction's object. *Text and Performance Quarterly, 11,* 190–206.

Donohue, T. R., Henke, L. L., & Meyer, T. P. (1983). Learning about television commercials:

The impact of instructional units on children's perceptions of motive and intent. *Journal of Broadcasting, 27,* 251–261.

Duhem, P. (1954). *The aim and structure of physical theory* (P. Wiener, Trans.). Princeton, NJ: Princeton University Press.

Durfee, H. A., & Rodier, D. F. T. (1989). The self and its language. In H. A. Durfee and D. F. T. Rodier (Eds.), *Phenomenology and beyond: The self and its language* (pp. 1–10). Dordrecht, The Netherlands: Kluwer Academic.

Dupre, J. (1993). *The disunity of science.* Cambridge, MA: Harvard University Press.

Dyke, C. (1993). Extralogical excavations: Philosophy in the age of shovelry. In J. Caputo & M. Yount (Eds.), *Foucault and the critique of institutions* (pp. 101–126). University Park: Pennsylvania State University Press.

Eagleton, T. (1980). *Literary theory.* Oxford: Oxford University Press.

Eagleton, T. (1990). *The ideology of the aesthetic.* Oxford: Basil Blackwell.

Eckhardt, B. R., Wood, M. R., & Jacobvitz, R. S. (1991). Verbal ability and prior knowledge. *Communication Research, 18,* 636–649.

Eco, U. (1976). *A theory of semiotics.* Bloomington: Indiana University Press.

Eco, U. (1984). *Semiotics and the philosophy of language.* Bloomington: Indiana University Press.

Eco, U. (1992). *Interpretation and overinterpretation.* Cambridge, UK: Cambridge University Press.

Edmondson, R. (1984). *Rhetoric in sociology.* London: Macmillan.

Ellis, R. (1986). *An ontology of consciousness.* Dordrecht, The Netherlands: Martinus Nijhoff.

Erickson, K. V., Fleuriet, C. A., & Hosman, L. A. (1993). Prolific publishing: Professional and administrative concerns. *Southern Communication Journal, 58,* 328–338.

Euske, N. A., & Roberts, K. H. (1987). Evolving perspectives in organization theory: Communication implications. In F. M. Jablin, L. L. Putnam, K. H. Roberts, & L. W. Porter (Eds.), *Handbook of organizational communication* (pp. 41–69). Newbury Park, CA: Sage.

Evans, J. St. B. T., Newstead, S. E., & Byrne, R. M. J. (1993). *Human reasoning: The psychology of deduction.* Hillsdale, NJ: Erlbaum.

Eyerman, R. (1981). *False consciousness and ideology in Marxist theory.* Stockholm: Almqvist & Wiksell International.

Faia, M. A. (1993). *What's wrong with social sciences?* Lanham, MD: University Press of America.

Fejes, F., & Petrich, K. (1993). Invisibility, homophobia, and heterosexism: Lesbians, gays, and the media. *Critical Studies in Mass Communication, 10,* 396–422.

Festinger, L. (1957). *A theory of cognitive dissonance.* Stanford, CA: Stanford University Press.

Feyerabend, P. K. (1988). *Against method.* London: Verso.

Feyerabend, P. K. (1989). How to be a good empiricist—a plea for tolerance in matters epistemological. In B. A. Brody & R. E. Grandy (Eds.), *Readings in the philosophy of science* (pp. 104–122). Englewood Cliffs, NJ: Prentice-Hall.

Fish, S. (1994). *There's no such thing as free speech.* New York: Oxford University Press.

Fishbein, M., & Ajzen, I. (1975). *Belief, attitude, intention, and behavior: An introduction to theory and research.* Reading, MA: Addison-Wesley.

238 ≡ References

Fisher, B. A. (1970). Decision emergence: Phases in group decision-making. *Speech Monographs, 37,* 53–66.

Fisher, W. R. (1987). *Human communication as narration: Toward a philosophy of reason, value, and action.* Columbia: University of South Carolina Press.

Fiske, J. (1987). *Television culture.* London: Methuen.

Foucault, M. (1970). *The order of things* (A. Sheridan, Trans.). New York: Random House.

Foucault, M. (1987). What is enlightenment? In P. Rabinow & W. M. Sullivan (Eds.), *Interpretive social science: A second look* (pp. 157–174). Berkeley and Los Angeles: University of California Press.

Fowler, D. D., & Hardesty, D. L. (Eds.). (1994). *Others knowing others: Perspectives on ethnographic careers.* Washington, DC: Smithsonian Institution Press.

Freeman, K. (1948). *Ancilla to the Pre-Socratic philosophers: A complete translation of the fragments in Diels, "Fragmente der Vorsokratiker."* Oxford: Basil Blackwell.

Frost, R., & Stauffer, J. (1987). The effects of social class, gender, and personality on physiological responses to filmed violence. *Journal of Communication, 37,* 29–45.

Fuchs, S. (1992). *The professional quest for truth: A social theory of science and knowledge.* Albany: State University Press of New York.

Fuller, S. (1993a). *Philosophy, rhetoric, and the end of knowledge.* Madison: University of Wisconsin Press.

Fuller, S. (1993b). *Philosophy of science and its discontents* (2nd ed.). New York: The Guilford Press.

Gadamer, H.-G. (1960/1989). *Truth and method* (J. Weinsheimer & D. G. Marshall, Trans.). New York: Crossroad.

Gale, G. (1979). *Theory of science.* New York: McGraw-Hill.

Gans, J. S., & Shepherd, G. B. (1994). How the mighty are fallen: Rejected classic articles by leading economists. *Journal of Economic Perspectives, 8,* 165–179.

Gaonkar, D. P. (1993). The idea of rhetoric in the rhetoric of science. *Southern Communication Journal, 58,* 258–295.

Garvey, W. D. (1979). *Communication, the essence of science: Facilitating information exchanges among librarians, scientists, engineers, and students.* New York: Pergamon Press.

Geertz, C. (1988). *The anthropologist as author.* Stanford, CA: Stanford University Press.

Gerbner, G., Gross, L., Morgan, M., & Signorielli, N. (1986). Living with television: The dynamics of the cultivation process. In J. Bryant & D. Zillmann (Eds.), *Perspectives on media effects* (pp. 17–40). Hillsdale, NJ: Erlbaum.

Gerbner, G., Morgan, M., & Signorielli, N. (1982). Programming health protrayals: What viewers see, say, and do. In D. Pearl, L. Bouthilet, & J. Lazar (Eds.), *Television and behavior: Ten years of scientific progress and implications for the 80s* (Vol. 2, pp. 291–307). Washington, DC: U.S. Government Printing Office.

Gergen, K. J. (1971). *The concept of self.* New York: Holt Rinehart & Winston.

Gergen, K. J. (1991). *The saturated self.* New York: Basic Books.

Gibson, J. J. (1966). *The senses considered as perceptual systems.* Boston: Houghton Mifflin.

Giddens, A. (1979). *Central problems in social theory.* Berkeley and Los Angeles: University of California Press.

Giddens, A. (1981). *A contemporary critique of historical materialism, Vol. 1: Power, property, and the state.* Berkeley and Los Angeles: University of California Press.

Giddens, A. (1984). *The constitution of society: Outline of thetheory of structuration.* Cambridge, UK: Polity Press.

Giddens, A. (1985). *A contemporary critique of historical materialism, Vol. 2: The nation-state and violence.* Berkeley and Los Angeles: University of California Press.

Giddens, A. (1987). Structuralism, post-structuralism, and the production of culture. In A. Giddens & J. H. Turner (Eds.), *Social theory today* (pp. 195–223). Stanford, CA: Stanford University Press.

Giddens, A. (1989). A reply to my critics. In D. Held & J. B. Thompson (Eds.), *Social theory of modern societies: Anthony Giddens and his critics* (pp. 249–301). Cambridge: Cambridge University Press.

Giddens, A. (1990). Structuration theory and social analysis. In J. Clark, C. Modgil, & S. Modgil (Eds.), *Anthony Giddens: Consensus and controversy* (pp. 297–316). Cambridge: Cambridge University Press.

Giere, R. N. (1983). Testing scientific theories. In J. Earman (Ed.), *Minnesota studies in the philosophy of science* (pp. 269–298). Minneapolis: University of Minnesota Press.

Gilbert, G. N. (1976). The transformation of research findings into scientific knowledge. *Social Studies of Science, 6,* 281–302.

Gilbert, G. N. (1977). Referencing as persuasion. *Social Studies of Science, 7,* 113–122.

Gillet, G. (1992). *Representation, meaning, and thought.* Oxford: Clarendon Press.

Glasser, T. L., & Ettema, J. S. (1993). When the facts don't speak for themselves: A study of the use of irony in daily journalism. *Critical Studies in Mass Communication, 10,* 322–338.

Glassner, B. (1990). Fit for postmodern selfhood. In H. S. Becker & M. M. McCall (Eds.), *Symbolic interaction and cultural studies* (pp. 215–243). Chicago: University of Chicago Press.

Goffman, E. (1959). *The presentation of self in everyday life.* Garden City, NJ: Doubleday.

Goldberger, N. R., Clinchy, B. M., Belenky, M. F., & Tarule, J. M. (1987). Women's ways of knowing: On gaining a voice. In P. Shaver & C. Hendrick (Eds.), *Sex and gender* (pp. 201–228). London: Sage.

Goldman, A. I. (1970). *A theory of human action.* Englewood Cliffs, NJ: Prentice-Hall.

Goldman, A. I. (1986). *Epistemology and cognition.* Cambridge, MA: Harvard University Press.

Goldman, A. I. (1991). *Liaisons: Philosophy meets the cognitive and social sciences.* Cambridge, MA: MIT Press.

Goodall, H. L., Jr. (1991). *Living in the rock n roll mystery.* Carbondale: Southern Illinois University Press.

Goodall, M. C. (1970). *Science, logic, and political action.* Cambridge, MA: Schenkman.

Goodman, N. (1978). *Ways of worldmaking.* Indianapolis, IN: Hackett.

Graff, G., & Robbins, B. (1992). Cultural criticism. In S. Greenblatt & G. Gunn (Eds.), *Redrawing the boundaries* (pp. 419–436). New York: MLA.

Gramsci, A. (1971). *Prison notebooks: Selections* (Q. Hoare & G. N. Smith, Eds. and Trans.). New York: International.

Green, B. S. (1988). *Literary methods and sociological theory.* Chicago: University of Chicago Press.

Greenblatt, S., & Gunn, G. (Eds.). (1992). *Redrawing the boundaries.* New York: MLA.

Griemas, J. A. (1990). *The social sciences: A semiotic view* (P. Perron & F. H. Collins, Trans.). Minneapolis: University of Minnesota Press.

Griffin, E. (1994). *A first look at communication theory* (2nd ed.). New York: McGraw-Hill.

Gross, A. G. (1990). Persuasion and peer review in science: Habermas's ideal speech situation applied. *History of the Human Sciences, 3,* 195–209.

Gross, A. G. (1990). *The rhetoric of science.* Cambridge, MA: Harvard University Press.

Grossberg, L. (1984). Strategies of Marxist cultural interpretation. *Critical Studies in Mass Communication, 1,* 392–421.

Grossberg, L. (1993a). Cultural studies and/in new worlds. *Critical Studies in Mass Communication, 10,* 1–22.

Grossberg, L. (1993b). *Cultural studies: What's in a name?* Salt Lake City: University of Utah, Department of Communication, B. Aubrey Fisher Memorial Lecture.

Gurnah, A., & Scott, A. (1992). *The uncertain science: Criticism of sociological formalism.* London: Routledge.

Gutting, G. (1989). *Michel Foucault's archaeology of scientific reason.* Cambridge: Cambridge University Press.

Habermas, J. (1984). *Theory of communicative action* (Vol. 1). Boston: Beacon Press.

Habermas, J. (1987a). *Theory of communicative action* (Vol. 2). Boston: Beacon Press.

Habermas, J. (1987b). *The philosophical discourse of modernity: Twelve lectures* (F. G. Lawrence, Trans.). Cambridge, MA: MIT Press.

Habermas, J. (1988). *On the logic of the social sciences* (S. W. Nicholsen & J. A. Stark, Trans.). Cambridge, MA: MIT Press.

Hall, A. R. (1994). *Science and society.* Aldershot, Hampshire, UK: Variorum.

Hall, J. R. (1992). The capital(s) of culture: A nonholistic approach to status situations, class, gender, and ethnicity. In M. Lamont & M. Fournier (Eds.), *Cultivating differences: Symbolic boundaries and the making of inequality* (pp. 257–285). Chicago: University of Chicago Press.

Hall, S. (1982). The rediscovery of "ideology": Return of the repressed in media studies. In M. Gurevitch, T. Bennett, J. Curran, & J. Woollacott (Eds.), *Culture, society, and the media* (pp. 56–90). London: Metheun.

Hammermesh, D. S. (1994). Facts and myths about refereeing. *Journal of Economic Perspectives, 8,* 153–163.

Hammersley, M. (1992). *What's wrong with ethnography?* London: Routledge.

Hanna, J. (1991). Critical theory and the politicalization of science. *Communication Monographs, 58,* 202–212.

Hanson, N. R. (1958). *Patterns of discovery.* Cambridge: Cambridge University Press.

Hanson, N. R. (1972). *Observation and explanation: A guide to philosophy of science.* London: George Allen & Unwin.

Harding, S. (1986). *The science question in feminism.* Ithaca, NY: Cornell University Press.

Harding, S. (1991). *Whose science? Whose knowledge? Thinking from women's lives.* Milton Keynes, UK: Open University Press.

Hardt, H. (1989). The return of the "critical" and the challenge of radical dissent: Critical theory, cultural studies, and American mass communication research. In J. A. Anderson (Ed.), *Communication yearbook* (Vol. 12, pp. 558–600). Newbury Park, CA: Sage.

Harnad, S. (Ed.). (1982). *Peer commentary on peer review.* Cambridge: Cambridge University Press.

Harré, R. (1983). *An introduction to the logic of the sciences.* New York: St. Martin's Press.

Harré, R. (1994). Is there still a problem about the self? In S. Deetz (Ed.), *Communication yearbook* (Vol. 17, pp. 55–73). Newbury Park, CA: Sage.

Harrison, B. (1991). *Inconvenient fictions: Literature and the limits of theory.* New Haven, CT: Yale University Press.

Hart, R. P., & Burks, D. M. (1972). Rhetorical sensitivity and social interaction. *Speech Monographs, 39,* 75–91.

Hawkes, T. (1977). *Structualism and semiotics.* Berkeley and Los Angeles: University of California Press.

Hebb, D. O. (1960). The second American Revolution. *American Psychologist, 15,* 735–745.

Heidegger, M. (1977). *Basic writings* (D. F. Krell, Ed.). New York: Harper & Row.

Heider, F. (1944). Social perception and phenomenal causality. *Psychological Review, 51,* 358–374.

Hekman, S. J. (1990). *Gender and knowledge: Elements of a postmodern feminism.* Boston: Northeastern University Press.

Helle, H. J. (Ed.). (1991). *Verstehen and pragmatism: Essays in interpretative sociology.* Frankfurt am Main: Peter Lang.

Hempel, C. (1952). *Fundamentals of concept formation in empirical science.* Chicago: University of Chicago Press.

Hempel, C. (1965). *Aspects of scientific explanation and other essays in the philosophy of science.* New York: Free Press.

Henderson, D. K. (1993). *Interpetation and explanation in the human sciences.* Albany: State University of New York Press.

Hess, P. H. (1988). *Thought and experience.* Toronto: University of Toronto Press.

Hesse, M. (1980). In defence of objectivity. In M. Hesse (Ed.), *Revolutions and reconstructions in the philosophy of science* (pp. 167–186). Brighton, UK: Harvester Press.

Hewitt, J. P. (1989). *Dilemmas of the American self.* Philadelphia: Temple University Press.

Hickson, M., III, Stacks, D. W., & Amsbary, J. H. (1989). An analysis of prolific scholarship in speech communication, 1915–1985: Toward a yardstick for measuring research productivity. *Communication Education, 38,* 230–236.

Hickson, M., III, Stacks, D. W., & Amsbary, J. H. (1992). Active prolific female scholars in communication: An analysis of research productivity. *Communication Quarterly, 40,* 350–356.

Hickson, M., III, Stacks, D. W., & Amsbary, J. H. (1993). Active prolific scholars in communication studies: Analysis of research productivity, Part 2. *Communication Education, 42,* 224–233.

Hiley, D. R., Bohman, J. F., & Shusterman, R. (Eds.). (1991). *The interpretive turn: Philosophy, science, culture.* Ithaca, NY: Cornell University Press.

Hirsch, E. D., Jr. (1967). *Validity in interpretation.* New Haven, CT: Yale University Press.

Hodge, R., & Kress, G. (1988). *Social semiotics.* Ithaca, NY: Cornell University Press.

Holmwood, J., & Stewart, A. (1991). *Explanation and social theory.* New York: St. Martin's Press.

Horkheimer, M. (1968/1972). *Critical theory: Selected essays* (M. J. O'Connell, Trans.). New York: Herder and Herder.

Horkheimer, M., & Adorno, T. W. (1944/1972). *Dialectic of enlightenment.* New York: Herder and Herder.

Huck, K. (1993). The arsenal on fire: The reader in the riot, 1943. *Critical Studies in Mass Communication, 10,* 23–48.

Husserl, E. (1907/1970). *The idea of phenomenology.* (W. P. Alston & G. Nakhnikian, Trans.). The Hague, The Netherlands: Martinus Nijhoff.

Huizenga, J. R. (1992). *Cold fusion: The scientific fiasco of the century.* Rochester, NY: University of Rochester Press.

Hume, D. (1748/1974). *An enquiry concerning human understanding.* New York: Doubleday.

Husserl, E. (1929/1964). *Cartesian meditations: An introduction to phenomenology (D. Cairns, Trans.). The Hague, The Netherlands: Martinus Nijhoff.*

Infante, D., Rancer, A. S., & Womack, D. F. (1990). *Building communication theory.* Prospect Heights, IL: Waveland Press.

Ingram, D. (1985). Hermeneutics and truth. In R. Hollinger (Ed.), *Hermeneutics and praxis* (pp. 32–53). Notre Dame, IN: University of Notre Dame Press.

Inyengar, S. (1979). Television news and issue salience: A reexamination of the agenda-setting hypothesis. *Journal of Communication, 31,* 395–416.

Isajiw, W. (1968). *Causation and functionalism in sociology.* New York: Schocken Books.

Jablin, F. M., Putnam, L. L., Roberts, K. H., & Porter, L. W. (1987). *Handbook of organizational communication.* Newbury Park, CA: Sage.

Jackson, M. (1989). *Paths toward a clearing: Radical empiricism and ethnographic inquiry.* Bloomington: Indiana University Press.

James, W. (1908). *Pragmatism: A new name for some old ways of thinking.* New York: Longmans, Green, and Co.

James, W. (1912/1922). *Essays in radical empiricism.* New York: Longmans, Green, and Co.

James, W. (1912/1943). *A pluristic universe.* New York: Longman.

James, W. (1890/1983). *The principles of psychology.* Cambridge, MA: Harvard University Press.

Jameson, F. (1972). *The prison-house of language: A critical account of structuralism and Russian formalism.* Princeton, NJ: Princeton University Press.

Jameson, F. (1981). *The political unconscious: Narrative as a socially symbolic act.* Ithaca, NY: Cornell University Press.

Jarvie, I. C. (1986). *Thinking about society: Theory and practice.* Dordrecht, The Netherlands: D. Reidel.

Jensen, K. B. (1986). *Making sense of the news.* Aahus, Denmark: Aahus University Press.

Jensen, K. B. (1991). When is meaning? Communication theory, pragmatism, and mass media reception. In J. A. Anderson (Ed.), *Communication yearbook* (Vol. 14, pp. 3–32). Newbury Park, CA: Sage.

Jicks, T. O. (1979). Mixing qualitative and quantitative methods: Triangulation in action. *Administrative Science Quarterly, 24,* 602–611.

Joas, H. (1993). *Pragmatism and social theory.* Chicago: University of Chicago Press.

Johnson, R. (1986–1987). What is cultural studies anyway? *Social Text, 16,* 38, 43.

Johnson, T., Dandeker, C., & Ashworth, C. (1984). *The structure of social theory: Strategies, dilemmas, and projects.* New York: St Martin's Press.

Kane, J. (1984). *Beyond empiricism: Michael Polanyi reconsidered.* New York: Peter Lang.

Kant, I. (1781/1964). *The critique of pure reason* (N. K. Smith, Trans.). London: Macmillan.

Katz, E., Blumler, J., & Gurevitch, M. (1974). Uses of mass communication by the individual. In W. P. Davidson & F. Yu (Eds.), *Mass communication research* (pp. 11–35). New York: Praeger.

Kazoleas, D. (1993). The impact of argumentativeness on resistance to persuasion. *Human Communication Research, 20,* 118–137.

Keller, E. F. (1982). Feminism and science. In N. O. Keohane, M. Z. Rosaldo, & B. C. Gelpi (Eds.), *Feminist theory: A critique of ideology* (pp. 113–126). Chicago: University of Chicago Press.

Kellermann, K. (1989). Coherence: A meaningful adhesive for discourse. In J. A. Anderson (Ed.), *Communication yearbook* (Vol. 12, pp. 95–129). Newbury Park, CA: Sage.

Kellermann, K., & Cole, T. (1994). Classifying compliance-gaining messages: Taxonomic disorder and strategic confusion. *Communication Theory, 4,* 3–60.

Kelley, H. H. (1973). The processes of causal attribution. *American Psychologist, 28,* 107–128.

Kerby, A. P. (1991). *Narrative and the self.* Bloomington: Indiana University Press.

Kerlinger, F. N. (1973). *Foundations of behavioral research* (2nd ed.). New York: Holt, Rinehart & Winston.

Kierkegaard, S. (1958). *Journals* (A. Dru, Trans.). London: Collins.

Kimball, R. (1990). *Tenured radicals: How politics has corrupted our higher education.* New York: Harper & Row.

Kohut, H. (1977). *The restoration of the self.* New York: International Universities Press.

Kolenda, K. (1990). *Rorty's humanistic pragmatism.* Tampa: University of South Florida Press.

Kourany, J. (1987). The validation of scientific knowledge. In J. Kourany (Ed.), *Scientific knowledge* (pp. 112–121). Belmont, CA: Wadsworth.

Kovacic, B. *New approaches to organizational communication.* Albany: State University of New York Press.

Kuhn, T. S. (1970). *The structure of scientific revolutions* (2nd ed.). Chicago: University of Chicago Press.

Kundera, M. (1984). *The unbearable lightness of being* (M. H. Heim, Trans.). New York: Harper & Row.

Lacan, J. (1968). *The language of the self: The function of language in psychoanalysis* (A. Wilden, Trans.). New York: Delta Books.

Lacan, J. (1977). *Ecrits* (A. Sheridan, Trans.). New York: W. W. Norton.

Lacan, J. (1988). *The seminar of Jacques Lacan* (J. A. Miller, Trans.). New York: Norton.

Lakatos, I. (1970). Falsification and the methodology of scientific research programmes. In I. Lakatos & A. Musgrave (Eds.), *Criticism and the growth of knowledge* (pp. 91–195). Cambridge: Cambridge University Press.

Landgrebe, L. (1981). *The phenomenology of Edmund Husserl* (D. Welton Ed.). Ithaca, NY: Cornell University Press.

Lanigan, R. L. (1988). *Phenomenology of communication.* Pittsburg: Duquesne University Press.

Lanigan, R. L. (1992). *The human science of communicology.* Pittsburg: Duquesne University Press.

Lasswell, H. D. (1927). *Propaganda technique in the World War.* New York: Knopf.

Latour, B. (1987). *Science in action.* Cambridge, MA: Harvard University Press.

Leaf, M. J. (1989). Singer, Kant, and the semiotic self. In B. Lee & G. Urban (Eds.), *Semiotics, self, and society* (pp. 171–192). Berlin: Mouton de Gruyter.

Leahey, T. R. (1994). *A history of modern psychology.* Englewood Cliffs, NJ: Prentice-Hall.

Lehrer, K. (1973). Skepticism and conceptual change. In R. M. Chisholm & R. J. Swartz (Eds.), *Empirical knowledge* (pp. 47–58). Englewood Cliffs, NJ: Prentice-Hall.

Lehrer, K. (1974). *Knowledge.* Oxford: Clarendon Press.

Lenin, V. (1960). *Selected works.* Moscow: Foreign Languages Publishing House.

Lenoir, T. (1993). The discipline of nature and the nature of disciplines. In E. Messer-Davidow, D. R. Shumway, & D. J. Sylvan, *Knowledges: Historical and critical studies in disciplinarity* (pp. 70–102). Charlottesville: University of Virgina Press.

Lévi-Strauss, C. (1967). *Structural anthropology* (G. Weidenfeld, Trans.). Chicago: University of Chicago Press.

Levin, J. D. (1992). *Theories of the self.* Washington, DC: Taylor & Francis.

Levine, G. (Ed.). (1992). *Constructions of the self.* New Brunswick, NJ: Rutgers University Press.

Lewis, C. I. (1946). *An analysis of knowledge and valuation.* La Salle, IL: Open Court.

Lewis, H. D. (1982). *The elusive self.* London: Macmillan.

Liebes, T., & Ribak, R. (1994). In defense of negotiated readings: How moderates on each side of the conflict interpret Intifada news. *Journal of Communication, 44,* 108–124.

Little, D. (1991). *Varieties of social explanation.* Boulder, CO: Westview Press.

Littlejohn, S. W. (1989). *Theories of human communication* (3rd ed.). Belmont, CA: Wadsworth.

Littlejohn, S. W. (1992). *Theories of human communication* (4th ed.). Belmont, CA: Wadsworth.

Livingston, P. (1988). *Literary knowledge: Humanistic inquiry and the philosophy of science.* Ithaca, NY: Cornell University Press.

Locke, J. (1690/1974). *An essay concerning human understanding.* New York: Doubleday.

Loges, W. E. (1994). Canaries in the coal mine: Perceptions of threat and media system dependency relations. *Communication Research, 21,* 5–23.

Longino, H. (1989). Can there be a feminist science? In A. Garry & M. Pearsall (Eds.), *Women, knowledge, and reality* (pp. 203–216). Boston: Unwin Hyman.

Longino, H. (1990). *Science as social knowledge.* Princeton, NJ: Princeton University Press.

Lukács, G. (1971). *History and class consciousness.* London: Merlin Press.

Lyotard, J.-F. (1984). *The postmodern condition: A report on knowledge* (G. Bennington & B. Massumi, Trans.). Minneapolis: University of Minnesota Press.

Macmurray, J. (1957). *The self as agent.* London: Farber & Farber.

Madison, G. B. (1988). *The hermeneutics of postmodernity.* Bloomington: Indiana University Press.

Mah, H. (1987). *The end of philosophy, the origin of "ideology."* Berkeley, University of California Press.

Mailloux, S. (1991). Rhetorical hermeneutics revisited. *Text and Performance Quarterly, 11,* 233–248.

Manganaro, M. (1990). Textual play, power, and cultural critique: An orientation to modernist anthropology. In M. Manganaro (Ed.), *Modernist anthropology: From fieldwork to text* (pp. 3–47). Princeton, NJ: Princeton University Press.

Mannheim, K. (1940). *Ideology and utopia.* New York: Harcourt, Brace & Company.

Manning, D. (1989). Ideology and political reality. In N. O'Sullivan (Ed.), *The structure of modern ideology* (pp. 54–88). London: Edward Elgar.

Marx, K. (1867/1930). *Capital* (P. Eden & P. Cedar, Trans.). New York: Dutton.

Mayhew, L. (1976). Methodological dilemmas in social science. In J. J. Loubser, R. C. Baum, A. Effrat, & V. M. Lidz (Eds.), *Explorations in general theory in social science* (pp. 59–74). New York: Free Press.

McCombs, M. E., & Shaw, D. L. (1972). The agenda-setting function of mass media. *Public Opinion Quarterly, 36,* 176–187.

McGuire, W. J. (1973). The yin and yang of progress in social psychology: Seven Koans. *Journal of Personality and Social Psychology, 26,* 446–456.

McLellan, D. (1986). *Ideology.* Minneapolis: University of Minnesota Press.

McPhail, M. (1994). The politics of complicity: Second thoughts about the social construction of racial equality. *Quarterly Journal of Speech, 80,* 343–357.

McPhee, R. D., & Tompkins, P. K. (Eds.). (1985). *Organizational communication: Traditional themes and new directions.* Beverley Hills, CA: Sage.

McQuail, D. (1987). *Mass communication theory: An introduction* (2nd ed.). Newbury Park, CA: Sage.

McQuail, D., & Windahl, S. (1993). *Communication models for the study of mass communication* (2nd ed.). New York: Longman.

Meadows, A. J. (1974). *Communication in science.* London: Butterworths.

Megill, A. (1991). Introduction: Four senses of objectivity. *Annals of Scholarship, 8,* 301–320.

Meltzer, B. N., Petras, J. W., & Reynolds, L. T. (1975). *Symbolic interactionism: Genesis, varieties, and criticism.* London: Routledge & Kegan Paul.

Mennell, S. J. (1974). *Sociological theory: Uses and unities.* New York: Praeger.

Mepham, J. (1979). The theory of ideology in *Capital.* In J. Mepham & D.-H. Rubin (Eds.), *Issues in Marxist philosophy* (Vol. 3, pp. 141–174). Brighton, UK: Harvester Press.

Merleau-Ponty, M. (1962). *Phenomenology of perception.* New York: Humanities Press.

Merton, R. K. (1937). The sociology of knowledge. *Isis, 75,* 493–503.

Merton, R. K. (1948). Discussion of Talcott Parsons' "The position of sociological theory." *American Sociological Review, 13,* 164–168.

Merton, R. K. (1957). *Social theory and social structure.* Glencoe, IL: Free Press.

Messer-Davidow, E., Shumway, D. R., & Sylvan, D. J. (1993). *Knowledges: Historical and critical studies in disciplinarity.* Charlottesville: University of Virgina Press.

Meyers, P. N., Jr., & Biocca, F. N. (1992). The elastic body image: The effect of television advertising and programming on body image distortions in young women. *Journal of Communication, 42,* 108–133.

Mirowski, P. (1989). *More heat than light.* Cambridge: Cambridge University Press.

Mitchell, D. B. (1994). Distinctions between everyday and representational communication. *Communication Theory, 4,* 111–131.

Morgan, M., & Gerbner, G. (1982). TV professions and adolescent career choices. In M. Schwarz (Ed.), *TV and teens: Experts look at the issues* (pp. 121–126). Reading, MA: Addison-Wesley.

Morley, D. (1980). *The "Nationwide" audience: Structure and decoding.* London: British Film Institute.

Morley, D. (1986). *Family television: Cultural power and domestic leisure.* London: Comedia.

Moscovici, S. (1991). Silent majorities and loud minorities. In J. A. Anderson (Ed.), *Communication yearbook* (Vol. 14, pp. 298–308). Newbury Park, CA: Sage.

Mueller-Vollmer, K. (Ed.). (1990). *The hermeneutics reader.* New York: Continuum.

Mullins, N. C. (1973). *Theories and theory groups in contemporary American sociology.* New York: Harper & Row.

Munch, R. (1987). *Theory of action: Toward a new synthesis going beyond Parsons.* London: Routledge & Kegan Paul.

Murphy, J. P. (1990). *Pragmatism: From Peirce to Davidson.* Boulder, CO: Westview Press.

Myers, G. (1990). *Writing biology: Texts in the social construction of scientific knowledge.* Madison: University of Wisconsin Press.

Myers, G. D. (1969). *Self: An introduction to philosophical psychology.* New York: Pegasus.

Nagel, E. (1961). *The structure of science.* London: Routledge & Kegan Paul.

Nelson, J. S., Megill, A., & McCloskey, D. N. (Eds.). (1988). *The rhetoric of the human sciences.* Madison: University of Wisconsin Press.

Nelson, J. S., Megill, A., & McCloskey, D. N. (1987). Rhetoric of inquiry. In J. S. Nelson, A. Megill, & D. N. McCloskey (Eds.), *The rhetoric of the human sciences* (pp. 1–18). Madison: University of Wisconsin Press.

Nelson, L. (1973). The impossibility of the "theory of knowledge." In R. M. Chisholm & R. J. Swartz (Eds.), *Empirical knowledge* (pp. 3–19). Englewood Cliffs, NJ: Prentice-Hall.

Nelson, L. H. (1990). *Who knows: From Quine to a feminist epiricism.* Philadelphia: Temple University Press.

Newcomb, H. M. (1991). On the dialogic aspects of mass communication. In R. K. Avery & D. Eason (Eds.), *Critical perspectives on media and society* (pp. 69–87). New York: The Guilford Press.

Newell, R. W. (1986). *Objectivity, empiricism, and truth.* London: Routledge & Kegan Paul.

Noelle-Neumann, E. (1991). The theory of public opinion: The concept of the spiral of silence. In J. A. Anderson (Ed.), *Communication yearbook* (Vol. 14, pp. 256–287). Newbury Park, CA: Sage.

Nöth, W. (1990). *Handbook of semiotics.* Bloomington: Indiana University Press.

O'Hanlon, R. (1988). Recovering the subject: Subaltern studies and histories of resistance in colonial South Asia. *Modern Asian Studies, 22,* 189–224.

O'Neil, J. (Ed.). (1976). *On critical theory.* New York: Seabury Press.

Osgood, C. (1963). On understanding and creating sentences. *American Psychologist, 18,* 735–751.

Outhwaite, W. (1987). *New philosophies of social science.* New York: St. Martin's Press.

Parsons, T. (1937). *The structure of social action: A study of social theory with special reference to a group of recent European writers.* New York: McGraw-Hill.

Parsons, T. (1951). *The social system.* London: Tavistock.

Pearce, W. B. (1994). Recovering agency. In S. Deetz (Ed.), *Communication yearbook* (Vol. 17, pp. 34–41). Newbury Park, CA: Sage.

Pearce, W. B., & Cronen, V. (1980). *Communication, action, and meaning: The creation of social realities.* New York: Praeger.

Peirce, C. S. (1960). *Collected papers* (Vol. 2; C. Hartshorne & P. Weiss, Eds.). Cambridge, MA: The Kelnap Press of Harvard University Press.

Pettersson, R. (1988). *Visuals for information.* Stockholm: Esselte Forlag.

Phillips, D. C. (1987). *Philosophy, science, and social inquiry.* Oxford, UK: Pergamon Press.

Phillips, D. C. (1992). *The social scientist's bestiary.* Oxford, UK: Pergamon Press.

Phillips, D. P. (1983). The impact of mass media violence on U.S. homicides. *American Sociological Review, 50,* 364–371.

Piaget, J. (1970). *Structuralism* (C. Muschler, Trans.). New York: Basic Books.

Plantinga, A. (1993). *Warrant: The current debate.* New York: Oxford University Press.

Polanyi, M. (1964). *Personal knowledge: Toward a post-critical philosophy.* New York: Harper Torchbooks.

Pollock, D., & Cox, J. R. (1991). Historicizing "reason": Critical theory, practice, and postmodernity. *Communication Monographs, 58,* 170–178.

Pollock, J. L. (1986). *Contemporary theories of knowledge.* Totowa, NJ: Rowman & Littlefield.

Popper, K. R. (1968). *Conjectures and refutations: The growth of scientific knowledge.* New York: Harper Torchbooks.

Popper, K. R. (1972). *Objective knowledge.* Oxford: Oxford University Press.

Popper, K. R., & Eccles, J. C. (1977). *The self and its brain.* Berlin: Springer-Verlag.

Potter, W. J., Cooper, R., & Dupagne, M. (1993). The three paradigms of mass media research in mainstream communication journals. *Communication Theory, 3,* 317–335.

Prelli, L. J. (1989). *A rhetoric of science.* Columbia: University of South Carolina Press.

Propp, V. (1968). *The morphology of the folktale.* Austin: University of Texas Press.

Putnam, H. (1983). Why reason can't be naturalized. In H. Putnam (Ed.), *Realism and reason* (pp. 229–247). Cambridge: Cambridge University Press.

Putnam, L. L., & Pacanowsky, M. E. (1983). *Communication and organizations: An interpretive approach.* Beverly Hills, CA: Sage.

Quine, W. V. O. (1966). *Ways of paradox.* New York: Random House.

Quine, W. V. O. (1953/1961/1980). *From a logical point of view* (2nd ed., rev.). Cambridge, MA: Harvard University Press.

Quine, W. V. O. (1981). Epistemology naturalized. In R. M. Chisholm & R. J. Swartz (Eds.), *Empirical knowledge* (pp. 59–74). Englewood Cliffs, NJ: Prentice-Hall.

Quinton, A. M. (1973). *The nature of things.* London: Routledge & Kegan Paul.

Rabinow, P., & Sullivan, W. M. (1987). *Interpretive social science: A second look.* Berkeley, University of California Press.

Radway, J. (1984). *Reading the romance.* Chapel Hill: University of North Carolina Press.

Reichert, J. (1977). *Making sense of literature.* Chicago: University of Chicago Press.

Richards, I. A. (1925). *Principles of literary criticism.* New York: Harvest-Harcourt.

Richards, I. A. (1936). *The philosophy of rhetoric.* London: Oxford University Press.

Richards, S. (1983). *Philosophy and the sociology of science: An introduction.* Oxford: Basil Blackwell.

Ricoeur, P. (1981). *Hermeneutics and the human sciences.* Cambridge: Cambridge University Press.

Ricoeur, P. (1992). *Oneself as another.* Chicago: University of Chicago Press.

Rochberg-Halton, E. (1986). *Meaning and modernity: Social theory in the pragmatic attitude.* Chicago: University of Chicago Press.

Rodrick, R. (1995). *A critical analysis of organizational empowerment.* Unpublished Ph.D. dissertation, University of Utah, Salt Lake City.

Rogers, E. M. (1962). *Diffusion of innovations.* New York: Free Press.

Rogers, E. M., & Dearing, J. W. (1988). Agenda-setting research: Where has it been? Where is it going? In J. A. Anderson (Ed.), *Communication yearbook* (Vol. 11, pp. 555–594). Newbury Park, CA: Sage.

Rogers, L. E. (1989). Relational communication processes and patterns. In B. Dervin, L. Grossberg, B. O'Keefe, & E. Wartella (Eds.), *Rethinking communication: Paradigm exemplars* (pp. 280–290). Newbury Park, CA: Sage.

Rogers, L. E., & Farace, R. V. (1975). Analysis of relational communication in dyads: New measurement procedures. *Human Communication Research, 1,* 222–239.

Rorty, R. (1979). *Philosophy and the mirror of nature.* Princeton, NJ: Princeton University Press.

Rorty, R. (1982). *Consequences of pragmatism.* Minneapolis: University of Minnesota Press.

Rorty, R. (1987). Science as solidarity. In J. S. Nelson, A. Megill, & D. N. McCloskey (Eds.), *The rhetoric of the human sciences* (pp. 38–52). Madison: University of Wisconsin Press.

Rorty, R. (1991a). *Objectivity, relativism, and truth.* Cambridge, UK: Cambridge University Press.

Rorty, R. (1991b). Inquiry as recontextualization. In D. R. Hiley, J. F. Bohman, & R. Shusterman, *The interpretive turn: Philosophy, science, culture* (pp. 59–80). Ithaca, NY: Cornell University Press.

Rosaldo, R. (1993). *Culture and truth: The remaking of social analysis.* Boston: Beacon Press.

Rose, D. (1990). *Living the ethnographic life.* Newbury Park, CA: Sage.

Rosenau, P. M. (1992). *Post-modernism and the social sciences: Insights, inroads, and intrusions.* Princeton, NJ: Princeton University Press.

Rosengren, K.-E. (1995). Substantive theories and formal models—Bourdieu confronted. *European Journal of Communication, 10,* 7–39.

Rosengren, K.-E., & Windahl, S. (1972). Mass media consumption as a functional alternative. In D. McQuail (Ed.), *Sociology of mass communications* (pp. 166–194). Harmondsworth, UK: Penguin Books.

Rosenthal, R. (1986). Media violence, antisocial behavior, and the social consequences of small effects. *Journal of Social Issues, 42,* 141–154.

Ross, A. O. (1992). *The sense of self: Research and theory.* New York: Springer.

Roth, P. A. (1987). *Meaning and method in the social sciences: A case for methodological pluralism.* Ithaca, NY: Cornell University Press.

Roth, R. (1993). *British empiricism and American pragmatism: New directions and neglected arguments.* New York: Fordham University Press.

Rouse, J. (1987). *Knowledge and power: Toward a political philosophy of science.* Ithaca, NY: Cornell University Press.

Russell, K. (1979). Science and ideology. In J. Mepham & D.-H. Rubin (Eds.), *Issues in Marxist philosophy* (Vol. 3, pp. 185–196). Brighton, UK: Harvester Press.

Sacks, O. (1993). A neurologist's notebook: To see and not see. *New Yorker, 69,* 59–73.

Said, E. W. (1983). *The world, the text, and the critic.* Cambridge, MA: Harvard University Press.

Sanday, P. R. (1981). *Male dominance and female power.* Cambridge: Cambridge University Press.

Sarup, M. (1993). *An introductory guide to poststructuralism and postmodernism* (2nd ed.). Athens: University of Georgia Press.

Sartre, J.-P. (1956). *Being and nothingness.* (H. E. Barns, Trans.). New York: Philosophical Library.

Sartre, J.-P. (1976). *Critique of dialectical reason: Theory of practical ensembles* (A. Sheridan-Smith, Trans.). London: New Left Books.

Saussure, F. de. (1910/1959). *Course in general linguistics.* New York: McGraw-Hill.

Scheler, M. F. (1924/1980). *Problems of a sociology of knowledge* (M. S. Frings, Trans.). London: Routledge & Kegen Paul.

Schoening, G. R. (1992). *Social action principles for theories and studies of mediated communiction.* Unpublished doctoral dissertation, University of Utah, Salt Lake City.

Schoening, G. T., & Anderson, J. A. (1995). Social action media studies: Foundational arguments and common premises. *Communication Theory, 5,* 93–116.

Schwanenberg, E. (1976). On the meaning of the general theory of action. In J. J. Loubser, R. C. Baum, A. Effrat, & V. M. Lidz (Eds.), *Explorations in general theory in social science* (pp. 35–45). New York: Free Press.

Scott, A. (1990). *Ideology and the new social movements.* London: Unwin Hyman.

Scott, J. C. (1990). *Domination and the arts of resistance.* New Haven, CT: Yale University Press.

Searle, J. (1969). *Speech acts: An essay in the philosophy of language.* Cambridge: Cambridge University Press.

Searle, J. (1975). The logical structure of fictional discourse. *New Literary History, 6,* 319–332.

Searle, J. (1994, January). *Philosophical issues in higher education.* Paper presented in the Colloquium Series, Humanities Center, University of Utah, Salt Lake City.

Segal, J. M. (1991). *Agency and alienation: A theory of human presence.* Savage, MD: Rowman & Littlefield.

Seidler, V. J. (1991). *The moral limits of modernity: Love, inequality, and oppression.* New York: St. Martin's Press.

Seung, T. K. (1982). *Semiotics and thematics in hermeneutics.* New York: Columbia University Press.

Severin, W. J., & Tankard, J. W., Jr. (1988). *Communication theories: Origins, methods, uses* (2nd ed.). New York: Longman.

Shapin, S. (1982). History of science and its sociological reconstructions. *History of Science, 20,* 157–211.

Sherif, M., & Hovland, C. I. (1961). *Social judgment.* New Haven, CT: Yale University Press.

Shotter, J., & Gergen, K. J. (1994). Social constructionism, knowledge, self, others, and continuing the conversation. In S. Deetz (Ed.), *Communication yearbook* (Vol. 17, pp. 3–33). Newbury Park, CA: Sage.

Sherrif, J. K. (1989). *The fate of meaning.* Princeton, NJ: Princeton University Press.

Sigman, S. J. (1987). *A perspective on social communication.* Lexington, MA: Lexington Books.

Silverman, K. (1983). *The subject of semiotics.* Oxford: Oxford University Press.

Simons, H. W. (Ed.). (1989). *Rhetoric in the human sciences.* Newbury Park, CA: Sage.

Skura, M. (1992). Psychoanalytic criticism. In S. Greenblatt & G. Gunn (Eds.), *Redrawing the boundaries* (pp. 349–373). New York: MLA.

Slack, J. D., & Allor, M. (1983). The political and epistemological constituents of critical communication research. *Journal of Communication, 33,* 208–218.

Snare, F. (1992). *The nature of moral thinking.* London: Routledge.

Sobchack, V. (1992). *The address of the eye.* Princeton, NJ: Princeton University Press.

Solomon, R. C. (1987). *From Hegel to existentialism.* Oxford: Oxford University Press.

Soper, K. (1986). *Humanism and anti-humanism.* La Salle, IL: Open Court.

Sosnoski, J. J. (1994). *Token professionals and master critics: A critique of orthodoxy in literary studies.* Albany: State University of New York Press.

Sparks, G. G., Spirek, M. M., & Hodgson, K. (1992, May). *Individual differences in arousability: Implications for understanding immediate and lingering emotional reactions to frightening mass media.* Paper presented at the annual meeting of the International Communication Association, Miami, FL.

Spirek, M. M., & Sparks G. G. (1993, May). *The impact of children's coping style on emotional reactions to a frightening movie.* Paper presented at the annual meeting of the International Communication Association, Washington, DC.

Spradley, J. P. (1980). *Participant observation.* New York: Holt, Rinehart & Winston.

Stevens, S. S. (1951). Mathematics, measurement, and psychophysics. In S. S. Stevens (Ed.), *Handbook of experimental psychology* (pp. 1–49). New York: John Wiley and Sons.

Stohl, C. (1993). European managers' interpretation of participation. *Human Communication Research, 20,* 97–117.

Strawson, P. F. (1950/1964). Truth. In G. Pitcher (Ed.), *Truth* (pp. 32–53). Englewood Cliffs, NJ: Prentice-Hall.

Suppe, P. (1974). The search for philosophic understanding of scientific theories. In P. Suppe, *The structure of scientific theories* (pp. 3–241). Urbana: University of Illinois Press.

Swanson, D. L. (1979). Political communication research and the uses and gratifications model. *Communication Research, 6,* 37–53.

Szahaj, A. (1990). Actuality of the Frankfurt School's critical theory of society: The Polish reception. In Ph. v. Engledorp Gastelaars, S. Magala, & O. Preuss (Eds.), *Critics and critical theory in Eastern Europe* (pp. 53–60). The Hague, The Netherlands: University Press of Rotterdam.

Tan, A. S. (1981). *Mass communication theories and research.* Columbus, OH: Grid.

Tavakol, M. (1990). *Sociology of knowledge: Theoretical problems.* Bangalore, India: Sterling.

Taylor, B. C. (1993). Fat Man and Little Boy: The cinematic representation of interests in the nuclear weapons organization. *Critical Studies in Mass Communication, 10,* 367–394.

Taylor, C. (1986). *Philosophical papers* (2 vols.). Cambridge: Cambridge University Press.

Taylor, C. (1991). The dialogic self. In J. F. Bohman, D. R. Hiley, & R. Shusterman (Eds.), *The interpretive turn: Philosophy, science, culture* (pp. 304–314). Ithaca, NY: Cornell University Press.

Teichman, J. (1988). *Philosophy and the mind.* Oxford: Basil Blackwell.

Terwee, S. J. S. (1990). *Hermeneutics in psychology and psychoanalysis.* Berlin: Springer-Verlag.

Thalheimer, A. (1936). *Introduction to dialectical materialism: The Marxist worldview* (G. Simpson & G. Weltner, Trans.). New York: Covici Friede.

Thibaut, J. W., & Kelley, H. H. (1959). *The social psychology of groups.* New York: John Wiley & Sons.

References ≡ 251

Tolman, E. C. (1930). *"Insight" in rats*. Berkeley and Los Angeles: University of California Press.

Tompkins, P. K. (1987). Translation organizational theory: Symbolism over substance. In F. M. Jablin, L. L. Putnam, K. H. Roberts, & L. W. Porter (Eds.), *Handbook of organizational communication* (pp. 70–96). Newbury Park, CA: Sage.

Toulmin, S. (1953). *The philosophy of science*. London: Hutchinson.

Toulmin, S. (1961). *Foresight and understanding: An enquiry into the aims of science*. Bloomington: Indiana University Press.

Trenholm, S. (1991). *Human communication theory* (2nd ed.). Englewood Cliffs, NJ: Prentice-Hall.

Trujillo, N. (1993). Interpreting November 22: A critical ethnography of an assassination site. *Quarterly Journal of Speech, 79,* 447–466.

Trujillo, N., & Ekdom, L. (1985). Sportswriting and American cultural values. *Critical Studies in Mass Communication, 1,* 262–281.

Tudor, A. (1982). *Beyond empiricism: Philosophy of science in sociology*. London: Routledge & Kegan Paul.

Turner, G. (1990). *British cultural studies: An introduction*. Boston: Unwin Hyman.

Turner, S. P. (1986). *The search for a methodology of social science*. Dordrecht, The Netherlands: D. Reidel.

Turner, V. W., & Bruner, E. M. (Eds.). (1986). *The anthropology of experience*. Chicago: University of Illinois Press.

Tyler, S. A. (1987). *The unspeakable discourse, dialogue, and rhetoric in the postmodern world*. Madison: University of Wisconsin Press.

van Fraassen, B. C. (1980). *The scientific image*. Oxford: Clarendon Press.

Van Maanen, J. (1988). *Tales of the field*. Chicago: University of Chicago Press.

Vidmar, N., & Rokeach, M. (1974). Archie Bunker's bigotry: A study in selective perception and exposure. *Journal of Communication, 24,* 36–47.

Wagner, R. (1981). *The invention of culture*. Chicago: University of Chicago Press.

Waldron, V. R. (1995). Is the "golden age of cognition" losing its luster? Toward a requirement-centered perspective. In B. R. Burleson (Ed.), *Communication yearbook* (Vol. 18, pp. 180–197). Newbury Park, CA: Sage.

Warnock, G. J. (1962). Truth and correspondence. In C. D. Rollins (Ed.), *Knowledge and experience* (pp. 11–20). Pittsburg: University of Pittsburg Press.

Watzlawick, P., Bavelas, J. B., & Jackson, D. D. (1967). *Pragmatics of human communication*. New York: W. W. Norton.

Weber, M. (1903/1949). *The methodology of the social sciences* (E. A. Shils & H. A. Finch, Trans. and Eds.). Glencoe, IL: Free Press.

Wegner, D. M., & Vallacher, R. R. (Eds.). (1980). *The self in social psychology*. New York: Oxford University Press.

Weiss, A. J., Imrich, D. J., & Wilson, B. J. (1993). Prior exposure to creatures from a horror film: Live versus photographic representations. *Human Communication Research, 20,* 41–66.

Wertsch, J. V. (1985). The semiotic mediation of mental life: L. S. Vygotsky and M. M. Bakhtin. In E. Mertz & R. J. Parmentier, *Semiotic mediation: Sociocultural and psychological perspectives* (pp. 49–71). New York: Academic Press.

Wexler, P. (1990). Citizenship in the semiotic society. In B. S. Turner (Ed.), *Theories of modernity and postmodernity* (pp. 164–175). London: Sage.

White, A. R. (1982). *The nature of knowledge.* Totowa, NJ: Rowman & Littlefield.

White, H. C. (1963). *An anatomy of kinship: Mathematical models for structures of cumulated roles.* Englewood Cliffs, NJ: Prentice-Hall.

White, M. (1992). Ideological analysis. In R. C. Allen (Ed.), *Channels of discourse, reassembled* (pp. 161–202). London: Routledge.

Whitley, R. (1984). *The intellectual and social organization of the sciences.* Oxford: Oxford University Press.

Will, F. L. (1974). *Induction and justification.* Ithaca, NY: Cornell University Press.

Williams, H. (1988). *Concepts of ideology.* Brighton, Sussex, UK: Wheatsheaf Books.

Williams, R. (1958). *Culture and society, 1780–1950.* Garden City, NJ: Doubleday.

Williams, R. (1973). *The country and the city.* New York: Oxford University Press.

Williams, R. (1981). *Culture.* London: Fontana.

Williams, R. (1991). Base and superstructure in Marxist cultural theory. In C. Mukerji & M. Schudson (Eds.), *Rethinking popular culture* (pp. 407–423). Berkeley and Los Angeles: University of California Press.

Wilshire, B. W. (1990). *The moral collapse of the university: Professionalism, purity, and alienation.* Albany: State University of New York Press.

Wilson, B. (1991). Children's reactions to dreams conveyed in mass media programming. *Communication Research, 18,* 283–305.

Wilson, B. R. (Ed.). (1970). *Rationality.* Oxford: Basil Blackwell.

Winch, P. (1958). *The idea of a social science and its relation to philosophy.* London: Routledge & Kegan Paul.

Wittgenstein, L. (1972). *On certainty* (G. E. M. Anscombe & G. H. von Wright, Eds., and D. Paul & G. E. M. Anscombe, Trans.). New York: Harper Torchbooks.

Wolin, R. (1992). *The terms of cultural criticism.* New York: Columbia University Press.

Wright, C. R. (1965). *Mass communication: A sociological perspective.* New York: Random House.

Yearly, S. (1981). Textual persuasion: The role of social accounting in the construction of scientific arguments. *Philosophy in the Social Sciences, 11,* 409–435.

Zemach, T., & Cohen, A. (1986). Perception of gender equality on television and social reality. *Journal of Broadcasting and Electronic Media, 30,* 345–358.

Zillmann, D., & Bryant, J. (1982). Pornography, sexual callousness, and the trivialization of rape. *Journal of Communication, 32,* 10–21.

Ziman, J. (1978). *Reliable knowledge.* Cambridge: Cambridge University Press.

Zimmerman, D. (1982). Are blind reviews really blind? *Canadian Sociology, 23,* 46–48.

INDEX

Sampling *(cont.)*
  epistemic value of, 171–172
  functional equivalence in, 171
  representativeness, 172, 174
  surrogacy, 133, 172, 174
Schoening, G., 216
Science
  archive of, 193–194, 220
  critique of, 32
  cycles in, 12n5
  disunity of, 30
  method of, 154n5
  multiple methodologies of, 32–33
  normalized, 6
  progressivism in, 116
  rationality in, 198n3
  revolutions in, 14
  self correction of, 118
  as social action, 136
  unity of, 15, 29–30, 130, 170–171
    and disunity of compared, 33
  value in, 155n20, 185n7, 191–193, 196–
    197, 208, 209, 210, 219–220
Scientific realism, 160
Semiosis, 38, 52, 62
Semiotic excess, 38, 55
Semiotic punctuation of reality, 37
Semiotic phenomena, 17, 55
Semiotics
  of action, 91, 136
  collective governance, 38
  encoding and decoding analysis of,
    63
  extension, 38
Semiotics and reality
  encoding and decoding, 51
  realm of interpretation, 51, 61–63
    comparisons, 60
  realm of production, 51, 59–61
    comparisons, 59
Shaw, D., 212–213
Significance
  as expression of authority, 144
  as scale, 144
Situated individual, 89–90
Social action theory, 152, 215–216
  Parson's work, 100n11

Social practice assumptions in measure-
  ment, 161–162
Sociological relativism, 115–116
Sociological determinism, 118
Sociology of knowledge, 186
Spiral of silence, 213–214
Statistical decision rules
  critique of, 175–176
  epistemic function of, 108
  uncertainty management, 175
Statistics, epistemic value of, 174–175
Structuralism, 71–72
  hermeneutics, 72, 73
  individual in, 72
  members of, 76–77n10
Structuralism and poststructuralism,
  100n9
Structuration theory, 214–215, 216
Subjectivity, 22–24, 58, 79–80
  and interpretation, 23–24
Symbolic interaction, proponents of,
  100–101n13

T

Taylor, B., 145–146
Theory
  background principles, 6
  components of, 2–3, 8
  evaluative tools of, 43
  families of, 9
  frames of, 5
  initiation practices of, 5
  normalizing texts, 6, 8
  paradigms, 8
  poaching, 7
  as practice, 8
  practical assumptions in, 159
  relation to methods, 8
  requirements for, 3
  as sign value, 148
Theory and method
  analysis of practice, 164–165
  fractures in claim, 165–166
  and knowledge, 184
  media effects example, 157–158